Shakespeare's Lyric Stage

Shakespeare's Lyric Stage

Myth, Music, and Poetry in the Last Plays

SETH LERER

The University of Chicago Press ✻ *Chicago and London*

The University of Chicago Press, Chicago 60637
The University of Chicago Press, Ltd., London

For more information, contact the University of Chicago Press, 1427 East 60th Street, Chicago, IL 60637.
Published 2018
Printed in the United States of America

27 26 25 24 23 22 21 20 19 18   1 2 3 4 5

ISBN-13: 978-0-226-58240-5 (cloth)
ISBN-13: 978-0-226-58254-2 (paper)
ISBN-13: 978-0-226-58268-9 (e-book)
DOI: https://doi.org/10.7208/chicago/9780226582689.001.0001

Library of Congress Cataloging-in-Publication Data

Names: Lerer, Seth, 1955– author.
Title: Shakespeare's lyric stage : myth, music, and poetry in the last plays / Seth Lerer.
Description: Chicago : The University of Chicago Press, 2018. | Includes bibliographical references and index.
Identifiers: LCCN 2018003418 | ISBN 9780226582405 (cloth : alk. paper) | ISBN 9780226582542 (pbk. : alk. paper) | ISBN 9780226582689 (e-book)
Subjects: LCSH: Shakespeare, William, 1564–1616—Technique. | Shakespeare, William, 1564–1616—Criticism and interpretation. | English drama—17th Century—History and criticism. | Dramatic monologues—History—17th century. | Music and literature—England—History—17th century.
Classification: LCC PR2995 .L47 2018 | DDC 822.3/3—dc23
LC record available at https://lccn.loc.gov/2018003418

∞ This paper meets the requirements of ANSI/NISO Z39.48–1992 (Permanence of Paper).

Contents

Preface

Shakespeare's late plays, wrote Samuel Taylor Coleridge in 1808, are "a different genus, diverse in kind, not merely different in degree—romantic dramas, or dramatic romances."[1] For the past two centuries, readers, directors, actors, and teachers have sought to hone the edge of just what makes these dramas different. Edward Dowden, in 1878, saw them as "Romances," concerned with "knitting together human bonds," rich with reunions of "parted kindred, the forgiveness of enemies, the atonement for wrong."[2] Some have thus focused on the plotlines of the plays: their arcs of spectacle and ceremony that heal (in the words of Sarah Beckwith) "the terrible world- and soul-destroying split" between the performing social body and the inner self, "a mind too lonely and inaccessible to be expressed."[3] Some have seen them largely as the products of the first decade of James I's rule, where court masque became the vehicle for affirmations of political and familial power, where the monarch sat simultaneously as spectator and object of spectatorship, and where the questions of a new Anglo-Scottish, "archipelagic" England were reshaping the relationships of art and patronage on a global stage.[4] Some have understood them as of and for a new interior performance space—in particular, the Blackfriars Theater, which enabled dramas "less concerned with the interaction of characters" than with a quality "more evenly lyrical, tend[ing] towards abstraction."[5] Finally, some have seen the distinctive feel of the last dramas as a matter of Shakespeare himself, of his self-generating and self-revising literary engine, turning in its final years to retrospection, regret, and farewell.[6]

Whatever scholars think, the plays continue to allure their audiences. Their complex female roles, their adventurous metaphors, and their inspirations for experimental dramaturgy speak, anew, to our early twenty-first-century sensibilities.[7] Recent productions of *The Tempest*, *Pericles*, *Cymbeline*, and *The Winter's Tale* have brought out the most imaginative of actors, directors, and designers. Today's London stages echo with what Lucy Munro calls the "odd uncertainty" of these plays, whose scenes, at times, "give the impression that they might explode beyond the stage's confines."[8] They balance, barely, on the edge (in Raphael Lyne's words) of "improbability and machination," their anxieties enabling "reflection and meditation on the power of the dramatist's hands."[9]

We may reflect and meditate along with Shakespeare, but I will argue that the ends of those activities—for us and for the characters within his fictions—lie in an awareness of the powerlessness of the literary craft. Shakespeare's late plays dramatize how poetry tries to resist patronage, how the machinations of the stage reveal the machinery behind illusion, and how increasingly improbable plots and resolutions test the faith and patience of an audience or reader. The plays may, again in Lyne's words, "excite wonder and reason," but they also baffle, irritate, and stun.[10] Something of this bafflement may stand behind Jonathan Bate's response to *Henry VIII*. Writing about the doomed Queen Katherine of Aragon, "rejected and arraigned," Bate sees her call for Orphic music at the opening of act 3 as something far different from the "sweet power" of the *Merchant of Venice* or the early poems. "Take thy lute, wench," she commands. "My soul grows sad with troubles." Her servant sings, but there is little consolation in her tale of Orpheus's power to make nature stop and listen. "In sweet music is such art." For Bate, this moment offers "metamorphic music . . . for a victim of history." It cannot change the world nor change her mood. Yet, still, the Queen desires song. It is an act of desperation. Bate announces: "Art is something you turn to when all else is lost."[11]

My book is a study of how drama turns to lyric art when faced with loss of purpose, pedigree, or power. Shakespeare's late plays explore the place of the aesthetic in the exercise of rule. They raise questions about the role of poetry and music in evoking an emotional response, and they dramatize that emotional response within the fiction of the stage performance. Moreover, in the performance of such scenes of lyric ravishment or musical attention, they illustrate the challenge of staging intimacy—that is, representing private moments before an audience.

These are the major features of the late plays that distinguish them from earlier works that may be full of song or magic. *Midsummer Night's Dream*, for example, interrogates the place of artistic performance in the maintenance of political control (whether that control is human or fairy). It shows us a commissioned spirit charged with stage-managing desire. But this is a world of fantasy: of fairy king and queen, of ancient Athenian lovers, of local rustics displaced into ravishment or lunacy. In *The Tempest*, there is magic on Prospero's island, but it is the magic worked by an all-too-human exiled duke. There are spirits and monsters, but we never see them fully manumitted from their master. There is ravishment of sound and sweet airs, but the poetry of this sublime dramatic moment is given neither to a human being nor to a spirit, but to Caliban. At such a moment, the central questions of my book emerge: what does it mean to have an emotional response to verbal and sonic art? What does it mean to give voice to that inner feeling before others? What happens when the audience for that voice is undeserving or unqualified to hear it?

"Sing and disperse" my troubles, Queen Katherine commands in *Henry VIII*, "if thou canst." This is the challenge of late Shakespeare: the challenge to perform and have effect, the challenge to move character and audience, fictional figures and historical groups. "Metamorphic music . . . for a victim of history." In the ten years leading up to *Henry VIII*, viewers would have lived through a Queen lost and a King found, a violent plot foiled, a plague come and gone, witches hunted, reason haunted, ships launched and not returned, and the first Prince of Wales in over sixty years suddenly dead. In some sense, all members of Shakespeare's audience were victims of history.

Much has been made of history in Shakespeare. But little has been said about the place of history in the making of the lyric genre and its contribution to the social function of poetry in narrative drama. Most critics, even after decades of historicist hegemony, strip history from lyric poetry, affirming it a formal practice better served by close rather than contextual reading.[12] But when it is a matter of "Shakespeare," formalism may not suffice. Do his verses truly remain freestanding objects of our delectation, guiding our understanding wholly through internal form and figure? Or are they counters in a currency of social and political exchange, whose shards of meaning must be recovered? Helen Vendler continues to aver that "any respectable account of a poem ought to have considered closely its chief formal features," and she prefaces her book about the Sonnets with this manifesto:

> Because the lyric is intended to be voiceable by anyone reading it, in its normative form it deliberately strips away most social specification (age, regional location, sex, class). A social reading is better directed at a novel or a play; the abstraction desired by the writer of, and the willing reader of, normative lyric frustrates the mind that wants social fictions or biographical revelations.[13]

What Vendler says about lyric poetry in general, I hold to be what Shakespeare's late plays are about, both dramatically and historically. They ask what happens when words voiceable by anyone become uniquely voiced by characters. What happens when an old familiar poem gels in the drama of a social reading? To read or hear the lyric performances within these plays is precisely to watch characters *as* performers and audiences—to see the fictions of their minds frustrated, torn between a powerful response to lyric beauty and the need for restitution.

In *The Tempest*'s Ariel, in Autolycus of *The Winter's Tale*, in Wolsey and Katherine of *Henry VIII*, in Cloten of *Cymbeline*, and in the various characters of *Pericles* and *The Two Noble Kinsmen*, Shakespeare dramatizes these tensions between the social and the aesthetic. These last plays bring together myth and music, past and present, poetry and politics, into a new lyrical history. Much of that history depends on new modes of performance and patronage emerging in the years around 1610. These include the return of the great lutenist John Dowland to James I's court and the dissemination of his music in printed form; the coalescing of royal masquery around the affirmations of the Jacobean family; and a new self-consciousness about the social and the mythic status of the poet, drawn from changing ways of reading Ovid and Chaucer in the first years of the seventeenth century. Out of these worlds emerges a distinctive understanding of the metamorphic nature of the lyric and, in turn, of the character (in all senses of that word) behind the recitation, writing down, and reading of poetry.

Unlike the early dramas shaped by sonnet, song, or serenade—for example, *Romeo and Juliet*, *Twelfth Night*, *Love's Labor's Lost*, *A Midsummer Night's Dream*—the late works create a sense of displaced lyric utterance, where set pieces of poetry and performance signal generational distance and cultural change. Words set to music come off as increasingly ironized, sung or said by characters that fail, or mock, or misplay their occasions. Lyric moments in the late plays invite listeners and readers to reflect back on these gaps of time and sensibility in their performances. Instead of marveling at Romeo's sonneteering or Oberon's purple passage work, we laugh at Autolycus and ache with Ariel. Orsino may open *Twelfth Night* with "If music be the food of love, play on," but by the time we get to Cloten's calls for song in *Cymbeline*, we wince at his vulgarity: "I am advised to give her music a-mornings, they say it will penetrate."

And yet, what follows Cloten's call is one of Shakespeare's

most exquisite songs. "Hark, hark, the lark at heaven's gate sings," is verse, as *Cymbeline*'s recent editor, Roger Warren, has claimed, full of "beauty and value."[14] Does Cloten get it? Do we? At moments such as this one—and these are, for me, the defining moments of the late plays—characters and audiences are torn, frustrated, unfulfilled. What interests me most in these plays is not when things go right but when they go wrong: when artifice fails, metamorphosis dissipates, and drama will not suffice. Lyric utterances should invite consolation, revelation, and connection. But more often than not, they don't.

I am concerned, then, with these tensions between feeling and control, growing out of the changing social roles of myth and music in the early seventeenth century. The works I study here rework the tales of Ovid's *Metamorphoses* to interrogate relationships of literature, the human body, and the body politic. His characters reveal the skill of art to transmute nature and the self. These are the metamorphic figures of the work, not simply men and women changed to birds or trees or flowers, but artists of the imagination. Orpheus is but the most famous of them all, and, much like many others in the *Metamorphoses* (Midas, Morpheus, Philomela, Proteus, Pygmalion), he illustrates how art transcends the artifices of impersonation. They show how the human body, masked or mutilated, sings and recognizes song for what it is. Ovid's tales narrate how the powerplays of families or factions seek (but do not always find) concord in a lyric clause.

Shakespeare's Ovidianism has long been a subject for the scholar.[15] But it is not a static thing, as if he had read Ovid once and used him in the same ways throughout his career. Later plays rework earlier ones; myths change according to their social context. Take, for example, Shakespeare's dead. Throughout his plays, they appear to come back to life. Juliet rises from her pallet, Falstaff stands up from the battlefield, Bottom surprises his friends by returning whole and hale. And then there are the ghosts: Caesar, old Hamlet, Banquo. But something changes as the career arcs. Cleopatra dies, only to lament how she will return, later, on a stage of boys and comedians. Innogen, disguised as the boy page Fidele, will come back to life in *Cymbeline*; yet Cloten, headless, will not rise again. Children gone for years will reappear, a statue will come alive, and men thought drowned will show up on the shore, all dry and clean as if nothing had happened. Progressively throughout the plays, it is as if Shakespeare considers almost everybody capable of metamorphosis. Will lovers turn to birds or trees? Will husbands seen in dreams return in waking life? Will exiles come home, crowned anew? Will we all wake up one day and find the dead Queen back upon the throne, as if her passing were a nightmare?

These changes hearken back to Orpheus himself. Not only could he pluck strings and cause the rocks and rivers to attend. He could try to bring back the dead. He went to rescue his lost love, Eurydice. Pluto had challenged him to play, and in that playing he won back her life. And yet, he failed to bring her to the surface, turning back in mistrust of the god and of himself. In the end, he is horribly transformed, ripped apart by the Maenads, his still singing head floating along a river.[16]

Ovid's tales of failed artistry increasingly had an impact on the Shakespeare of the Jacobean years. In the late plays, he returns to those episodes to show the ineffectiveness of art, even when we turn to it in despair. Readers since Coleridge are right: there is something unique about these final works. I argue that this uniqueness comes from their handling of the metamorphic music behind Ovid's work—a new sense that maybe all will not be well, that artistry cannot, ultimately, bring the dead home and that, perhaps, with a Midas on the throne, the lyre will take second place to pipes.

To understand the Orphic on the stage and at the court, I turn to the life and work of John Dowland (1563–1625), the great lutenist of the Elizabethan 1590s, who spent the better part of a decade with the King of Denmark, and then returned to England in 1606, eventually gaining his coveted place as one of James's musicians in 1612.[17] A well-known composer and player, a sought-after teacher, and, in Denmark, a courtly advisor/diplomat, Dowland, in the recent formulation of the scholar Michael Gale, had come to be seen as a figure "in the public eye rather than merely as [a] professional musician."[18] His correspondence was collected with that of some of the most prominent men of the age, and (again in Gale's words) he "acutely harnessed the power of print in order to advance his professional status."[19] Dowland was a musical celebrity; and yet, his celebrity status changed as he moved courts and countries. Shakespeare knew his music, and they moved in interlocking social and artistic circles. Both shared in the late Elizabethan fascination with the melancholic humor of the courtly lover. Dowland's repeated songs of loss and sorrow, his plangent tunes, his pungent harmonies and intervals—all have been heard as background music, as it were, to the inwardness of Jacques or the black cloak of Hamlet's seeming.[20]

But there is much more to Dowland's relationship to Shakespeare than a couple of characters or courtly fashion. Dowland not only produced poems set to music but also published books of his songs, prefaced by elaborate and self-conscious writings about art and artistry. He developed a new and textured self-consciousness about performance, authorship, and craft. He pressed old myths into the service of new social critique. He disseminated a cogent set of ideas about the place of the performing self in a changed society.[21] Much had, in fact, changed since he left England, and it took him years upon returning to secure a place at James's court. During that time, he lived among the players and composers in the area around Blackfriars, and their shared presence, as Tiffany Stern has suggested, contributed to the "new fascination with music evinced by the Blackfriars plays."[22]

Dowland was one among many musicians. But he was—based on his reputation and his publications—the most self-conscious and self-mythologizing of those artists. He figured himself, in Kirsten Gibson's words, "a modern descendant of the Orphic genealogy and in so doing claim[ed] for himself and his art classical validity and prestige."[23] And yet, after such vaunted claims, he fell the farthest of them all. He had the most varied and variable of careers. He comes to represent, I argue, the political impotence of artistic craft—as if Orpheus had decided to return, again, to Pluto for a job. True skill is devalued; patrons are not what they appear; clothes do not make the man. By 1612, in what would be his final printed volume, *The Pilgrimes Solace*, Dowland could write that he found "strange entertainment since my returne," and that lutenists are not what they once had been. Quoting an adage Shakespeare himself had used in his plays, Dowland announces that the cowl does not make the monk: *Cucullus non facit Monachum*. What does it mean to dress the part? Do costumes change us? And, if the cowl does not make the monk, what does it say about the robes of office or the crowns of kings?[24]

In the end, Shakespeare's life of performance ended not with a whimper but a bang. The famous story of the playhouse burning down at the start of *Henry VIII* stands not simply as an irony in theater history. It also stands as a moment in the theater we ourselves have scripted for the life of Shakespeare. Whatever the validity of the account, we want to see the cannon roar and costumes burn, as if the end of Shakespeare's career were to be found in a loss no metamorphosis could bring back. The burning of the Globe becomes a moment of high meta-drama, as if to announce to us that all was done and what we find, after this moment, is but a collection of collaborations and half-scripts, with Shakespeare as a sideman to Fletcher or Wilkins.

My first chapter charts these cultural encounters with the changing habits of performance, reading, criticism, and mythology. Behind these encounters lies a theoretical assessment of the key terms of my study: the nature of lyric poetry and performance; the impact of Chaucer and Ovid on the period; the status of music as both something heard and something coming to be seen on printed pages.[25] The last of my preliminary moves explores the place of these late plays in the First Folio. While recognizing the largely contingent quality of that book's selection and arrangement, I argue for an overarching critical coherence to its prefatory matter: that set of editorial addresses and commendatory poems that not only celebrate its author but also guide its reader. These "paratexts" draw on a set of interpretive idioms, mythic images, and authorial ideals that are themselves explored throughout the plays. There may be much about the book that looks back to the years of their performance. But there is much, too, about the moment of its publication. I see in the First Folio a sense of retrospection, compilation, and review. For all the chance and change behind its publication, I make a case for the meaningful place of its late plays—*The Winter's Tale*, *Henry VIII*, and *Cymbeline*—as the final works of their respective generic sections. If there is a quality of "lastness" to these plays, it may be as much a matter of bibliography as biography.

For this reason, primarily, I organize this book by plays and range them in the order of their printing. I want to convey something of a double sense of the late dramas: as works performed as well as read, as texts that survive in a bound book (or, as in the case of *Pericles* and *The Two Noble Kinsmen*, in free-circulating quartos). I am not inattentive to the habits of performance on the Jacobean stage. But I am fascinated by the ways in which those performances and printed texts provoked written responses by contemporaries. Figures such as Simon Forman, Henry Wooton, and the anonymous annotator of a copy of the Folio now in the Mesei University Collection in Japan became my guides to reading. They record, they garble, they interpret. At stake is not their transparent ability as witnesses to words and actions. At stake, for me, is how they shape their witnessing into occasionally creative acts of narrative or figurative rephrasing.

Theirs is a world of trying to make sense of the increasingly complex language of the late plays and of the various performance practices of the time. Theirs is, as well, a world of likes and dislikes, and their criticism has (much like that of their contemporaries) a powerfully affective quality. It is that sense of affect that I wish to find not only among audiences and readers but also within the fictions of the plays themselves. These are dramas of many things, but they are often dramas of interpretation. Taking and mistaking speeches, hearing and judging lyrical performances, watching and recounting actions: these are, in my account, the moments when the plays ask what it means to listen, see, and feel.

The commentaries of Shakespeare's contemporaries say as much about themselves as they do about their subject. So, too, of course, do all critical responses. My book will say much about my own sensibilities. Throughout my research, writing, and teaching, I have focused on the histories of literacy and the making of a reading self. A concern with vernacular self-consciousness runs (as one reviewer once commented) like a red thread throughout my work on early English literature, the history of the language, children's books, and the institutions of scholarship. Much of that work emerged as a dialogue between the historical recovery of literary taste and the personal expression of my own.

Some may find, in that dialogue embedded here, an uneasy synthesis. Rereading what I have written, I see, at times, an essay wrestling against the ropes of a monograph. I cannot but see my own world, as a university professor in the early twenty-first century, in the patronage fortunes of Dowland, the seeming irrationality of Leontes, the intrigues of Wolsey, the appetites of Cloten, and the elegies in *Pericles* and the *Two Noble Kinsmen*. Most men may flatter themselves a Prospero in the classroom. I found myself an Ariel among administrators. What is the place of the aesthetic in the exercise of rule? That question has been one I have asked about the place of the humanities in the modern university curriculum. It is one I asked of donors when I was a dean charged with fund-raising for the arts. It is one we could ask at any moment of our time.

I have tried to write a book of scholarship. It has emerged, perhaps, as an elegy for the imagination, both old and new. As such, it can share in our modern turn that recognizes research as a form of autobiography and that brings to the fore the personal motives for professional choice.

A Note on Texts, Editions, and Critical Traditions

The plays on which I focus all appear in only one early text. *The Tempest*, *The Winter's Tale*, *Henry VIII*, and *Cymbeline* were first printed in the First Folio of 1623. *Pericles* appeared in quarto in 1609, was reprinted six times through 1635, and was later incorporated into the Third and Fourth Folios. *The Two Noble Kinsmen* appeared in quarto in 1634 and was reprinted in the Beaumont and Fletcher folio edition of 1679. In the absence of competing early texts, the modern editor's task should seem straightforward. It has not been so. Editions of the plays first printed in the First Folio have dealt with matters of lineation, of redistributing poetry and prose, of spelling and punctuation, and of stage direction. As I will occasionally discuss, the activities of compositors and scribes (especially Ralph Crane) have compelled modern editors to question what is Shakespeare and what is the work of his transmitters (such questions are especially acute for the plays with extensive stage directions, massed entries, and frequent uses of parentheses and other idiosyncrasies of punctuation). For those plays generally accepted as collaborations—*Henry VIII*, *Pericles*, and *The Two Noble Kinsmen*—editors have often interceded to distinguish Shakespearean and non-Shakespearean sections, to modernize, and to emend.

I began work on the late plays with the exemplary Oxford editions of Stephen Orgel: *The Tempest* (Oxford: Oxford University Press, 1986), and *The Winter's Tale* (Oxford: Oxford University Press, 1996). The Shakespeare that emerges from these editions is one of willful verbal density, of constant concern for the actor's challenge in performance, and of imaginative command of classical and continental source material. The texts that emerge from these editions are ones marked by understatement and contingency. Their place in the First Folio, for Orgel, largely hinges on the chances of transmission and transcription. There is little claim for an intended thematic or political placement of these or of any other plays in the volume. Other editors have been less reticent. Others, too, have been prepared to argue and emend. One of the questions, then, that I will raise throughout this book is how the placement and appearance of the plays in the First Folio has meaning: to early readers, to later scholars, and to us.

For purposes of consistency, I will use these and the other Oxford editions as my basic texts for quotation: Stanley Wells and Gary Taylor, general editors, *William Shakespeare: The Complete Works* (Oxford: Oxford University Press, 1986). Specifically, for the other First Folio late plays, I use *King Henry VIII*, ed. Jay L. Halio (Oxford: Oxford University Press, 1999); and *Cymbeline*, ed. Roger Warren (Oxford: Oxford University Press, 1998). But I have found much to challenge and accept in the New Cambridge Shakespeare editions of *King Henry VIII*, ed. John Margeson (Cambridge: Cambridge University Press, 1990); and *Cymbeline*, ed. Martin Butler (Cambridge: Cambridge University Press, 2005). These editions reflect a set of textual positions different from those of the Oxford ones. They offer fuller historical frameworks, they indulge (at times) in more extensive annotation, and they make a clearer set of distinctions, especially in stage directions, between what is the First Folio's and what is the editors'.

Editions of *Pericles* have either been so aggressively intrusive (the Oxford edition incorporating material from George Wilkins's prose version of the story as part of a "reconstruction" of a putative original) or resignedly hands off (the Cambridge edition going so far as to question collaborative authorship itself, and to restore readings from the quarto) that I have opted to quote directly from the 1609 quarto. Finally, Lois Potter's revised Arden edition of *The Two Noble Kinsmen* incorporates such a wealth of critical material and engages so fully with the editorial issues of the text that I have used it rather than the older Oxford edition of Eugene Waith.

No one can work on John Dowland without the foundational work of Diana Poulton, and I have relied on her scholarship (as well as that of others who have qualified and challenged her research) for my understanding of Dowland as an artist highly self-aware of the relationships of patronage to personal expression. Quotations from the lyrics set to Dowland's music are from David Nadal's editions (with their slightly modernized spelling), *Lute Songs of John Dowland: The Original First and Second Books Including Dowland's Original Lute Tablature* (New York: Dover, 1997) and *John Dowland's Lute Songs: The Third and Fourth Books with Original Tablature* (New York: Dover, 2002).

Throughout this book, I have tried to attend to representative traditions of criticism and scholarship. My notes seek to record my debts to critics whom I follow and to those I do not. In particular, I have been attracted to the lineage of critical approach (or sensibility) that may be traced from Emrys Jones through Jonathan Bate, Colin Burrow, and Raphael Lyne. Such an approach, by and large, seeks an aestheticized engagement with the classical tradition and a recognition of the late plays as returning to and recasting idioms and issues of the early ones. In addition to these critics, I have been moved by Anne Barton's "Leontes and the Spider," an unrivaled anatomy of the making and unmaking of linguistic meaning and personal interiority, not just in *The Winter's Tale* but throughout the late plays. Much recent work on early modern musicality (especially that of David Lindley, Joseph Ortiz, Linda Austern, and Amanda Eubanks Winkler) has directed me away from older, even sentimentalizing, impressions of a Shakespeare songbook to a more social and contingent sense of voice and lyric in the plays. The research of Tiffany Stern on playhouse habit (of both performers and audiences) reveals a fluid world of day-to-day production in Shakespeare's time. Finally, the increasing body of scholarship on Shakespearean lexicography speaks to my own training in historical linguistics. The work of Simon Palfrey and of David Crystal (very different in approach and purpose though they are) pushes me to see, in individual word histories and usages, a drama of making meaning in a culture that, as Stephen Orgel has averred, often valued a "poetics of incomprehensibility" in its rhetorical brio.

Quotations from the First Folio are from the facsimiles available online at internetshakespeare.uvic.ca.

Quotations from Arthur Golding's English translation of Ovid's *Metamorphoses* are from the 1567 printing (London: W. Seres), available online at http://www.perseus.tufts.edu/hopper/text?doc=Perseus%3Atext%3A1999.02.0074.

I abbreviate references as follows:

OED: *The Oxford English Dictionary*, revised third edition, available online at www.oed.com.

PMLA: *Publications of the Modern Language Association of America.*

SQ: *Shakespeare Quarterly.*

Concordance: Concordance of Shakespeare's Complete Works, available online at http://www.opensourceshakespeare.org/concordance/.

1

Myth, Music, and Lyric

Even though the word "lyric" appears nowhere in Shakespeare's verse or drama, it is clear that by the close of the sixteenth century his own and his contemporaries' writings were responding to an idea of lyric poetry as something classical in resonance, musical in origin, and emotively moving in effect. The word comes from "lyre," the instrument of Orpheus and Apollo long associated with celebratory poetry of heightened diction or distinctive verbal craft. With the increasing availability of Greek and Latin literature, the absorption of Aristotle, the renewed attention to Horace, and the commerce in critical theory with Europe, the word "lyric" entered the English language in the 1580s in the wake of a self-conscious classicizing of its heritage. George Puttenham, in his *Arte of English Poetry* of 1589, looked back on "Lirique Poets" of antiquity: Pindar, Anacreon, and Callimachus in Greek, and Horace and Catullus in Latin. These were the poets of "pleasure," the "melodious poets," whose writings were often accompanied by musical instruments.[1]

But intended musical performance did not necessarily stand behind every poem called a lyric. What came to matter more and more to readers of the later sixteenth century were genealogies of poetry in which the idea of the lyric participated in a history of literary ennoblement. Sir Philip Sidney, in his *Defence of Poesy* of 1583, had said as much, scripting an inheritance of vernacular verse from Chaucer through Surrey to Spenser keyed to excellence, nobility, and beauty. The Earl of Surrey's "lyrics," he writes, have "many things tasting of a noble birth, and worthy of a noble mind." Lyric poetry may reflect a higher power or a higher birth, but in addition it makes something better of its reader. Poetry enhances us, and there is something that anticipates, in these remarks, what critics of a later century would see as the sublime: the raising up of emotion and sensibility. William Webbe caught some of this notion in his *Discourse of English Poetry* of 1586. Working from Horace's *Ars Poetica*, Webb averred that "Sometime the lyric riseth aloft," and it is clear that, by the early seventeenth century, to call a poet "lyric" was to praise not just skill or form, but heritage and effect. The term increasingly became associated with such modifiers as "delicate" and "sweet," with certain poets coming to epitomize its form and function.

But at the heart of lyric form and function are not only legacies of classical performers or the class-shaped codes of courtly conduct, but also the dramas of impersonation. Lyrics may be performances, but they sustain—both often in their content and in their culture—a fiction of performance. The rhetorical trope of prosopopoea centered on "creating a character and performing another's voice."[2] Puttenham rephrased it as "Counterfait in personation," and a species of fiction-making.[3] Lyric performance is, itself, a kind of impersonation, and at the heart of that word lies *persona*, the Latin term for the actor's mask. To speak in verse, whether on the stage or in the bedroom, was to take on a sense of "person," to assume a character. That lovely moment in *Midsummer Night's Dream*, when Peter Quince misspeaks his stage direction—"he comes to disfigure, or to present, the person of Moonshine" (3.1.55–56)—brilliantly exposes the frisson of speaking in another's voice. For every impersonation is not just a figuration but a *dis*-figuration, a making wrong, a counterfeiting in "personation." To write a poem is, in some sense, always to disfigure oneself: to personate, to put a mask before the speaking face. This imagery, so central to early modern poetics, has been revived by the twenty-first-century critic David Orr. Lyric poems, he avers, "don't have characters, they are characters—and characters with an oddly doubled aspect. We hear the voice of the poem, but we also understand that we're hearing a filtered version of the poet's own voice. . . . The poet isn't so much taking on a character as donning a mask."[4]

This question of donning a mask, the question of how dramatic a lyric poem may be, lies at the heart of both our own critical assessments of the genre and the early modern practices of poets and editors. Jonathan Culler has summarized a broad inheritance of critical approaches, noting that for all of their apparent voice and drama, lyric poems do not "offer representations of speeches by fictional characters but memorable writing to be received, reactivated, and repeated by readers."[5] In this formulation, he is not that far from Helen Vendler's notion of this kind of poetry "voicable by anyone reading it." With each of those readings, a given lyric may take on a different social purpose, and it is this quality of lyric poetry that made it possible for early editors, anthologists, and publishers to bring together pre-existing texts into new frames of meaning and occasion.

Such anthologizing of short poetry had been practiced from antiquity onward, and much of our surviving classical and medieval vernacular verse comes to us already contextualized in compilations. The idea of the anthology controls much of early English notions of the literary.[6] Not only were short poems brought together into compilations; longer poems were themselves often read as anthologies of a sort, capable of being broken up and rearranged for individual needs (such were the practices with Chaucer's, Gower's, and Lydgate's long poems well into the sixteenth century). Even with the advent of print, the anthologistic impulse controlled much of literature's dissemination, marketing, and critical reception. Often, when individual copies of major, authored poems were produced, readers would bind them together into personal collections (*Sammelbände*, in the term used by bibliographers), creating clusters of books, each of which came to voice a social purpose or a historical narrative. Texts have their meaning in the codex or the compilation. They are, to some degree, already voiced, already playing roles in assemblies of love, devotion, praise, plea, and desire.[7]

This sense of lyric poems stripped of character or voice ignores the ways in which these works come down to us. What histories of editing and compilation do is constantly refigure these ways, creating in effect not brand-new characters, but layers or echoes of voice and reference. To read selections, say, from Chaucer in a medieval manuscript is to read poems cobbled out of or extracted from earlier works. They are old texts put to new purposes. Their history echoes behind them.

Sixteenth-century anthologists and printers exploited these echoes. The compilers of the Devonshire Manuscript of verse in the 1530s, for example, selected stanzas out of pre-existing poems (Chaucer's *Troilus and Criseyde*, most prominently) and made them into new assemblies of amorous conversation.[8] In the mid-1550s, Richard Tottel brought together poems from the age of Henry VIII—most famously those of Wyatt and Surrey—to make courtly verse available to a new generation and a new class.[9] The readers of his *Songes and Sonnetts* (now known as *Tottel's Miscellany*) experienced the verse of an earlier generation in a new way: in print, in regularized spelling and meter, and in a particular order keyed to authorship. Whatever the original environments of these poems may have been, in Tottel's book they exist for what he called the "profit and pleasure" of his readership. Each poem has a title now descriptive of a social, biographical, or historical occasion: "The louer comforteth himself with the worthiness of his love"; "Complaint of a dying louer refused upon his laidies uniust mistaking of his writing"; "Of the louers unquiet state." These titles do to lyrics precisely what Vendler says we should not do to them. They create a "social fiction" or a "biographical revelation" for each poem, and in the process they make this book a record of historical performances. The poems of the volume leave the worlds of court and courtesy and enter the marketplace of books and buyers.[10] They come together in new ways, and we may read their sequence, along with bibliographer Paul Marquis, as tracing, now, "the plight of the persona from the private world of courtly love to the public world of politics and religion."[11]

Tottel's volume had an immense impact on the social and aesthetic sensibilities of readers and writers for the half century since its first edition appeared in 1557. It shaped a taste for commercially produced, printed anthologies of verse that similarly gave a social fiction to aesthetic artifacts. One of the most popular of such publications was *The Passionate Pilgrim* of 1599: a collection of songs, sonnets, ballads, and brief narratives put together by William Jaggard, with William Shakespeare prominently displayed as the author on its title page.[12] Even though only five of this volume's eighteen poems are unquestionably by Shakespeare (two sonnets and three excerpts from *Love's Labour's Lost*), the entire book has a "Shakespearean" feel to it: what Colin Burrow describes as a quality that gives its readers "just enough to enable them to believe they are by Shakespeare if they really want to."[13]

The commercial and aesthetic contexts for *The Passionate Pilgrim* remain transparent: the cultural commodity of Shakespeare's name, the print shop opportunities for bringing out popular verse, the broader climate of poetic identity in the late Elizabethan years. But this book also represents the problem of what I call the displaced lyric. Jaggard's volume, in its printing and reprintings, takes previously circulating poems, removes them from their earlier narrative or dramatic contexts, and creates new sequences for the reader. As I have noted, this action in itself is nothing new. What is different about Jaggard's volume is that it juxtaposes lyrical and dramatic excerpts into new sequences of narrative impersonation. Open the volume and find what we now would recognize as a version of Shakespeare's Sonnet 138, "When my love swears that she is made of truth." Then we will find a version of Sonnet 144, "Two loves I have, of comfort and despair." But then we find Longueville's sonnet to Maria from *Love's Labour's Lost*, "Did not the heavenly rhetoric of thine eye," and all is different. Today, we read these first gestures for the fact that they are Shakespeare's. And yet, for the early reader, before the Sonnets had been published, just in the wake of *Love's Labour's Lost* printing in 1598, these moves create a sense that we are reading something more akin to narrative than excerpt—that the voices of the Sonnets and the play have been displaced, removed, and reimpersonated into something else. To paraphrase Peter Quince, they come disfigured, to present the person of the "Passionate Pilgrim."

Throughout this volume, Shakespeare's texts interact with others to contribute to a broader sense of what a lyric sensibility had come to be by the end of the sixteenth century. At stake is not just Shakespeare's impact on potential sales, or our modern judgments of his verse against that of the largely anonymous compeers in the volume. At stake is that this is a book that makes an argument about what lyric is: about its impact on the reader or the listener, about the place of music in poetic performance, and about the idea of authorship itself. *The Passionate Pilgrim* does not just simply collect texts. It dramatizes them. It takes performances by literary characters and dramatic personae and presents them, anew, as fresh scripts for presentation. The heart of the volume is a set of counterfeits, a series of imagined acts of performing another's voice.

It is precisely this increasing sense of performing in another's voice that makes the lyric moments within plays so acutely difficult and challenging. By the early 1600s, Shakespeare himself had begun dramatizing its effects. Lyric moments in *Romeo and Juliet*, or *Midsummer Night's Dream*, or *Twelfth Night*, or *Love's Labour's Lost*, seem straightforward: ordered stanzas of heightened language, addressed in dramas of appeal or praise. But when we come to *Hamlet*, things have changed. Now, poems and letters come to others, stripped of their original voices. Texts are disfigured, some by Hamlet, some by others. *Hamlet* is of course a play of impersonations, and it has long been seen as a watershed for Shakespeare. Nothing seems the same after it. Gender, genre, sentence, and soliloquy all seem irrevocably different. One area that has been little explored, however, is its new relationship of lyric utterance to dramatic action. *Hamlet* is a play of old texts in new voices, of poems and letters intercepted and reread, of songs sung by those unqualified to sing them.[14]

Take, for example, that remarkably complex and layered moment in act 2 when Polonius opens Hamlet's letter to Ophelia and reads and interprets it before the King and Queen. Polonius reads, "To the celestial and my soul's idol, the most beautified Ophelia." Then he interrupts: "That's an ill phrase, a vile phrase, 'beautified' is a vile phrase." And he goes on. He reads the poem Hamlet wrote—to us, a strangely conventional bit of rhyming, full of echoes of old styles, most notably those of the lovers in *Love's Labour's Lost.* "Doubt thou the stars are fire . . ." He reads. But he also impersonates.

Polonius avows, "I will be faithful." His is a protest about not political fidelity to court but textual fidelity to poem. He is faithfully reading what has been written, faithful to this script. Here is the courtier as an actor: the man who, later in act 2, will recall how he had himself played Julius Caesar, the man who sees all forms of politics as performance. "He will not miss this chance to perform," notes Marvin Rosenberg. "Polonius may well try to act Hamlet's letter in the accent and manner of the young man himself. Olivier's old Polonius read the poem like a young lover."[15]

This scene illustrates how lyrics come, increasingly in Shakespeare's later work, to signal generational distance. We hear the lover, not in his own voice, but in that of an old man—an actor, using Hamlet's script now, giving us a taste of how he might have played a lover in his youth. So, too, at the play's close, we hear an old song in another old man's mouth. In act 5, Hamlet shows up at the cemetery, to hear the Gravedigger recall a lyric from his youth.[16]

> In youth when I did love, did love
>   Methought it was very sweet
> To contract—O—the time for—a—my behove,
>   O, methoutht there—a—was nothing—a—meet.

These garbled, halting lines, as generations have known, draw on "The aged lover renounceth love" from Tottel's *Songes and Sonettes*, and the Gravedigger's two subsequent forays into song come from the same poem. Scholars have identified the differences between Shakespeare's version and the text printed in Tottel, and the poem itself (attributed to Lord Thomas Vaux) circulated in at least two other versions in late sixteenth-century collections.[17] But there is more to this association than source-mongering. It dramatizes, once again, the displacement from one to another. Tottel's book, nearly half a century in circulation by the time of *Hamlet*, represents an earlier generation of literary performance: one held up, now, as fodder for tired clowns, rather than for aspirant courtiers. Tottel himself had dug up treasures (as he put it in his preface) hoarded away by others. The Gravedigger unearths the skulls of courtiership. With each verse, we imagine, he throws up another skull, until, of course, he gets to Yorick's. And when Hamlet picks up the skull, reflecting on the passage of time and the loss of youth, he shows us all that time has passed—that the gambols and gibes, the songs and flashes of merriment, are not just buried in the ground with Yorick but past purpose in the present. Taken in all its parts—the shards of Tottel's *Songes and Sonettes*, the reflections on the courtly life, the understanding that a generation has now passed—this episode distances the present world of the play of *Hamlet* from the past world of earlier Tudor performance. The culture of courtly song has now been buried with the courtier's skull, only to be exhumed for sad nostalgia.

Hamlet is a turning point in Shakespeare's lyric theater. After it, there is an increasingly ironic distance in lyrical performance. The Fool's songs in *Lear* ring uneasily in the ear. In *Macbeth*, the Witches' poetry stages itself as a performance for the audiences in the play (indeed, some of that poetry was probably by Middleton, whose songs were later included in the play's text and performances). The quality of lyrical anxiety and self-conscious theatrical distance emerges full force in *Antony and Cleopatra*, as the queen—played at this moment by one of the great boy actors of the company—dies, lamenting that her future will be the province of "scald rhymers," and "quick comedians," with a "squeaking Cleopatra" left to "boy my greatness."

By the time we get to the last clutch of plays, these ironic displacements shape the dramas of exile and return, performance and politics. This is the feature of the plays' emerging sense (to return to Raphael Lyne's formulation) of their own artifice. We watch their characters enter, not comically or parodically as in *Midsummer Night's Dream*, but all too seriously, to disfigure the persona they inhabit. Poems and songs come together in new anthologies of indecision or regret. Ariel's is a songbook of anticipating what it would be like to no longer be someone else's instrument. Autolycus is in the business of selling copies of old tunes to unsuspecting buyers. The rustic brothers in *Cymbeline* wish to sing, but their voices can only crack. And in *Henry VIII*, when Queen Katherine calls forth her wench, she will sing of an Orpheus who had once changed the world; but now, no song can stay the executioner.

Mythic Lyricism

It is that Orphic figure that increasingly controls the songsters and the poets of the late plays. If there is an increasing sense of displacement and impersonation in the early modern anthology, and if Shakespeare himself deployed that sense of displacement in his later dramas, then there is as well an increasing sense of the mythical displacement of these lyric terms. What does it mean to evoke Orpheus in song? How can we look back to an ancient, mythic figure as a model for social performance in an all-too-fallen world? What is the nature of command performance in a hall so strangely resonant of Pluto's Hell?

These questions had been asked throughout the *Metamorphoses*, the collection of mythic tales and histories that constituted a map for the medieval and the early modern literary imagination. At the heart of Ovid's book of changes is the sense that literature itself works changes on the world. Orpheus's lyre can halt rivers and turn beasts into a willing audience. Stories can make ordinary things seem magical and strange. In the telling of a tale, the dead may come alive. Many parts of the *Metamorphoses* were taken in this critical, self-conscious way. The story, for example, of Tereus and Philomela became a narrative of literary craft itself, stanched by violence but emerging, still, in spite of muteness. The figure of Proteus, the shape-changer, came to be seen as an avatar of art. Pygmalion's skill brings stone to life. Ovid's technique, wrote Jonathan Bate, "is to slide from one story to the next in a process of repetition and variation that embodies the neo-Pythagorean theory of constancy and change."[18]

For Ovid, the power of poetic myth is the power of the myth of poetry. What makes the *Metamorphoses* so compelling for later writers as a source or stimulus is not just its collection of arresting characters. It is precisely the way in which such characters participate in the production and social reception of poetry itself. Nowhere in the *Metamorphoses* is such participation so much a part of the literary drama of the text as book 11. This book, beginning with the death and dismemberment of Orpheus, its segue into tales of Midas's avarice and his choice of Pan over Apollo, and its sustained account of Ceyx and Alcyone (the lovers separated, animated, dreamt of, and ultimately united in death as birds)—this book may be taken as an Ovidian *ars poetica*. It offers tales of poetry gone bad, of performers and performances misheard or misjudged, of characters maimed and mutilated, of literary drama pressed into the service not of civic wholeness but of social fracture.

Book 11 begins with song. Its first word is *carmine*, the songs of Orpheus that calmed the beasts and woodlands and that so infuriated the Maenads:

> Carmine dum tali silvas animosque ferarum
> Threicius vates et saxa sequentia ducit . . . (11.1–2)

The women throw their spears and stones at Orpheus, and while his music can deflect them at first, he is overwhelmed by their own clamor of flutes, drums, and howls. Orpheus succumbs to their attack, and they come at him with the very things of earth that he had once subdued: the rocks, the clods of dirt, the branches of the trees. They steal the plowshares of the nearby farmers, kill their oxen, and kill the poet. Now, the things of earth themselves cry out: the birds, the trees, the rivers. The Maenads dismember Orpheus, letting his head and lyre float downstream out to the sea.

This opening stands as a model for the later stories in book 11. The tales of Midas, too, are tales of conflict between art and artifice—between things of nature and of culture and the touch that would transform them into useless gold. So, too, the story of Midas misjudging musical performance, preferring Pan's pipes to Apollo's lyre, results in a transformation of the body—here, the god giving the king a set of ass's ears to match his foolish taste. Subsequent tales similarly adumbrate the ways in which the artistry of word can change the self and the world. Mercury's son Autolycus, for example, will briefly enter as a character who can turn black to white and white to black. His dramatic transformation into the balladeer at the close of Shakespeare's *Winter's Tale* will emerge as one of both literary and social metamorphosis.

The last sections of book 11 are taken up with the stories of King Ceyx and his Queen, Alcyone. Ceyx himself is a tale-teller, offering at first an extended elegy for his brother, Daedalion. Then, he is a seafarer, traveling to the oracle at Delphi on a ship that will be drowned in a great tempest. Alcyone, lost and alone, prays to Juno, who sends her messenger into the Cave of Sleep to rouse Morpheus and have him impersonate Ceyx in a dream to the Queen, offering closure and, ultimately, metamorphosis itself. For with Alcyone dead of grief, the two lovers are ultimately transformed into shorebirds, and their image prompts the book's final story of Aesacus of Troy: lovesick, despondent, throwing himself off a cliff but turned into a diving bird by Tethys, who takes pity on him.

Poetry for book 11 is an embodied thing, something that emerges from and changes irrevocably the human bodies that produce and hear it. Its presiding deity is Morpheus, whose Cave of Sleep becomes a site of the poetic imaginary. Modern scholars have long noticed the "metapoetic" quality of book 11's tales. They center on the nature of literary representation, the power of narrative, and the artistry of impersonation. Philip Hardie summarizes: "in the workings of Morpheus in the Ceyx and Alcyone story we have perhaps the most powerful of all of Ovid's figurations of his own poetic ambition."[19]

Hardie has his medieval and Renaissance precursors. For European artists, the tale came to be read as a story not only of love lost but of imaginative fiction made. Morpheus presided over sleep and dreaming, narrative imagination and the plastic arts. Annibale Caro, a friend of Michelangelo and designer of the Cardinal Allesandro Farnese's great villa, imagined Morpheus at the center of an elaborate pictorial decoration for the villa's bedroom. He instructed the artist: "Morpheus is called by Ovid the artificer and maker of figures; and therefore you will show him in the act of making masks of various appearances, placing some of them at his feet."[20] Morpheus the mask-maker recalls the personae behind lyric performances, and he evokes the arts of acting, too. As Colin Burrow has shown, his scenes have the "richest afterlife" of any in Ovid's poem, with their "energetic defense of the imitative arts," compelling readers to "think of what it is to imitate both living people and past literatures."[21]

For Geoffrey Chaucer, Ovid's tale of Ceyx and Alcyone compelled just that. His first major poem, *The Book of the Duchess*, began with the narrator trying to fall asleep, trying to recover an imaginative space for writing, and he turns to Ovid and to this tale for solace.[22] This tale formed the mythic, if not allegorical, spine for a poem about death's acceptance and the poetry of mourning, and Chaucer told the story of Ceyx lost and returning in a dream as something of a romance of deferred desire. He told it, though, stripped of its metamorphic end. Here, King and Queen do not come back to life as birds, but simply disappear—the poem's narrator breaks off, falling asleep over his book before the final resolution. What we have instead of metamorphosis is moral allegory (a key feature of medieval Ovidian reading)—and yet it is moral allegory newly inflected with feeling and desire. Chaucer's characters, here, call and weep and cry. They enact something of their story, and in his brief telling we may find the seeds of later drama.

Shakespeare knew Chaucer well, especially after the publication of Thomas Speght's editions of 1598 and 1602.[23] *A Midsummer Night's Dream* echoes the *Canterbury Tales* and the *Legend of Good Women*. *Troilus and Cressida* reworks Chaucer's own poem on the pair. *The Tempest* hints of *The Franklin's Tale* magic in Prospero. *The Two Noble Kinsmen* returns to *The Knight's Tale*.

Chaucer's version of Ceyx and Alcyone also haunts Shakespeare as foil for fantasy, and it would haunt Arthur Golding as he expanded the inherent theatricality of this myth into something reaching into tragedy.

Golding's "Englishing" of the *Metamorphoses* was published in complete form in 1567 and reprinted in 1575.[24] His version moved beyond the older, medieval allegorical moralizations to create a set of stories stressing social types and personal motives.[25] Golding's version of Ceyx and Alcyone is of a piece with this new emphasis, presenting Morpheus as an artist, actor, and deceiver:

> . . . the feyner of mannes shape, a craftye lad.
> None other could so conningly expresse mans verrye face,
> His gesture and his sound of voyce, and manner of his pace,
> Togither with his woonted weede, and woonted phrase of talk.
> (11.736–39)

Morpheus's sons, too, dwelling with him in the Cave of Sleep, take on shapes: one mimicking a bird, or beast, or snake; another taking on the illusions of earth, stones, rivers, trees. The scope of all creation that would halt at Orpheus's songs now reappears, here, as impersonations and illusions of a comparable cunning. Morpheus stands as an avatar of acting itself, a god of impersonations. His subsequent appearance as Ceyx is fraught with a performer's anxieties—in Colin Burrow's words, his lines to Alcyone are those "of an uneasy actor who is not quite sure that he lives up to the part he is playing."[26] Such meta-theatrics was not lost on his early modern English audiences. Golding's idioms resonate with the archetypes of artifice, feigning, cunning, craftiness, and false seeming that populated the English drama of the court and commercial theater. In *The Tempest*, Alonso sees Prospero's conjuring through Golding's verbal lens:

> I cannot too much muse
> Such shapes, such gesture, and such sound expressing,
> Although they want the use of tongue, a kind
> Of excellent dumb discourse. (*Tempest*, 3.3.36–39)

Throughout book 11 of the *Metamorphoses*, Shakespeare and his contemporaries would have seen dramatizations of poetic craft and narrative performance. These scenes appear with such force in the last plays that this book emerges as an anchor point for their distinctive drama: Orpheus's dismembered head echoing behind Cloten's decapitation; Midas's bad literary criticism facing the listeners of poetry and song in *Cymbeline*, *The Tempest*, and *The Winter's Tale*; the great storm separating Ceyx and Alcyone inflecting the opening of *The Tempest*; Autolycus showing up, with his Mercurian genealogy, in *The Winter's Tale*; and Orpheus himself the subject of the song performed to soothe the heart of Katherine of Aragon in *Henry VIII*.

In the last works, Orpheus and Midas haunt and Morpheus presides. Heads roll, fools listen. Someone is always sleeping. Someone comes back impersonating someone else. Shapes change in vision or in darkness only to vanish with the sun. Morpheus animates a simulacrum of the dead King Ceyx. How do we bring the dead before the audience? Shakespeare's last plays reach, as it were, into the Cave of Sleep to recall figures from not just a historical but also a Shakespearean past: echoes of earlier plays and poems, evocations of the tastes of his youth, or characters that his contemporaries would have barely, but just barely, known.

The tale of Ceyx and Alcyone provided early modern readers with set pieces of reflection on the arts of impersonation. But it, too, had provided dramas of shipwreck and storm that would have resonated with the emerging awareness of just how precarious this new and global world was soon to be. *The Merchant of Venice* hinges on the fears of lost ships, while Sonnet 87—rich with a newly energized vocabulary of investment, debt, and return—imagines the beloved's great gift that "comes home again, on better judgment making": a complex image synthesizing notions of ownership and economic return, as well as seafaring anticipation. Readers have long seen storm and rescue shaping Shakespeare's drama, no more so than in *The Tempest* itself, but few have sought to find the inspiration of that storminess in Ovid. King Ceyx sets off on his voyage and, in Chaucer's phrasing,

What that he
Was in the see thus in this wise,
Such a tempest gan to rise
That brak her mast and made it falle,
And cleft her ship, and dreinte hem all,
That never was founde, as it telles,
Bord ne man, ne nothing elles. (*Book of the Duchess*, 68–74)[27]

Golding's version develops this scene to give a new and distinctively dramatic cast to the scene, complete with theater-like oratory:

Anon the Mayster cryed: Strike the toppesayle, let the mayne
Sheate flye and fardle it to the yard. Thus spake he, but in vayne,
For why so hideous was the storme uppon the soodeine brayd,
That not a man was able there to heere what other sayd.
And lowd the sea with meeting waves extreemely raging rores.
(11.557–610)

The storm's roar contests with the noise of "crying men and boyes," and for nearly a hundred lines of Golding's verse, the ship flails against the sea. The men yell, cry, and pray, and we can hear the very tumult of their terror:

All arte and conning was to seeke. Theyr harts and stomacks fayle:
And looke, how many surges came theyr vessell to assayle,
So many deathes did seeme to charge and breake uppon them all.
One weepes: another stands amazde: the third them blist
dooth call
Whom buryall dooth remayne. To God another makes his vow,
And holding up his handes to heaven the which hee sees not now,
Dooth pray in vayne for help. (11.619–25)

Finally, the sea breaks the ship, the men are lost, and Ceyx himself, drowning in the darkness, lifts his voice one last time to praise his queen:

. . . But cheefly in his mouth his wife Alcyone was.
In hart was shee: in toong was shee: he wisshed that his corse
To land where shee myght take it up the surges myght enforce:

And that by her most loving handes he might be layd in grave.
In swimming still (as often as the surges leave him gave
To ope his lippes) he harped still upon Alcyones name,
And when he drowned in the waves he muttred still the same.
(11.653–59)

Here, Golding brilliantly transforms the drowning king into a kind of Orpheus, his mouth and lips still moving, harping on Alcyone's name. It is that verb, "harp," that transforms the sinking king into the poet, a verb unique to this English version that creates, in metaphor, a transformation all its own.[28]

It is precisely this distinctive phrasing that links Ceyx's story with the tales of Orpheus and Midas earlier in book 11, and it is precisely Golding's powerfully evocative verse that makes this scene not just one of violent seas and drowning men but one of human speech. Ceyx, in death, already finds himself transformed, harping and muttering, sinking down, while Morpheus soon will rouse himself to move up from the realm of sleep to speak Alcyone's name.

. . . In shewing of this shipwrecke Morphye so
Did feyne the voyce of Ceyx . . . (11.773–74)

Golding's translation enables a reading of the tale of Ceyx and Alcyone as one of speech and drama, with the theater of impersonation and the theatrical effects of the storm already embedded in the story.

With all these voices and effects, Shakespeare's *Tempest* opens as if in the middle of this myth, with calls of the men, the crying of the master, and the commands of the Boatswain:

Down with the topmast! Yare! Lower, lower! (1.1.34)

Like Ceyx's shipmates, these men cry and pray, and just as they will think of their beloveds and their relatives (one thinks of his "brother and his parents," and calls to mind his "house and wife"), so too the men of *The Tempest* cry: "Farewell, my wife and children! Farewell, brother" (1.1.60–61).

Of course, we know that all has not been lost, and that Prospero, through his Ariel, staged the storm and saved the men. Now, it is Ariel who "flamed amazement" instead of the hostile sea that has the lightning "set the waves on fyre" and give "lyght within the ship." Ceyx's shipmates stand "amazed" in Golding's Ovid; in Shakespeare, amazement is something put on by the magus and his servant:

> Be collected.
> No more amazement. Tell your piteous heart
> There's no harm done. (1.2.14–16)

The Tempest opens, then, by setting out the stage of Ovid's storm, and it transforms the tragic loss of king and husband into a domestic restitution. None are drowned, the ship is safe. Even their clothes are dry.

Ovid's story moves across these realms to show the power of poetic evocation, with Golding's translation acutely bringing out the theater of these episodes: the drama of the storm and shipwreck, the rhetoric of dying men, and then the impersonations of Morpheus himself, stage creature, feigning voice and face.

> None other could so conningly expresse mans verrye face,
> His gesture and his sound of voyce, and manner of his pace,
> Togither with his woonted weede, and woonted phrase of talk.
> (11.737–39)

Morpheus performs, but these moments in the *Metamorphoses* are not just about performing but about commissioning performance: Juno commands her Iris, Iris pleads with Sleep, and Sleep sends Morpheus. Throughout these scenes the idea of performance is inseparably linked to the idea of commission, patronage, command.

That, too, is what Shakespeare learned from Ovid: the sense that every voice has been commanded, that artists and their audiences place both their imaginations and their bodies on the line, that what we see not only in our dreams but in our days may well be only feigned appearances. Shakespeare's mythic lyricism exploits the tension between the creative artist and patron, between the musician's ability to move the listener and that listener's own resistance to that power.

And while his last plays hearken back to Chaucer and to Golding, they increasingly frame those echoes in a new politics of Ovidian lyricism. Orpheus would have had a new place in a court, with James himself as something of a musical monarch, bringing concord to his realm:

> Behold, how like another Orpheus, Amphion, and Arion, he draweth to the true knowledge of God, very salvage Beasts, Forrests, Trees, and Stones, by the sweet Harmony of the Harp; the most fierce and wilde, the most stupid and insensed, the most brutish and voluptuous, are changed and civilized by the delectable sound of his Musick. The which may transport and ravish our eares . . .

This praise, from George Marcelline's *Triumphs of King James the First of 1610*, distills the language of power and ravishment into an aesthetics of rule. It makes the figure of the lyricist political, and Orpheus's taming of the wild emerges as a new way of imagining James himself, taming the "brutish" of his kingdom.[29]

Such a taming would have been a local and a colonial project, and in his *Minerva Brittania* of 1612, Henry Peacham images England's conquest of Ireland as an Orphic one. The lyre plants itself on Irish soil (in a framed emblem on the page), and Peacham writes:

> Now since I breathed by thy Roiall hand,
> And found my concord by so smooth a tuch,
> I give the world abroade to understand,
> Ne're was the musck of old Orpheus such,
> As that I make, by meane (Deare Lord) of thee,
> From discord drawne, to sweetest unitie.

As Joseph Ortiz has argued, the poetic speaker is Ireland herself, and the musical imagery becomes not an old medieval morality, but a new "allegorization of royal power." New concord comes, here, not as the poet stills beasts and rivers. It comes through kingship. The smooth touch—a repeated term of praise throughout Elizabethan writings on performance—changes now, as the

Royal hand does not so much pluck strings as sit upon the land. "James orders the musical state," Ortiz writes, "in a way that resembles musical consonance," and when we look at artists who, themselves, were famous for their touch and concord, we can see how the old verities of sweetness fail, and new concords of power fill the air.[30]

John Dowland, Orpheus, and Ravishment

No musician of Shakespeare's time was more renowned for his touch and tone than John Dowland. The arc of his brilliant, challenging career traces the shifting fashions among poetry and song in early modern England. But it also charts the shifting sense of Orpheus and the Ovidian myths behind him. He provides a backdrop for the later Shakespearean sense of artistry and patronage, performance and preferment.[31]

Dowland was born in 1563, and by his early thirties he was famous for his skill and sensibility. Thomas Campion provided the opening Latin poem for the *First Book of Songes and Ayres*, published in 1597: "Famam, posteritas quam dedit Orpheu / Dolandi melius Musica dat sibi" ("The renown which posterity gave to Orpheus, / The music of Dowland better gives to herself"). And in the preface to the volume, Dowland placed himself as heir to "Linus, Orpheus, and the rest."[32] This Orphic Dowland certainly contributes to the rising status of the musician in print, and it dovetails with a range of panegyrics that were emerging to privilege this lutenist not just as maker or performer, but as author of his own persona.

Two years before that publication, Dowland served as subject of extended praise by Campion. In his 1595 *Poemata*, Campion reflected on Dowland's absence from England (perhaps due to royal prejudice against his recusant Catholicism, perhaps due to courtly cost-cutting, perhaps due to his own desire to widen his musical horizons), and he recalled his prowess:[33]

Ad Io. Dolandum.
O qui sonora coelites altos cheli
Mulces, et umbras incolas astrae Stygis,

Quam suave murmur? Quale fluctu prominens,
Lygia madentes rore dum siccat comas,
Quam suave murmur flaccidas aures ferit,
Dum lenis oculos leviter invadit sopor?
Ut falce rosa dissecta purpureum caput
Dimittit, undique foliis spargens humum,
Labuntur hei sic debiles somno tori,
Terramque feriunt membra ponderibus suis.
Dolande misero surripis mentem mihi,
Excorsque cordae pectus impulsae premunt.
Quis tibi deorum tam potenti numine
Digitos trementes dirigit is inter deos
Magnos oportet principem obtineat locum.
Tu solus offers rebus antiquis fidem,
Nec mirror Orpheus confidens Rhodope super
Siquando rupes flexit et agrestes feras.
At O beate siste divinas manus,
Iam iam parumper siste divinas manus,
Liquescit anima, quam cave exugas mihi.

To John Dowland

O you who on the sonorous chelys charms those in high heaven
And the shades of gloomy Styx,
How sweet is your murmur? When emerging from the waves
Lygia began to dry her wet hair,
How sweet the murmur when her notes strike our fainting ears
And when quiet sleep steals over our eyes?
As the rose cut by the knife drops its purple head,
Shedding its petals on the ground,
Even so, alas, my weakening muscles fail
And my limbs fall of their own weight.
O Dowland, unawares you steal my poor mind,
The strings you pluck overwhelm my breast.
The god who with such divine power directs your trembling fingers
He should hold the highest place among the great gods.
You alone have the power to restore faith in antiquity.
I do not wonder that bold Orpheus could move the rocks
And wild creatures on Rhodope.
But O, you blessed one, stay your divine hand,

Now, now for a moment stay your divine hand.
My soul liquefies, do not draw it from me yet.

From the beginning, we are in the world of classical mythology. The instrument on which he plays here is not a lyre or a lute but a *chelys*, a rare word from Greek originally meaning the shell of a tortoise and, by extension, the rounded shape of a lyre or a harp.[34] Hermes, the legend went, had found, on the banks of the Nile, a tortoiseshell strung with the tendons of the desiccating animal, and the wind blowing through them made a rapturous sound. The music of that instrument charms both the heavens and the underworld, its sound a sweet murmur. That word, *murmur*, takes us back to the strains of Orpheus in Ovid, and again the sweet murmur appears to put us all to sleep. Listening to this magical music, the poet's limbs fail, and he swoons. Dowland appears to steal away the mind, to ravish away consciousness, and as the Latin poet seems to fall asleep, he avows that not even Orpheus himself could have such power to move rocks and beasts. *Liquescit anima*, my soul liquefies, and as if it were some liquor newly brewed, the poet asks that Dowland stay his hand and not yet tap it from the body.

This is a powerfully metamorphic moment. Campion's verb is not simply "charm," as we would render it in English, but *mulces*, from *mulceo*, meaning to stroke or lightly touch, soothe, caress, flatter, and by implication, then, to charm.[35] It is a word of palpable physicality, a word that calls attention to the fingers of the lutenist, bringing his instrument to sweetness through his touch. Behind that verb lie buried resonances of sweet fluids, honey in particular, a drink as soothing as a soft touch. Such sweetness turns us all to liquid, and Campion's poem brilliantly develops these associations, giving us a sense of Dowland's music as transforming us to water.

There is myth, but there is also sex. The image of the drooping rose and its splayed petals is as much an image of deflowerment as of rapture. The raining down of golden liquid onto human bodies resonates with the familiar mythological image of Zeus taking the form of golden rain to impregnate Danae. *Liquescet anima*—the liquid imagery, the sense of stroking hands, the loss of physical control, all point to something of a moving detumescence of desire at the end of Dowland's playing.

Stories of ravishment are stories that always return to myths of sex and power. Behind each nightingale's sweet song is the story of Philomela attacked and mutilated by Tereus. Behind the music of Orpheus is the memory of his last hours, ripped to shreds by the Maenads, his disembodied head still singing, floating down the river to the sea. Behind the changing of the seasons is the tale of Proserpina stolen off by Pluto. Think, now, of that episode in book 5 of Ovid's *Metamorphoses* when Cyane, in grief over the "ravishment of Proserpine" (Golding's phrase), cries herself into water, dissolving in her own tears: *primaque de tota tenuissima quaeque liquescunt.*

> For these same slender parts
> Doe quickly into water turne, and afterward converts
> To water, shoulder, back, brest, side: . . . (5.538–40)

Campion's language is the language of ravishment and the language of metamorphosis. Indeed, here, they may be two sides of the same coin, as both signal the transformation of the self through grief, desire, or submission. In the Cyane episode in the *Metamorphoses*, ravishment and metamorphoses are similarly paired.

So, too, are they in late Shakespeare. Those plays walk a fine line between the aesthetic and sexualized sense of ravishment. Art, Jonathan Bate has noted, is something we turn to when all else is lost. But this is more than sentiment. It is the sense that in a world of Jacobean kingship, in a world where the ruler was spectator and always object of spectatorship, in a world in which, by the year of Shakespeare's last dramatic endeavors, a royal son was newly dead, a daughter had been married off to someone far away, and the king himself had increasingly retreated into solitude and inarticulateness—in that world, art is something that can restore, in memory or myth, a sense of what things used to be like. It lives in a privileged space not simply of nostalgia but of a productive memory, when the past could come back, however fleetingly, in costume or in song in staged fictions.

There is, of course, a history to such ravishment—a history going back to Thomas More's imagination of *Utopia*, where music (in the phrasing of the book's first English translator, Ralph Robinson) "tickleth and moveth oure senses," and where its sounds could "wonderfully moue, stire, pearce and enflame the hearers myndes." That history developed, throughout the sixteenth century, into the idea that music somehow compelled the listener into states of feeling.[36] By Dowland's time, such an idea had been honed into a fine instrument of criticism, as well as performance.

The Passionate Pilgrim reprints a sonnet by Richard Barnfield that relies on this idea of ravishment and rapture to praise Dowland's accomplishment. His sonnet begins, "If music and sweet poetry agree," and the finest example he can find of such agreement is Dowland himself. Echoing Campion's Latin phrasings, Barnfield writes:

> Dowland to thee is dear, whose heavenly touch
> Upon the lute doth ravish human sense.[37]

In his praise of Edmund Spenser that follows these lines, Barnfield announces that this poet, like he himself, "lov'st to hear the sweet melodious sound / That Phoebus' lute, the queen of music, makes." Much like Campion, liquefied in rapture, Barnfield, too, finds his watery response to music:

> And I in deep delight am chiefly drowned
> When as himself to singing he betakes.

It is this powerful association among ravishment and drowning, sleep and water, that sustains the mythic axes along which Dowland would play and be received. Throughout his lyrics, Dowland associates the sleep of sweet unreason with a tearful, watery end.

> Come, heavy Sleep the image of true Death:
> And close up these my weary weeping eyes:
> Whose spring of tears doth stop my vitall breath.[38]

Sleep comes in this lyric as the "image" of death—its apparition, its *imago*. The call is to a personified deity, the Sleep of Ovid's realm of Morpheus, and like that metamorphic god, sleep takes on a persona or an image. This sleep should stanch the crying poet, but the poet is not simply weeping. He lives in a world where breath has become water. Dowland's persona lives in tears. "Hope oft doth hang the head, and Trust shed teares," he laments at one point (*First Booke*, 3), and further in that poem he notes that his beloved's doubt and distrust would mask her eyes with "clouds," and make the heavens dark, "Or with thy tears dissolve them into rain." "Burst, burst forth my tears," begins another lyric (*First Booke*, 8). "Go christall eares, like to the morning showers," starts another, before circling back to sleep:

> So let your drops of pittie be addres'd
> To quicken up the thoughts of my desert,
> Which sleeps to sound whilst I from her depart. (*First Booke*, 9)

To read through Dowland's lyrics, or to listen to their settings, is to watch the poet liquefied into distress, crying himself like Ovid's Cyane into water. That tearfulness, of course, reaches its apotheosis in his most famous of compositions, *Lachrimae*, a pavan originally for his lute but, throughout the late Elizabethan and Jacobean periods, transformed by other musicians into arrangements that would come to crystallize that melancholy of the age. His musical motif—the four descending notes in the minor—became one of the most famous melodic tropes of the age. The motif was as common and as meaningful as any of the many rhetorical tropes of verbal trickery, and Dowland's contemporaries recognized it as such. Such devices create the effect of heightened emotion, and the Lachrimae motif supported words both secular and sacred. Dowland's own publication of 1604, *Lachrimae, or Seaven Teares Figured in Seaven Passionate Pavans*, made the music available not only as performance pieces but as a cultural artifact.[39]

By the second decade of the seventeenth century, *Lachrimae* was everywhere. It had become such a familiar bit of music that dramatists and poets (ranging from Beaumont and Fletcher to

Thomas Overbury) alluded to it, cited it, and even parodied it in their writings.[40] Well into the 1630s, a reference to *Lacrimae* would signal heightened artistry, or emotional release. Much like the Orpheus of his imagination, Dowland himself could change the world. "Come thou and charme these rebels in my brest," he invites sleep, as if somnolence could, much like Orpheus, charm all discord away (*First Booke*, 20). In "Flow my tears," the lyric set to the *Lacrimae* tune, the singer mourns "exiled for ever," where "night's black bird her sad infamy sings." The singer welcomes the "shadowes that in darkness dwell." His voice is now reduced to "tears and sighes and groans" (*Second Booke*, 2).

Such lines locate the singer in an Orphic Hell, and part of the price for playing Orpheus is precisely this sense of grim entrapment. But by the end of the first Jacobean decade, things have changed. Poetizing of this sort had grown stale—in Steven May's words, "as out of fashion as the codpiece."[41] Even Dowland recognized the difference. His later publications increasingly reveal a sense of how impotent his arts of metamorphic music had become. Just weeks before Elizabeth's death, Dowland published what he called *The Third and Last Booke of Songes*. It opens with this dazzling, self-mythologizing "Epistle to the Reader."

> The applause of them that iudge, is the incouragment of those that write: My first two books of aires speed so well that they haue produced a third, which they have fetcht far from home, and brought euen through the most perilous seas, where hauing escapt so many sharpe rocks, I hope they shall not be wrackt on land by curious and biting censures. As in a hiue of bees al labour alike to lay vp honny opposing them selves against none but fruitless drones; so in the house of learning and fame, all good indeuourers should striue to ad somewhat that is good, not malicing one an other, but altogether bandying against the idle and malicious ignorant. My labours for my part I freely offer to euerie mans iudgement, presuming, that favour once attayned, is more easily encreased then lost.[42]

It is a brilliant performance. Almost Baconian in its aphoristic opening, the Epistle immediately associates production with applause. The fortunes of his first two books, like Dowland's fortunes themselves, express themselves through the romance tropes of sea voyage, as if the story of Ceyx and Alcyone had shaped a life lived through the perils of sharp rocks. Orpheus himself had not escaped such terrors, for his own head floated down the river to the sea before wrecking on land and being attacked by a snake—a figure of curious and biting censure if ever there was one. Finally, reaching back to one of the oldest cultural similes in the West—the industry of bees—Dowland sees life among the learned and famous as a life of shared striving. The idle and malicious ignorant will find their own likes and dislikes. Offering himself to every man's judgment, Dowland presents his book of music much like a classical figure might offer up his artistry for a demanding judge: whether it be the gods of the underworld for Orpheus or Apollo before Midas.

Dowland's Epistle bubbles with these tropes, allusions, echoes, and imaginations. A decade later, however, they have settled to a simmer, as he reflects on years of wandering and lack of success. The opening Epistle to the reader of his *Pilgrimes Solace* from 1612 notes how he has, himself, "lien long obscured from your sight," performing "kingly entertainment in a forreigne climate." He has, though, "held up my head within this Horizon," and has received fame throughout the "most famous Cities beyond the Seas." He goes on, noting that performance practices in England have declined. "Divers strangers from beyond the seas" have come into the kingdom. But little do they realize that "skill lyeth not in their fingers ends." Music is about more than mere technique, and in the publishing of this new book, Dowland presents a collection of songs designed not only to delight and please, but to instruct the player and the listener in critical and aesthetic judgment.

Much like a character out of romance, Dowland scripts out a plotline of performance, reception, and value that hews to the tropes of an Ovidian poetics and that makes art's life into a sea voyage of both praise and peril. It is as if Orpheus were to announce: I have returned from darkness, entertaining a king in the most foreign of climes. Much good it would have done him.

And so Dowland must aver that, unlike the dismembered old musician, he can still hold his head up. Seas are not media of pain and loss, but of fame. And yet, still, he has come home to a court whose tastes have changed, whose lutenists think skill lies only in their fingertips and not in souls.

Dowland was not alone in feeling something changed. Henry Peacham, whose *Minerva Britannia* had, as I mentioned earlier, articulated a new political and social Orpheus for James's empire, considered Dowland as part of this new world.[43] In contrast to the emblem portrait of the Orphic lyre planted securely in Irish soil, Peacham has an image of Philomel, the bird alone, sitting in silence, aging and ignored. The image comes with a dedication to *Ioannes Doulandes*, and read against Dowland's own remarks, they complement the vision of an artist all-too-soon forgotten.

> How few regard thee, whome thou didst delight,
> And farre, and neare, came once to hear thee sing.

Peacham's lines take us to the artist in his winter, and for this old Philomel there is no final metamorphosis. *Annos ludendo hausi* is the epigram to Peacham's stanzas: I used up my years in playing. But Peacham's verb means more than use or squander. From the Latin *haurio*, it means to drain, to drink, to draw, or to deplete by use or by ingestion. The tears behind his songs, the liquefaction of the listening soul, the overarching imagery of sea and sorrow—all of these images return here at the moment when we see the artist drained of patronage or power.

Dowland would return to James's court in 1612. His modern biographer, Diana Poulton, thinks his final years "peaceful enough," and his contemporary, William Webbe—who had defined the lyric as rising aloft in his *Discourse* of 1596—could write a poem in 1624 commending Dowland as one of "our rare Artists." But as far as we can tell, these last years were spent less as a star than as a sideman. He is last recorded as a member of the consort that played for the funeral of James I on May 5, 1625.[44]

Dowland may seem, himself, a metamorphic figure: an artist whose fortunes moved from patronage to penury. He may have seen himself in that way. In 1603, when he dedicated *Lacrimae* to Anne of Denmark, he asked her to vouchsafe her protection to "these showers of Harmony, least if you frown on them, they bee Metamorphosed into true teares."[45] Again, the language of the metamorphic. From Campion's praise of Dowland liquefying souls, to his own praise of Queen Anne's power to transform showers of harmony into true tears, and finally to resignation at the sight and sound of lutentists who can do little more than pluck—along this arc lies, I will argue throughout this book, a vision of the sonic arts to move, if not to ravish. In tune with Shakespeare's fictive performers, Dowland assays relationships between the aesthetic and the social. Poetry and song can change the world; but so can royal patronage. Like so many of Shakespeare's later characters, Dowland moves between worlds of sleep and water, dreams and drowning, tiredness and tears. His listeners share much with those of *The Tempest*, *Cymbeline*, *The Winter's Tale*, and *Henry VIII*. They all will witness lyric spectacles that will release or rescue them. They all will, some successfully, some not, attempt to hold their heads up after lying long obscured from sight.

The First Folio and the Last Plays

So, too, did Shakespeare's editors seek to return him, headfirst, into readers' hands. The publication of the First Folio represents many features of the Jacobean literary world: the work of scribes and copyists, manipulations of the printer, the chances and contingencies of manuscript inheritance and artistic ownership. But what it also represents is a sustaining of the myths of art. To read the prefatory texts before its plays is to return, again and again, to the Ovidian imaginary, to places of metamorphosis, dismemberment, realization, and rebirth. The First Folio is central to a study of the late plays. It remains their only early text. It offers information on the ministrations of the scribe and copyist in shaping something readable out of performance history. It presents them, tantalizingly, in privileged places in the book. But the First Folio offers more than an assembly of plays. It offers a mythopoetics for their understanding.[46]

The First Folio has not lacked for critical and bibliographical analysis. For all its claims to be the work of Shakespeare's mind and hand, the Folio emerged as a profoundly collaborative project. John Heminge and Henry Condell, former members of the King's Men, provided the overarching aegis for the book, collecting texts, arranging rights, and preparing the opening Epistles to its patrons and its readers. William and Isaac Jaggard were the father-and-son printers who prepared the book itself, the former having published *The Passionate Pilgrim* and, with Thomas Pavier, prepared a set of quarto editions of some of the plays in 1619. Edward Blount was the well-educated stationer who entered into the association with the Jaggards to produce the Folio, and it was at his bookshop that the book was offered first for sale in November 1623. Ralph Crane is perhaps, now, the best known and most closely studied of the scribes who prepared texts of the plays. His idiosyncratic spellings, taste for elaborate stage directions, use of parentheses and punctuation to organize Shakespeare's complex syntax, and preference for "massed entries" and lists of characters are clear in at least seven of the First Folio's play texts. Martin Droeshut prepared the famous portrait of the playwright at the opening. Ben Johnson wrote the opening sonnet "To the Reader," as well as the extended panegyric poem after Heminge and Condell's Epistles. Other writers, far less well known now, contributed commendatory verses, while the compositors and inkers and correctors and apprentice "devils" that actually made the books remain, by and large, anonymous to us. And then there are the actors, listed in the prefatory pages, with Shakespeare's own name first, followed by the famous Richard Burbage.

There is, quite simply, so much stuff before we actually get to any of the plays that we may well wonder what the purpose of these prefatory lists, addresses, and encomia might be. Certainly, there was a commercial purpose to the whole thing: this was a book to be sold, a book designed to be attractive to the buyer, trading on the fame of Shakespeare, on the claim that it presented "true originall copies" of the plays, and that it contained all of them. Heminge and Condell enjoin those in doubt to read the author's work: "Reade him, therefore; and againe, and againe." But only if the reader buys the book can it be read: "the fate of all books depends on your capacities, and not of your heads alone, but of your purses." Read Shakespeare, but "whatever you do, buy."[47]

Given the elaborate preparation for the plays themselves, it may come as a surprise to learn just how contingent, unplanned, and messy the book seems. A product of the print shop of the early seventeenth century, the book shares with its contemporaries a production technique in which types might break in mid-print run and in which corrections could be made after previous copies had been printed and sold. Each individual copy may be thought of as a unique artifact. Collating these copies reveals scores of differences, some of them only recently seen as textually and critically significant.

While it is organized into three generic sections, Comedies, Histories, and Tragedies, the order in those sections is hardly consistent. The History plays, for example, range themselves not in the order of Shakespeare's creation but in order of their historical content. They create, in essence, a dramatic history of English kingship, from King John to Henry VIII, rather than a trajectory of Shakespeare's royal imagination from Henry VI onward. The first play in the Folio, and the first of the Comedies, is *The Tempest*. It has been argued that it appears there not because of its place in the trajectory of Shakespeare's works or because of its formal features, but because it simply came to the compilers in excellent textual shape. The appearance of *The Winter's Tale* as the last of the Comedies has been seen as similarly contingent. The text of the play did not arrive until the others had been set in type, and the blank page between the start of this play and the end of *Twelfth Night* shows how it may have been a late edition. *Cymbeline* may be the last of the tragedies because the editors wanted to fill in that section. *Troilus and Criseyde* does not appear in the table of the contents because its text arrived late.[48]

For all its title page's claims for a fidelity to true and original copies, the First Folio is a messy thing. But I believe we draw the line too far into chance. I would not contest arguments about the contingency of the First Folio's compilation.[49] I do contest the belief that this contingency renders any meaningful reading of the plays' order impossible. The book that emerged from the press in 1623 was a material object, and the simple fact that it began with *The Tempest*, or that each of its sections ended with a particular play, could not but have an impact on its *reader*. Emma Smith, in a recent review of the production and early reception of the Folio, notes that, while "sequence . . . carries interpretative consequences in the Folio arrangement of the history plays . . . it is not clear whether the other categories are ordered according to some meaningful pattern." Reading the plays in their printed order might shape, she suggests, a critical response. Even if there was "no purposeful sequence to the plays" in their printing, "the order of the plays might have consequences for readers."[50]

Other reassessments of the Folio, while recognizing the contingencies of its compilation, have nonetheless sought to explain the place of certain plays in its assembly and, more generally, to find a bibliographical and, perhaps, even a critical set of reasons for its ordering.[51] What emerges from these researches is the recognition that each section of the book is bracketed by plays not previously published, or late, or printed from a transcript by Ralph Crane. Thus, the Comedies begin with *The Tempest* and end with *The Winter's Tale* (both of which fit all three of those criteria). The Histories begin with *King John* (new in the Folio, though most likely based on an earlier printed play) and end with *Henry VIII* (both previously unpublished and written late in the career). And the Tragedies begin with *Coriolanus* (unpublished and relatively late) and end with *Cymbeline* (unpublished, late, and printed from a Crane text).

This inquiry does not explain everything. It does not trump the argument that the History plays are arranged chronologically by subject rather than by date of composition. It does not supersede more critical (or even sentimental) arguments about

The Tempest as the first play. It does not undermine the claims that *Cymbeline* has something of a larger political purpose as the final play. What it does enable is a new set of approaches to what A. W. Pollard saw, in 1909, as an "appearance of deliberation" in the Folio's arrangement.[52]

Where do we locate that deliberation? What effect does the *Tempest*'s first appearance have on readers? Is *The Winter's Tale* truly a comedy, and if so, how does it close off its section? *Henry VIII* may complete the historical sequence of the English monarchs, but does it offer any other possibilities? *Cymbeline* is the last of the Tragedies, and the final play in the volume. Can there be anything more than speculation to the view of, for example, Leah Marcus, who suggests that its final placement in the book is significant, political, and ultimately Jonsonian? "With its climactic scenes invoking the image of Emperor Augustus and the *Pax Romana*, *Cymbeline*, like the final entry in Jonson's *Workes*, resonates with Golden Age ideas as they surfaced in Jacobean political panegyric. The play's anomalous placement in the folio could have been engineered by Ben Jonson, who sometimes performed similar generic violations for rhetorical purposes in his own dramatic work . . . There is more than one way in which the peculiar placement of *Cymbeline* can be understood."[53]

I want to rise to these suggestions, not to speculate on what we cannot know, but to excavate the guidelines and instructions that the Folio explicitly offers its readers. In the course of my individual chapters on the plays, I will look closely at their placement in the Folio, and there is tantalizing evidence from early readers, annotators, and critics about an emerging sense of lateness or of lastness in their placement. But the importance of this book for studying the late plays in particular extends beyond its placement of the works, or that it remains the only text for them (it is the only text for eighteen of the plays). The importance of the book for studying the late plays lies in its evocative and meaningful critical language. Its prefatory epistles and assemblies of commendations do provide a sense of what this book may be. The content of these paratexts is commercial and critical; but it is also aesthetic, social, and mythological. It places the occasion of the printing in a broader, imaginative context—a context shaped by ideas of the artist and the nature of embodied artistry.

In the same year of the Folio's publication, Henry Peacham published *The Compleat Gentleman*, his guide to educative reading and social performance for the aspirants of Jacobean life. His instructions hold little that is new—Peacham was clearly synthesizing decades of advisory material from handbooks, letters, poems, and courtly convention—but his opening injunction bears repeating. "Ere you begin a book," he counseled, "forget not to reade the Epistles; for commonly they are best labored and penned."[54]

And if we read the opening Epistles to the Folio, we would find, much as any gentleman of Peacham's purview might, a printed volume, commercially produced, and framed as a memorial to its author. The First Folio is a book that stands on the axes of poetry and the body. Behind much of my argument is that set of Ovidian poetic figures maimed and deformed in pursuit of literary judgment. Orpheus will be dismembered by the Maenads, his disembodied head still singing as it floats to the sea. Midas will have his ears elongated into those of an ass for choosing Pan's pipes over Apollo's lyre. And Ceyx and Alcyone will, in the classic Ovidian metamorphosis, be turned into seabirds, joined in love and song. This sense of an embodied poetics becomes a commonplace of literary history, but its dead metaphors revive in the preface to the First Folio.

> It had bene a thing, we confesse, worthie to have bene wished, that the author himselfe had lived to have set forth, and overseen his owne writings; but since it hath bin ordain'd otherwise, and he by death departed from that right, we pray you do not envie his Friends, the office of their care, and paine, to have collected & publish'd them; and so to have publish'd them, as where (before) you were abused with diverse stolne, and surreptitious copies, maimed, and deformed by the frauds and stealthes of injurious impostors, that expos'd them: even those, are now offer'd to your view cur'd, and perfect of their

> limbes; and all the rest, absolute in their numbers as he conceived them. Who, as he was a happie imitator of Nature, was a most gentle expresser of it. His mind and hand went together: (A3)

Dead and unable to preside over his own texts, Shakespeare hovers over this volume like a lost Orpheus, his editors now charged with ministering over "maimed and deformed" copies and presenting texts now "cur'd and perfect of their limbes." Shakespeare, the "happy imitator of Nature," is gone; his book remains; and if you do not like him, "surely you are in some manifest danger, not to understand him." How like the charge to Midas are these lines, how like the claims that Cloten will make in *Cymbeline* that, if Innogen does not like the music he has staged, there is something wrong with her ears? The preface teases us with images out of antiquity and asks us to choose wisely. Like travelers to the Cave of Sleep, we come upon a Morpheus, a happy imitator of Nature, and this book presents his imitations cured and perfect in their limbs.

The book restores the broken body of the text, much as Ben Jonson's poem will attempt to bring the poet back, almost as in an act of literary necromancy (First Folio, A5):

> My Shakespeare, rise; I will not lodge thee by
> Chaucer or Spenser, or bid Beaumont lye
> A little further, to make thee a roome:
> Thou art a Moniment, without a tombe,
> And art alive still, while thy Book doth live,
> And we have wits to read, and praise to give.

How can we not hear Prospero behind these lines, conjuring the creatures of his book? How can we not recall the metamorphic statue in *The Winter's Tale*, or the seemingly dead Innogen of *Cymbeline* (a boy actor, playing a girl, posing as a boy) waking up? These are Morpheus-like experiences, recognitions that the corpse may live, that the past comes alive again in verse, and that our challenges as readers are to hold the memory of our understanding against our new visions of the revived. How can we not read Jonson's praise of this revivified Shakespeare against the laments of helpless Dowland?

> Thus, wedded to my woes, and bedded in my tomb,
> O, let me, living, living, die, till death doth come, till death
> doth come.[55]

The Folio becomes a book of the dead, a collection of plays made by a man who, on every page, we know has passed.

Heminge and Condell have a sense of this reviving repetition in their preface. For their point is not just that we read Shakespeare or find the memory of performance in the bound book. It is that we *reread* him. "Reade him, therefore, againe and againe." It is this sense of repetition that returns us to the Ovidian book of changes: every reading is a new reading; every encounter with the text changes it. Embedded in this urge to repeat is the theme that Jonathan Bate had found in the Pythagorean last book of *Metamorphoses* and in Shakespeare's poetic fascinations with iteration and difference. Every repetition is a renewal. And in that act of repetition lies the temporality of the First Folio: its status not as object or memorial, but as a goad to constant action, as a book that prompts us to reread, and in that rereading, to locate ourselves in the arc of past and present, to see how both Shakespeare and we have changed from time to time. "The *Metamorphoses* works so well as poetry," Bate writes, "because when its characters undergo transformations, the language takes the reader along too."[56] Shakespeare's last plays, I argue here, similarly work to take the reader along in their language and transform him or her. Again, in Bate's words, they script "the metamorphosis of art into life."

In these worlds of Jacobean Ovidianism, the First Folio becomes a book of metamorphoses. It is a book that purports to take a mangled past and transform it into something new, whole, and beautiful. Its claims for rigorous fidelity to copy may be advertising; but they are also meditations on just what a copy is. What does it mean to replicate, impersonate, or act? This is a book that begins with the picture of an author and a literary meditation on how well it may present his self. There is much here that is conventional. But there is much here, too, that is Shakespearean. Think of *The Winter's Tale*, when Paulina argues with Leontes that his little girl by Hermione is, in spite of his protestations, his alone. "This brat is none of mine," he spits out, and Paulina avows:

It is yours;
And, might we lay th'old proverb to your charge,
So like you, 'tis the worse. Behold, my lords,
Although the print be little, the whole matter
And copy of the father—eye, nose, lip,
The trick of's frown, his forehead, nay, the valley,
The pretty dimples of his chin and cheek, his smiles,
The very mould and frame of hand, nail, finger.
And thou good goddess Nature, which hast made it
So like to him that got it, if thou hast
The ordering of the mind too, 'mongst all colours
No yellow in't, lest she suspect, as he does,
Her children not her husband's. (2.3.95–107)

Bringing together printing and impression, siring and sentence, Paulina tells a story of inheritance as if it were a form of proofreading. Her careful reading of the faces of the father and the daughter has about it all the blazonizing eroticism of a sonnet or of *Venus and Adonis*. She moves, carefully, from eye, to nose, to lip, to frown, to forehead, dimples, chin, and cheek. And with the attentions of hand and nail and finger, we move not only to her description of Leontes, but to Nature herself, who shapes creation with her own hands. A reader of this play in the First Folio would have been well prepared for such phrasing: Ben Jonson's claims about the portrait capturing the face, or about the engraver's "strife with Nature to out-doo the life," or Heminge and Condell's claims that their edition, now, offers texts "curd, and perfect of their limbes." There is a genealogy to Shakespeare's works as much as to Leontes's child. To the brothers Philip and William, the earls of Pembroke and Montgomery, to whom the book is dedicated, Heminge and Condell present themselves as collectors of the plays: "and done an office, to the dead, to procure his Orphanes, Guardians." Like characters out of a late romance, they take these orphaned works and give them guardianship. At the close of *The Winter's Tale*, Leontes will address Florizel, commending his legitimacy:

> Your mother was more true to wedlock, prince,
> For she did print your royal father off,
> Conceiving you. (5.1.123–25)

Motherhood, here, is like the printing press itself, running off copies of a true original. The Folio itself, "published according to the true original copies," garners its legitimacy by investing in precisely these now-social metaphors of genealogy and reproduction.

Bodies whole and broken, metamorphosed, brought to life, or sired and acknowledged—all fill the opening feints of the First Folio. Hands are everywhere: from the "country hands" of Heminge and Condell's Epistle, to Shakespeare's own hand (which, supposedly, never made a blot), to the hands of audiences that begin Hugh Holland's poetic praise of Shakespeare: "Those hands, which you so clapt, go now, and wring / You Britaines braue, for done are Shakespeares dayes."

Holland returns to the Ovidian mythologies of bodily remaking. The Thespian Spring is now "turn'd all to tears"; "Phoebus clouds his rays." The body dies, but the lines of verse live on: a commonplace, but one that goes back, ultimately, to the Ovid of the *Amores*, where he imagined his own verses outliving the work of kings. Lawrence Digges, in his commendatory poem, picks up this allusion explicitly, attributing it to "Naso" himself. For while this book, he states, will outlast "Brasse and Marble" (recall Shakespeare's own refraction of this idiom in Sonnet 55, "Not marble, nor the gilded monuments of time"), it has the power to revive the dead: "eu'ry Line, each Verse / Here shall reuiue, redeeme thee from thy Herse." To read these lines against their sources is to see them as cliché. To read them as an introduction to the plays themselves, however, is to see them as a guide. Revive, redeem: the dead come back to life. As I have said, there is a sense throughout the plays of characters returning from their seeming death. In the late plays, such returns take on new strangeness. And in the final poem of the Folio's introduction, John Mabbe's brief lines to Shakespeare's memory, we find old clichés invigorated into statements for the plays themselves: "We thought thee dead." How many times have characters announced this claim? How often are we, the audience, reminded of the fact that no one truly dies onstage? In Mabbe's words:

> An Actors Art,
> Can dye, and liue, to acte a second part.
> That's but an Exit of Mortalitie;
> This, a Re-entrance to a Plaudite.

And so, we turn the page and find the list of actors. Their names come back to us, their second act now in a book that will revive them. They did for Lucius Cary, the early seventeenth-century owner of a copy of the Folio, now in the Glasgow University Library. Cary, whom Emma Smith identifies as the annotator of this copy, was scribbling in its margins within a decade of the book's publication, and he comes upon the list of actors with what Smith calls "apparent reminiscences."[57] He writes the word "know" beside the names of Robert Benfield and Joseph Taylor; "by report" by Burbage; "by eyewitness" by John Lowen. Cary may well be setting out, as Smith implies, his personal engagement and investment in the legacy of Shakespeare's troupe. But he is also taking up the invitation to record those we thought dead.

An actor's art can die and live to act a second part. Just think of Prospero, dismissing the performers of his masque:

> These our actors,
> As I fortold you, were all spirits, and
> Are melted into air, into thin air. (4.1.148–50)

Lucius Cary heard these lines, marking them in his copy with a marginal "ap," for the Latin *approbo*: "I approve." Smith notes this marking, but brushes it off: "This is a rightly famous passage that could probably be found in any modern list of Shakespeare quotations."[58] But what had made it famous? What led someone like Cary to approve it?

The lines become a marker of Shakespearean identity because they share in a history of metamorphic language: in a history of visions, of impersonations of dead kings or ancient spirits. Like Morpheus roused to impersonation out of the Cave of Sleep, our actors come and go, put on a mask, and then retire. King Ceyx lives again in dreams. But kings can live again Shakespeare's lines.

It is this story of poetic power that I wish to tell here: the tension between a character (to return to Peter Quince) disfiguring the moonlight and each line of verse reviving and redeeming someone from the hearse. These are the stories of the *Metamorphoses*, of John Dowland, of the First Folio, and of the clutch of Shakespeare's final plays. These are the stories of a post-Elizabethan England: stories of masque and marvel, shipwreck and return; a world in which a word such as "redeem" would come increasingly to mean a return on investment and a maturation of a bond. We cannot truly know why Shakespeare left the London stage, or why these late plays, still, have a mysterious hold on our post-Romantic, postmodern, postliterate sensibilities. But we can follow Shakespeare's actors and collectors to take up the orphans they have brought together. We can read him, and read him again, and when we turn the page after the Names of the Principall Actors, we remain still in worlds of vivid memory and change, worlds where a stage direction can revive the past and make us think of entering again with plaudits.

2

An Elegy for Ariel

The *Tempest* first appeared in a performance for King James at Hallowmass, November 1, 1611.[1] As played at Whitehall, it was very much an indoor show: a court piece for an audience of royals and invitees by the troupe dubbed, since James's ascension, the King's Men. Two years later, they staged the play again, this time to celebrate the wedding of James's daughter, Elizabeth, to the Elector Palatinate. A court play, and yet not a play of court, for while it was played at Whitehall and, perhaps, composed originally for the Blackfriars Theater, there is no reason it could not have been a Globe play, too (Prospero's famous mention of the "great Globe" provoking years of speculation).[2] And while it offers up all of the spectacles so increasingly beloved of King James's circle—magic, masque, and majesty—it hovers insecurely as a truly Jacobean play. Ben Jonson, famously, dug deep into its reputation in the Induction to his *Bartholomew Fair* of 1614, mocking its "rare discourse" and its display. The 1616 text of Jonson's *Every Man in His Humor* offers snide asides to storms and monsters and those plays where the "Chorus wafts you o'er the seas."[3]

By the time the *Tempest* would open the First Folio, it had already been a product of such critique and allusion. Thomas

Tomkis's *Albumazar* of 1615 offers clear echoes, and *The Sea Voyage* of John Fletcher and Philip Massinger (acted by the King's Men in 1622) explicitly indebts itself to Shakespeare's play right from its opening.[4] Readers would have come to the play through the scrim of such reception, and they would have come to it, as well, with an elaborate set of stage directions (by far, the most elaborate of any in the Folio). Such directions, now attributed to the scribe Ralph Crane, may recall the specifics of a performance practice but, within the Folio itself, they evoke visions in the reader's mind.[5] For all of our desire to see it as the most transparently autobiographical of Shakespeare's plays, *The Tempest* comes into print already mediated. For all of our admiration of its formal control, linguistic adventurism, and poignant characterization, it remains an insecure thing, caught between the memories of kingly audience and the fifteen shillings of the Folio's first buyers.

Those buyers would have opened to a carefully prepared, well-edited, and closely proofread text. They would have come to it after pages of praise of Shakespeare and his actors, injunctions to read him and read again. Some may have recalled Jonson's criticisms. Some may have seen, by 1623, a story that had spawned many storms onstage. They, and we, may have sought to excavate its earliest appearance. But it remains clear that there remains a gap of time and taste and tension in the years between its first performance and its printing.

There is a gap, too, I will argue, between the idioms of its inhabitants and the tastes of its audience and readers, a gap of years but also sensibilities. It is precisely in that gap that I see its displacement of the lyric, its reliance on old tunes and tropes, its mythic power and its musical allure. Left on his island for nearly two decades, Prospero maintains the old habits of the court. His artistry commands his servant-actors, Ariel and Caliban—the former evoking an idealized boy of the Elizabethan stage, the latter reminiscent of an antic and uncontrolled clown. For all of its allusions to a new world, and for all of its Jacobean literary feel, *The Tempest* is a play out of joint with its time.[6] Nothing is real, nothing is straightforward. Prospero's masque is not a true, courtly masque. Rather, it is a simulacrum of a masque, one step removed from what Ben Jonson, Robert Campion, and Inigo Jones were staging for James's court.[7] It is as if its audience had landed on an island out of phase with everyday reality, a place trapped in time, run by its own rules. Yes, Miranda grows and Prospero ages. But Ariel and Caliban seem trapped in the amber of its landscape—the one an eternal adolescent, the other an enduring monster. In such a world, the songs are echoes.

I read the *Tempest* as a play of such displacements. I see its storms as far less meteorological than mythical. I hear its music less as something of its own but of another time. I feel its focus less in the old man who would retire to his dukedom than in the boy who, freed of service, anticipates a life among the bees.

For what catches my eye and ear in Shakespeare's play is less the instructing Prospero than his attendants, less the magician than the manservant. Here lies the problem of what I call its mythic lyricism: the sense that every voice has been commanded, that artists and their audiences place both their imaginations and their bodies on the line, and that what we see not only in our dreams but in our days may well be only feigned appearances. Throughout the play, characters are moved by forms of artistry, and *The Tempest* exploits the tension between the creative artist and the patron, between the musician's ability to move the listener and that listener's own resistance to that power.

Few courtly poets and musicians had the opportunity to voice their motives as much as John Dowland, and I want to place his narratives of service, travel, skill, and sadness against those embedded in *The Tempest*. His writings, as I have already suggested, invest in old familiar fears and fables: the need for applause, the storm and shipwreck, and the idea that, at our best, we are like the bees. "As in a hiue of bees al labour alike to lay vp honny opposing them selves against none but fruitless drones; so in the house of learning and fame, all good indeuourers should striue to add somewhat that is good." These words from his *Third Book of Songes and Ayers* (1602/1603) ring in the ear to any listener of

Dowland's songs. The bees are everywhere—in love, in service, and in shapely creation—much as they were everywhere in early modern myth and science. They stand for ingenuity and civic achievement. But in Dowland in Ariel, they stand as figures for aesthetic freedom.

Throughout his lyrics, songs, and prefatory prose, Dowland shares with *The Tempest* a language of artistic service, musical effect, and mythological allusion. He was the lutenist of sleep and sorrow, and for many of his listeners, he could transport them almost out of their earthly bodies. Dreaming, ravished, even (figuratively) liquefied with his lyric prowess, Dowland's listeners share much with the audiences in *The Tempest.* Ferdinand and Caliban, Gonzalo and Alonzo, Miranda and the clowns all witness lyric spectacles that release or rescue them. They move between the worlds of sleep and water, dreams and drowning, tiredness and tears.

The Tempest is a play possessed by tensions between power and aesthetics, and while I will find those tensions in the courts of Dowland's ache, I find it too in Ovid's dreams. It is, perhaps, Shakespeare's most Ovidian play, not simply in its borrowing of tropes and speeches but in its overarching metamorphoses.[8] As in the other late plays, book 11 of the *Metamorphoses* haunts its texture, though here it is Ceyx and Alcyone (that great tale of sleep and water) rather than Orpheus or Midas who shadow its motifs.[9] With its story of the king and queen separated by sea travel, its naturalistic depiction of the tempest that drowns Ceyx and his shipmates, and its account of Juno sending her messenger, Iris, to the Cave of Sleep, the episode chimes with the plots and ploys of *The Tempest.* One way of reading Shakespeare's play is as a comically restorative retelling of this tale. Drowned royalty remain alive, shapes shift in dream and vision, and a messenger of air does bidding to let everybody know that in this island world all has been rounded by a sleep. Iris herself appears in the play, not to wake a sleeping god or pass on news of sorrow, but to lead a celebration of a marriage. The masque-like feel to Ariel's great show takes on not just a courtly but a truly

Ovidian quality, as mythic goddesses and nymphs conjure a new, domestic metamorphosis.

The tale of Ceyx and Alcyone works with the lyricism of John Dowland to create a poetic language of both ravishment and change. Music and poetry, maritime travail and unsettled dream, the lassitude of men and the business of bees, all enable us to place Shakespeare's contemporary and his creation side by side: two poet-singers, asking if it had been well done, challenging us to find our own souls transformed by the work of divine hands.

Myth and Storm

Mine is an elegy for Ariel, and I begin with one of the most sensitive of critical encounters with his singing, David Lindley's opening to *Shakespeare and Music.* Lindley begins his book by exploring the dramatic possibilities of Ariel's first song to Ferdinand in act 1, scene 2.[10] Ariel (according to the stage directions, "invisible, playing and singing") performs the exquisite lyric "Come unto these yellow sands," and Ferdinand wonders from where it came. "I'th air, or th'earth?" Lindley teases out the impact of this scene: its basic, dramatic purpose of moving the narrative along and getting Ferdinand where Prospero wants him to be; its enigmatic textual condition in the First Folio, with the unclear directions and line assignations; and its place in the larger arc of song and performance in the play as a whole, with its temptations to imagine particular "instrumentation or vocal style," and the challenges to our understanding of "what ideological freight" its verbal codes had carried.

Lindley makes clear that, at this moment in *The Tempest,* Ariel's position is as a commissioned servant. "We are accustomed," he writes,

> to the notion that a theatrical character who sings is, in some way or another, giving voice to their own emotions: yet in Shakespearean drama, almost all performed songs are rendered by professionals and servants who do not articulate their own feelings so much as sing to, or on behalf of others. Those who sing directly "for themselves" are generally drunk, mad, in their dotage, or socially subversive.[11]

We can see Ariel clearly among the first kind here, those whose job it is to perform for an embedded audience within their plays. Feste in *Twelfth Night* comes to mind, as do Touchstone in *As You Like It*, the Fool in *Lear*, and the courtly singers in *Henry VIII* and *Cymbeline*. For the latter group, there are, most famously, the Gravedigger in *Hamlet*, Ophelia, the clownish drunkards of *The Tempest*, the love-besotted Benedick in *Much Ado About Nothing*, and the fairies and rustics in *Midsummer Night's Dream*.

But by the end of *The Tempest*, things have changed. Ariel stands at the cusp of freedom, Prospero has abjured his magic, and the onetime servant now sings as much for himself as any theatrical character who would give voice to emotion:

> Where the bee sucks, there suck I,
> In a cowslip's bell I lie;
> There I couch when owls do cry;
> On the bat's back I do fly
> After summer merrily.
> Merrily, merrily shall I live now
> Under the blossom that hangs on the bough. (5.1.88–94)

Lindley calls it "an utterly solipsistic song," a celebration of the spirit's impending freedom, a song that has an impact on the audience outside the play's fiction as much as within it. "Why, that's my dainty Ariel!" Prospero commends him when he finishes. "I shall miss thee."[12]

Ariel may well be one of the very few, if any, characters in Shakespeare's plays that moves from patronized to self-generated performance. He may have been cast for his distinctive skills in voice and instrument. But by the play's end, he has said farewell to boyish roles and looks forward to living "merrily." Ariel's is an actor's life, and his final words in the play are those of an actor asking for approval: "Was't well done?" (5.1.240). This is a play that closes with requests for affirmation and approval: for Prospero's blessing on Ariel's show, for the audience's comparable praise and release of Prospero himself, and with the range of characters within the play assembled to forgive, or judge each other. Alonso ends by longing "to hear the story of your life," making himself a willing audience for what we imagine to be Prospero's post-island recitation—and, in the process, affirming that he will be a far more attentive and approving one than impatient Miranda had been at the play's beginning. The meta-theatrics of *The Tempest* have been bruited for centuries, and in these final moments readers have wished to find Shakespeare himself retiring from the stage.[13]

> But release me from my bands
> With the help of your good hands. (5.1.327–28)

Prospero's asking for applause recalls, of course, Puck's epilogue in *Midsummer Night's Dream*, "give me your hands, if we be friends," and at such a moment it is as if this late play has taken us back to the comedy of a decade and a half before—that the presiding aegis of this daydream has called for closure, and the final words are left not to the playful servant but the master, as if we had been bid farewell, in the earlier play, by Oberon.[14]

This powerful tension between master and servant, played across the arts of lyric, music, and the theater, runs throughout both the plays. But nowhere, I believe, do we see the release of literary servitude as explicitly as in *The Tempest*. Many still like or want to believe that the play is Prospero's and that his story, somehow, helps explain Shakespeare's own enigmatic retreat from the theater in the early 1610s.[15] But what if we were to see this play as Ariel's: to see it not as a fable of retirement but as a fantasy of manumission? Ariel represents poetry patronized. He speaks, almost until his very last, only when spoken to, commanded, or provided with a script. "What shall I do? Say what: what shall I do" (1.2.300). He is the poet striving to emerge from actor's prompts, the lyricist and singer who has spent a lifetime under courtly care and can now, at the play's end, intuit an afterlife of freedom.

Throughout *The Tempest*, that work goes on in a drowsy wetness. People fall asleep and wake. Those drowned appear to live again. From its opening, the storm feels more like a bad dream than a real disaster, and Prospero's magic moves along the axes of sleeping and drowning, waking up and rescuing. His arts put

Miranda to sleep and rouse her when he wants; he wrecks the ship, but lets the nobles find themselves awake with clothes as dry as when they left; fathers and sons are feared drowned, only to be resurrected. There is a sense, throughout the play, that both sleep and water are more than conditions of the body but are realms of art.

I have already limned the contours of this reading. Ovid's story of Ceyx and Alcyone, especially in Golding's implicitly theatrical retelling, sets the stage for any tale of shipwreck and return. The terrors of those mythic sailors—"Strike the toppesaile," "harts and stomachks fayle," "One weeps: another stands amazed"—come back in *The Tempest*'s opening words: "A tempestuous noise of thunder and lightening heard." This stage direction takes the reader to the world of the Ovidian storm. For what Ovid gives us, by way of Golding, is noise: no man could hear the cries of another; there are "ratling ropes," "crying men and boyes," "flushing waves and thundering ayre." One need not have been in the theater to imagine such sounds: "swelling surges," "Hideous flusshing." "The Gallye being striken gave as great a sownd," in Golding's English, like a battle ram of steel or the roar of a lion. And there is lightning too.

> Howbee't the flasshing lyghtnings oft doo put the same to flyght,
> And with theyr glauncing now and then do give a soodeine lyght.
> The lightnings setts the waves on fyre. (11.603–5)

"To prayers, to prayers!" cry Shakespeare's mariners, much as they do in Golding's Ovid: "To God another makes his vow . . . Doth pray in vayne for help" (11.623–25). "Farewell, my wife and children! Farewell brother." And again, in Golding: "The thought of this man is uppon / His brother and his parents whom he cleerely hath forgone. / Another calles his house and wyfe and children unto mynd" (11.625–27).

The Tempest seems, at first glance, to begin where the story of Ceyx and Alcyone leaves off. There may have been much at the Blackfriars or Whitehall to evoke such sounds and shocks. But we need not have been there to see all this vividly. This is, first and foremost, a *literary* storm, a tempest out of poetry and myth.[16] Golding had found the English words to make that storm seem vivid to a local audience, and there is a sense throughout *The Tempest* as we have it in the Folio that we are not so much remembering a play as reading such a tale.

We read this, too, not just in Ovid's voice, or Golding's English, but through a woman's eyes. Queen Alcyone saw Ceyx off, a "chillness" striking to "her very bones," her face pale, crying, imagining his fate:

> To think uppon the sea dooth cause my flesh for feare to quake.
> I sawe the broken ribbes of shippes alate uppon the shore.
> And oft on Tumbes I reade theyr names whose bodyes long before
> The sea had swallowed. Let not fond vayne hope seduce thy mynd,
> That Aeolus is thy fathrinlaw who holdes the boystous wynd
> In prison, and can calme the seas at pleasure. When the wynds
> Are once let looce uppon the sea, no order then them bynds.
> Then neyther land hathe priviledge, nor sea exemption fynds
> Yea even the clowdes of heaven they vex, and with theyr meeting
> stout
> Enforce the fyre with hideous noyse to brust in flashes out.
> (11.492–501)

Her husband leaves, and Alcyone lies down in her bed. And to that bed comes Morpheus, now called by Juno, in the shape of the dead Ceyx, "Pale, wan, stark naakt." She sobs, wakes from her dream, and cries, "By shipwrecke he is perrisht: I have seene him." She cries until her heart is sore, and "Her sorrow would not suffer her to utter more."

Alcyone sees Ceyx in her mind and in her dreams, and so, too, does Miranda see the shipwreck:

> The sky, it seems, would pour down stinking pitch,
> But that the sea, mounting to th' welkin's cheek,
> Dashes the fire out. O, I have suffered
> With those that I saw suffer: a brave vessel—
> Who had, no doubt, some noble creature in her—
> Dashed all to pieces! O, the cry did knock
> Against my very heart—poor souls, they perished. (1.2.3–9)

It is as if Shakespeare displaced the vision of the wife on to the girl; as if Miranda saw in her mind's eye what Alcyone saw and suffered. In Golding's lines:

> . . . the raging sea did rowle about so fast:
> And all the heaven with clowds as black as pitch was over cast,
> That never nyght was halfe so dark. (11.635–37)

The pieces of the story, like the bits of a shattered boat, wash up on Prospero's island, a fragment of old Ovid, a story of sea storm and a noble creature lost, now transformed into theater by an old man. "There's no harm done."

Or is there? Prospero's island is a place of constant harm, of brusque injunctions to his spirit servant, of cruel torment to his monster, of insensitive tests of strength and will and patience set upon his child and the visitors. Each character, in his or her own way, suffers under Prospero's stagy yoke, and one might well ask whether there is always harm done in the making of a play. Golding's Ovid acutely brings out both the theater and the anguish of these episodes: the drama of the storm and shipwreck, the rhetoric of dying men, and the impersonations of Morpheus himself, stage creature, feigning voice and face.

> None other could so conningly expresse mans verrye face,
> His gesture and his sound of voyce, and manner of his pace,
> Togither with his woonted weede, and woonted phrase of talk.
> (11.737–39)

Morpheus performs, and the theme of performance runs through Ovid's tale much as it runs through Shakespeare's. But so does the terror. For these moments in the *Metamorphoses* are not just about performing but commanding performance: Juno compels Iris, Iris pleads with Sleep, and Sleep sends Morpheus. The sleeping god is none too happy with his task, and when he shows up in the Queen's dream, he announces himself:

> Most wretched woman, knowest thou thy loving Ceyx now
> Or is my face by death disformd? behold mee well, and thow
> Shalt know mee. (11.760–62)

Colin Burrow has perceptively seen this speech as "the opening lines of an uneasy actor who is not quite sure that he lives up to the part he is playing."[17] We can equally well see these lines as central to *The Tempest*, a play brimming with uneasy actors not sure of their master's, or their audience's, approval. "Was't well done?" Ariel's last words in the play take us back to this image of the artist as an actor, to Morpheus as commanded performer, and to the range of harms done on and off the stage. Prospero's boy has spent his time anxious about living up to parts in which he has been cast.

But those words take us back to the beginning. After the storm and shipwreck, after the daughter's nightmare and father's lesson, Ariel is called, and he appears, not just to praise his master but to tell, again, his myth. When Prospero asks if he has "Performed to the point the tempest that I bade thee," Ariel responds with his own version of the storm.

> I boarded the King's ship; now on the beak,
> Now in the waist, the deck, in every cabin,
> I flamed amazement. Sometime I'd divide
> And burn in many places; on the topmast,
> The yards and bowsprit would I flame distinctly,
> Then meet and join. Jove's lightning, the precursors
> O'th' dreadful thunder-claps, more momentary
> And sight-outrunning were not; the fire and cracks
> Of sulphurous roaring the most mighty Neptune
> Seem to besiege and make his bold waves tremble,
> Yea, his dread trident shake. (1.2.196–206)

This is, by this point, the third version of the play's beginning: the first enacted, the second dreamt, and now this one remembered and retold. There is as much of Golding's Ovid in this tale as in the others.

> One weeps; another stands amazde . . .
> The lightnings setts the waves on fyre. Above the netting skippe
> The waves, and with a violent force doo lyght within the ship.
> (11.622; 625–26)

Ariel retells this scene as a scene of artistic performance. We had already been plunged deep into the sound-world of the story: "A tempestuous noise of thunder and lightening heard." Everyone is yelling. So is the storm. "A plague upon this howling!" cries the Boatswain. "They are louder than the weather of our office." Miranda's dream is one of sight and sound. But it is an internalized response to sense; what matters here is how things "seem" to Miranda, how she herself felt them, how it knocked against her heart. Ariel's story, however, is one completely visualized. His job is to amaze the eyes. His literary task is to create a language of evocative imagery. His job, in short, is to make something we have barely seen completely visible.

That is the job of art. He shapes his speech not simply to impress his master but also us. For this is clearly a performance, a description of actions to amaze one audience—those on board the ship—and that, in their retelling, must amaze us. "Not a soul," he says, "but felt a fever of the mad." That is what theater, poetry, and music must do—to make us feel the fever, to bring us to the brink of drowning and, at the last moment, wash us up all dry on someone else's shores.

Sleep and Water

John Dowland and his circle knew this well. Remember Thomas Campion, whose Latin poem on his Orphic skills recalled Lygia walking from the waves and avowed that, when Dowland played, the listener's limbs fell, minds were stolen, and the soul was liquefied. *Liquescit anima.* Remember, too, Richard Barnfield's sonnet in *The Passionate Pilgrim*, where Dowland's "heavenly touch . . . doth ravish human sense." Much like Campion, liquefied in rapture, Barnfield finds his watery response to music:

> And I in deep delight am chiefly drowned
> When as himself to singing he betakes.

Dowland's had been a world of liquid metamorphoses. His lyrics conjure up a world of tears. The verb "dissolve" holds special power for him. Things change, and that constellation of what he would sing as "teares and sighes and groanes" had powerfully informed the late Elizabethan mood.

These three words shape, too, Shakespeare's early forays into anguish. Throughout his first poems and first plays, they mark their laments. Queen Margaret, in *Henry VI, Part 2*, could well be quoting Dowland when she eulogizes the Duke of Gloucester: "And for myself, foe as he was to me, / Might liquid *tears* or heart-offending *groans* / Or blood-consuming *sighs* recall his life" (3.2.59–61, emphases mine). The three words concatenate in *The Rape of Lucrece*: "If ever man were moved with woman moans, / Be moved with my tears, my sighs, my groans"; and again, "When sighs and groans and tears may grace the fashion / Of her disgrace . . ." (638–39; 1371–72). The words show up, in sequence, in *Richard II*, in *Twelfth Night*, and in *Two Gentlemen of Verona*. They are the currency of love's abandonment: the markers, for a late Elizabethan audience, of that Dowlandian melancholy that had become the emotive fashion of the age.

What happens when these idioms show up in later plays? What happens when the fashion for the black bile has passed and tears and groans and sighs no longer signal love or loss? These words have become old idioms. They are displaced on to reporting rather than to feeling. And *The Tempest* marks them clearly. There, the word "groans" shows up not to distinguish the loss of love or pangs of desire, but, instead, to note the cries of Ariel himself, pent in the pine tree before his release ("thou didst vent thy groans," 1.2.280). As Prospero reminds him, "Thy groans / Did make wolves howl" (1.2.287–88). So, too, the "sighs" in the play reserve themselves for Ariel, who in response to Prospero affirms that everyone has safely survived the tempest and the King's son was left "cooling the air with sighs" (1.2.222). And the word "tears" appears but once in the play, when at the end, Ariel describes old Gonzalo crying. Here, however, the tears are not the marker of emotion but, instead, the occasion for Ariel's own poetic skill, a prompt for simile rather than sense:

> His tears run [. . .] down his beard, like winter's drops
> From eaves of reeds. (5.1.16–17)

Here, it is Ariel who is the voice and vehicle for tears and sighs and groans. But they are things reported or remembered, now. *The Tempest* takes these old tropes of lyric dolor and distances them, displaces them from action or emotive life and places them securely in the past of narrative or memory. An older language resurfaces to mark generational distance. The allusive wording of the lyric distances the play's fiction from its feeling. Ariel is the servant but he is, as well, the messenger, and in his mouth the language of the old songs becomes strangely distant, displaced, different.

For Dowland, that was the language of sleep and water, and *The Tempest* transforms the allusions, images, and metaphors of his world into narrative. What is a set of tropes in the songs is a set of actions in the play. Look at act 2, when Ariel puts all but Sebastian and Antonio asleep. The waking courtiers debate whether they are indeed awake and dry. "What? Art thou waking?" Sebastian asks, thinking the language of his compeer "sleepy."

> This is a strange repose, to be asleep
> With eyes wide open. (2.1.211–12)

And when Antonio avows that he is "more serious than my custom," Sebastian seems to dare him to say something moving or convincing:

> Seb: Well? I am standing water.
> Ant: I'll teach you how to flow.
> Seb: Do so—to ebb
>   Hereditary sloth instructs me. (2.1.218–21)

This strange and allusive interchange makes human action into liquid, turning metaphor into matter. "Ebbing men," Antonio replies, "indeed, / Most often do so near the bottom run" (2.1.224–25). The conversation then soon turns to a man who may well be at the bottom, Ferdinand, the King's son: "'Tis as impossible that he's undrowned / As he that sleeps here swims" (2.1.235–36).

Sleep and water are the venues for the lyrical imagination, but here they are the sites of politics. Only with their companions asleep and with Ferdinand thought drowned can Antonio and Sebastian conspire to unseat the King, and only then must Ariel return to wake Gonzalo and the others and prevent the plot.

> *He sings in Gonzalo's ear*
> While you here do snoring lie,
> Open-eyed conspiracy
> His time doth take.
> If of life you keep a care,
> Shake off slumber, and beware.
> Awake, Awake! (2.1.298–303)

To wake the sleeping was the charge of Juno's messenger, sent to the Cave of Sleep so that Alcyone could learn her husband's end. In Ovid, it is an episode of ease and suggestion: Iris appeals to the god of Sleep quietly and directly. For Chaucer, whose *Book of the Duchess* rewrote this scene into burlesque, Juno's messenger (now a man) screams at the god and blows a trumpet in his ear:

> This messager com fleynge faste
> And cried, "O how! Awake anoon!"
> Hit was for noght; there herde hym non.
> "Awake!" quod he, "whoo ys lyth there?"
> And blew his horn right in here eere,
> And cried, "Awaketh!" wonder hye. (178–83)

Much has been made of Chaucer's transformation of this episode into domestic comedy, and much, too, has been made of the repeated calls to "Awake" in this poem: from these shouts, to the ghostly image of Ceyx telling Alcyone to "Awake" and realize that he is dead, to the Chaucerian narrator's own awakening at the poem's close.[18] It may be a rube's Ovid, but it may, too, be Shakespeare's, as the tone of Chaucer's episode inflects the tone of this scene in *The Tempest*. Its messenger of air calls upon an authority to awake, but now it is for purposes of restoring political, rather than domestic or amorous, alignment. Impersonators seek their vengeance, and if Antonio and Sebastian would be false kings in their dreams, it is left to Gonzalo to bring them back to earth. But still they lie. Gonzalo wakens with a start, and then the others, and Alonzo turns to his would-be usurpers and asks:

> Why, how now, ho! Awake? Why are you drawn?
> Wherefore this ghastly looking? (2.1.306–7)

Here, it is not the dead who come back, "ghastly" in their guise, but the all-too-living, and Alonzo's vision of his courtiers echoes that of Alcyone, woken by the image of her husband's speaking corpse (in Golding's English):

> Both with her crying so,
> And flayghted with the image of her husbands gastly spryght,
> She started up;

The co-conspirators make up a story: there was a noise, something terrible, did you hear it? Alonzo heard nothing, Gonzalo but a humming. The point of this interchange is that it takes the imagistic building blocks of Ovid's tale, filtered through Chaucer, and rebuilds them into political threat. The tale of Ceyx and Alcyone bubbles beneath the surface of *The Tempest*, from its opening storm through its anxieties about the drowned ruler, to its reflections on the metamorphic power of desire. Here, at this moment of usurper's threat, shards of the story return to make what once was love into suspicion.

Dowland, as well, had called upon his love to rise and come:

> Awake, sweet love, thou art return'd;
> My heart, which long in absence mourn'd,
> Lives now in perfect joy . . . (*First Booke*, 19)

Think of this lyric as a tale of Ovidian restoration, of love sleeping once but now returned whole, where the mourning heart now lives again. Sleep and waking, morning and life. Such are the axes of this aching lyric, a lyric made richer by awareness of its mythic resonances.

Thy happiness will sweeter prove,
Rais'd up from deep despair.

Raised from the depths, love will return. All of these images surround the language of *The Tempest*: the lyricality of love, the mythic sense of loss, the language of the lover/king impersonated in a dream.

Caliban's Ravishment

But Ariel and his beached noblemen are not alone. Caliban, too, can feel the ravishment of sound. His is a poetry of earlier, Elizabethan lyric beauty now transmuted into memories—as if he had awoken from a dream of benign queenship to find himself entrapped under an unforgiving monarch. He is a monster stuck remembering a world of how things used to be:

And then I loved thee
And showed thee all the qualities o'th'isle,
The fresh springs, brine pits, barren place and fertile— (1.2.336–38)

Like an untutored Orpheus, Caliban guards the memory of his aesthetic shore. The wood he bears, however, is not the enchanted and enchanting lyre of a hero but the firewood of a servant. Unlike Orpheus or Dowland, Caliban cannot still the animals or move the rocks. Nature besets him, and he offers up a catalogue of bad creation out to get him. Prospero's spirits

set upon me,
Sometime like apes that mow and chatter at me,
And after bite me; then like hedgehogs, which
Lie tumbling in my barefoot way . . .
sometime am I
All wound with adders, who with cloven tongues
Do hiss me into madness. (2.2.8–14)

It was such an adder that had bitten unsuspecting Eurydice, and such a snake that, long after Orpheus was dead and dismembered, finally ate his head that had washed up on its shore. Nothing is liquid, evanescent, rapturous for Caliban. Read against Orpheus and Dowland, he is resolutely anti-metamorphic, as if nothing could transform him into air or liquid beauty.

Except when he remembers. There was a time before Prospero and, he asserts to his visiting clowns, there will be a time "when Prospero is destroyed." Then they may have, in Stephano's words, "my music for nothing." And so, to tutor his new audience, Caliban gives them a tour of the island's sounds:

> Be not afeard, the isle is full of noises,
> Sounds, and sweet airs, that give delight and hurt not.
> Sometimes a thousand twangling instruments
> Will hum about mine ears; and sometime voices,
> That if I then had waked after long sleep,
> Will make me sleep again, and then in dreaming
> The clouds methought would open and show riches
> Ready to drop upon me, that when I waked
> I cried to dream again. (3.2.133–41)

How like an old Elizabethan he appears. His words—sounds, sweet airs, delight—draw on the lexicon of affect from the 1590s, a lexicon exemplified in Richard Barnfield's verse:

> Thou lov'st to hear the sweet melodious sound
> That Phoebus' lute (the queen of music) makes.

Sweet was a word that took off in that lyric era; it shows up countless times in lyrics, panegyrics, introductions, plays. Sweet airs were everywhere. Henry Peacham would recall the musician Luca Marenzino (admired by Dowland, dead in 1599) as excelling in "delicious Aire and Sweet Inuention." Dowland's own lyrics would hearken back to lines of Philip Sidney, "O sweet woods the delight of soliarinesse," while the poet Patrick Hannay, writing in the early 1620s, would look back to Marlowe to inflect his lines, "Or nimbly on a Lute light notes out finde, / Which with sweet airs my charming voice did grace."[19] Even in these Jacobean writings, sweet airs are a memory of something gone before.

Caliban's is the ravishment of old sounds. Even the instruments have an archaic feel to them. His "twangling instruments" recall the English of Thomas Phaer's 1558 translation of the *Aeneid*, when Aeneas comes upon the long-dead Orpheus in the underworld, still playing his lyre.[20]

> And Orpheus among them stands, as priest in trayling gowne
> And twancling makes them tune, with notes of musike seuerall
> seuen,
> And now with Yuery quill, now strings he strikes with fingers euen.

This is the background music of the dead, a moment out of an old-fashioned Virgil brought back to the ears of these strange, mock-Virgilian travelers. And, if we had any doubt that Phaer's diction was, by Shakespeare's time, old-fashioned, if not arch, we should recall that moment in the early *Taming of the Shrew*, when Hortensio stands dazed after he has been banged on the head with a lute:

> And there I stood amazed for a while
> As on a pillory, looking through the lute,
> While she did call me "rascal fiddler"
> And "twangling Jack." (2.1.148–51)

Hortensio becomes a fool's Orpheus, and Caliban, struck by the music by his ears, hears "twangling" instruments as one might well see stars. Caliban's poetry *is* poetry; but it is old verse, reminiscent of a time before Prospero, of a time of sweet airs that give delight—words of a gone court and a lost lute. Much as Campion would give himself to Dowland's slumber, so Caliban would succumb to sleep anew and dream again.

So many of us, now, want Caliban to be the unimpeded artist of this colony, want him to be the earliest anticipation of an imperial future, that we miss his echoes of the past. Douglas Brewster has suggested that the monster's antics would recall the jumps and starts of Will Kempe, that star clown who had left Shakespeare's Chamberlain's Men in 1599 and who was still, two decades later, remembered for his "hey" and "hey de gay" in his songs. Caliban's own exultant "heigh day" may well smell of the clown, but he gives off the aura of the lyricist as well.[21]

But he cannot sustain that aura for long. Instead of liquefying soul through flowing tears of love, he nearly drowns in the imported liquor of his shipwrecked drunkards. Instead of fingers making music out of strings, his fingers grub the earth: "And with my long nails will dig thee pig-nuts." And when the drunkards come upon that gift of splendid clothing, and Caliban begs them to leave off, he imagines a strange and anti-metamorphic consequence. They will, he fears, "all be turned to barnacles, or to apes / With foreheads villainous low" (4.1.249–50). But Stephano is unmoved: "Monster, lay to your fingers" (4.1.251). Lay to your fingers. An old command for music now bids the monster steal. A phrase that could have conjured beauty from a string now presses itself into parody. Caliban—earthbound, fingers in the dirt—emerges as a kind of anti-Ariel, a servant always on the verge of rebellion, a listener to music that moves him, but that he cannot reproduce.

And yet, like Ariel, like Prospero, Miranda, and practically every character in the play, he remembers things and tells their story. For, as we read on, we see the story repeating itself. The storm is witnessed and retold; Prospero's exile and his daughter's rearing are rehearsed; Ariel's imprisonment, Caliban's freedom, and the aristocrat's experiences all become subjects for review and reminiscence. As we read, *The Tempest* more and more becomes a play attempting to retell its pasts.

Strange Entertainments

I think that this is what the stage directions do. Increasingly, as the play progresses, they elaborate on what one may have seen before. Increasingly, they resonate with the words of the characters themselves. Ariel's own account of his storm-show, Prospero's commands, Caliban's tour of the island's soundscape—the characters speak more and more like stage directions, and it seems clear that, in the Folio text of the *Tempest*, a kind of dialogue emerges between the actor's lines and those of the directions. Ralph Crane's elaborate directives may have the feel of description or evocation. But what they increasingly have the feel of is that of a character within the play. They pick up, sensitively and with clear awareness, its Ovidianism of the play, its resonances to contemporary musical performance, and its sense of character at work.

Without them, we would not know that Ariel sings in Gonzalo's ear. Without them, we would not know that Ariel enters, on two occasions, "playing"—bearing what must be an instrument of song, a lute, and with that instrument emerging as the icon of a lyric self.[22] These are vital stage directions, as they signal Ariel's association with the courtly and the mythic: Orpheus, of course, but also all those boys who played the singers in the early plays. Those boys were playing girls, and girls and their lutes show up over and over again: from *The Taming of the Shrew*, through *Henry IV*, through *Titus Andronicus*. *Henry VIII* will have Katherine call for her servant-girl to play, and in that wonderfully challenging and unique stage direction from the First Quarto of *Hamlet*, Ophelia will enter, "playing on a Lute."[23] I stress this sense of Ariel the player, brought out in the stage directions—a boy actor well versed in the arts of song, an image of the courtly and controlled on this rare island.[24]

The play's stage directions offer not just information; they present interpretation, judgment, and affect. They fill with adjectives and adverbs. At the banquet in act 3, scene 3, there is "solemn and strange music," "strange shapes," and "gentle actions." Ariel makes them disappear with a "quaint device." After he vanishes "in thunder," there is "soft music." These are not just directions for performance. They are distillations of the key words of the play. The word "strange" appears nineteen times in *The Tempest*, more than in any other play ("strangely" appears four times, and "strangeness" twice).[25] Everybody seems to use it, describing everything from fate and fortune, to the sounds and sights of the island, to Caliban's shape, to inner feelings and outer appearances. Prospero, broken off in concentration from his masque in act 4, starts and speaks, and his conjured creatures vanish "to a strange hollow." And at the play's end, Alonzo—a spectator to all this magic, much like us—repeats over and over: things move "From strange to stranger," "This as strange a maze as e'er men trod," "This is a strange thing as e'er I looked on," and, in his last words of the play, "I long / To hear the story of your life, which must / Take the ear strangely."

Everything in *The Tempest* takes the ear strangely. We see and hear displacements of old songs and sorrows. The language of Orphic lutenists hovers around the play like a sea mist. We have a storm, but it is far more an Ovidian than an Atlantic one. Thunder is everywhere, but it is mostly in the stage directions and the mind. And, as Alonzo stares at all this strangeness, he and Shakespeare's audience would well have been reminded of Dowland's own strangeness, played in court and published in his songbooks.

> Now cease my wand'ring eyes,
> Strange beauties to admire,
> In change least comfort lies,
> Long joys yield long desire. (*Second Booke*, 13)

These opening lines from a lyric in *The Second Book of Songs or Ayres* may well stand as an epigraph for the whole play—a play of wandering eyes, strange beauties, changes, and characters who, as much as Miranda, constantly admire.

But so too would Dowland's later feeling of estrangement resonate with courtly life. In the Epistle to his *Pilgrimes Solace* of 1612, reflecting on his return to an England he had left over a decade earlier, he recalls how he came back from a "forraine climate," where his music had been published and praised, even though there he had "beene a stranger." Now, back in England, things are different: "so haue I againe found strange entertainment since my returne." Dowland goes on to complain about changes in musical styles at the Jacobean court, vocal singers who are mere technicians, lutenists who have no deep appreciation for their music, artists who have come from abroad without a sense of old traditions. "Moreouer that here are and daily doth come into our most famous kingdome diuers strangers from beyond the seas, which auerre before our own faces that we have no true methode of application or fingering of the Lute."

Dowland captures evocatively this sense of estrangement from the present. Things are different in this kingdom now: different because time has passed, but different also because strangers have come in. Part of what he is responding to is a changing set of musical tastes and techniques in the 1610s. But part of what he is responding to, as well, is the condition of a new global sensibility: a world in which everyone, ultimately, is a stranger, new to court and arrived from beyond the seas. This language captures, I think, the pervasive sense of strangeness on Prospero's island, a strangeness that is as much aesthetic as it is political or social. What Dowland and Antonio capture is this new world where things appear to move from strange to stranger. In change least comfort lies, and Dowland's lyric, much like Ariel's, chimes in the ear to show us that with every change is something strange.

> Nothing of him that doth fade,
> But doth suffer a sea-change
> Into something rich and strange.

In the Kingdom of the Bees

And in the end, the fantasy for the performer lies not on a distant shore but in familiar leas. Imagine a world without change. Ariel, stage-dresser to his master at the play's close, returns once again to sing. "Where the bee sucks, there suck I . . ." Music for this song, and for Ariel's earlier "Full fathom five," survives, attributed to Robert Johnson, lutenist to King James and, by the 1610s, one of the most successful court musicians of the era. He and Dowland moved in the same circles. They most likely lived near each other in the Blackfriars district. His songs show up in plays by Fletcher and Webster. His star rose as Dowland's fell. In 1613, both men contributed to the "Masque of the Middle Temple and Lincoln's Inn," performed at Whitehall in 1613. Records show that Johnson was paid forty-five pounds for "songs and music." Dowland was paid two pounds ten shillings as one of the lutenists. Ariel's tune may have been up-to-date. But his lyrics hearken back to older times. For, in the image of the bee, he returns to a central motif of both Dowland and the classicists—an image that helps us review the longing of his character for both political and artistic autonomy.[26]

Since antiquity, the bee has stood as the central figure for both civic industry and learning. Bee similes define the collaborative work of city building from Virgil on, and by the early modern period the study of bees had become the purview of the natural as well as the political scientist.[27] Bees, in their social organization, came to be understood as part of a royalty. While scientists did not confirm the queenship of the bees until the middle of the seventeenth century, the idea of a "bee king" was a commonplace, and the production of both honey and wax came to be appreciated as a fact of nature and a figure for society. Bees were political as well as artistic creatures, and Ariel's last poem brings both worlds together to imagine a life unbounded.

So too for Dowland, the bee stands as a fulcrum on which social and aesthetic balance. Recall his comment in the Epistle to his *Third Book of Songs and Airs*: "As in a hiue of bees al labour alike to lay vp honny opposing them selves against none but fruitless drones." But Ariel does not imagine a life of the hive. What he imagines, instead, is something more akin to Dowland's lyric from his *Third Book*:

> It was a time when silly Bees could speak,
> And in that time I was a sillie Bee,
> Who fed on Time until my heart gan break,
> Yet neuer found the time would fauour me.
> Of all the swarme I onely did not thriue,
> Yet brought I waxe and honey to the hiue.
>
> Then thus I buzd, when time no sap would giue,
> Why should this blessed time to me be drie,
> Sith by this Time the lazie drone doth live,
> The waspe, the worme, the gnat, the butterflie,
> Mated with griefe, I kneeled on my knees,
> And thus complaind unto the King of Bees.

My liege, Gods graunt thy time may never end,
And yet vouchsafe to heare my plaint of Time,
Which fruitlesse Flies have found to have a friend,
And I cast downe when Atomies do clime,
The king replied but thus, Peace peevish Bee,
Th'art bound to serve the time, the time not thee. (*Third Booke*, 18)

This poem had been well known long before Dowland set it to music. Some twenty versions of it have survived, most of which attribute it to the Earl of Essex. Historians have sought an allegory of Essex's own exile and his fraught relationship with Queen Elizabeth.[28] By the time Dowland published his setting, Essex was dead and the Queen nearly so, and some have therefore sought a more personal resonance to its lines. Diana Poulton speculates that "the poem also reflects precisely the image—fortune's victim—that Dowland was coming to associate with himself, and in setting the lines . . . he must have experienced the bitterness of his own exiled condition."[29]

We need not speculate on politics or personality here. The poem speaks for itself. It imagines a beast-fable past in which bees had the power of language, where the narrator presents himself as an impoverished and unrequited lover—a bee who, no matter how hard he works, cannot receive the favor of the age. The poem plays on a sustained pun between "time" and "thyme": the former representing the past age and life of service, the latter representing the herb on which the bees fed and made honey. To bring out this wordplay, I have quoted the poem not from a modernized edition but from its original printing, where both words are spelled "time." It is a poem of service and complaint, desire and power. Imagining a king of the bees, the poet becomes a supplicant, complaining to his monarch. I am cast down, the speaker complains, "when Atomies do clime"—that is, while even the smallest of creatures advance. And the King responds:

Peace peevish Bee,
Th'art bound to serve the time, the time not thee.

At the purely botanical level, the King's words counsel: you are the servant of the thyme plant; do your service; the plant does not serve you. More broadly, it is a statement about the rightness of hierarchy: serve nature, nature does not serve you. But, at the level of the poem's overarching wordplay, the King's comment is a claim for bondage. You are bound to serve the time.

The *OED* records the phrase "to serve time" as a phrase of prison life from the late nineteenth century. But "time" and "serve" are frequent in early modern English collocations, and they run through Shakespeare. A phrase such as "when time shall serve" means, in effect, when the time is right or when things come to fruition. "That time serves still," says the first lord in *Timon of Athens*; "the time now serves not to expostulate," says Proteus in *Two Gentlemen*. "When time shall serve, but let the herald cry," says Edgar in *Lear*. To serve the time is to be subject to the passage of things, to be part of a larger hierarchy of nature and power. Ariel himself enters and exits the play with service. "Remember I have done thee worthy service," he asserts early in his first appearance (1.2), and his penultimate lines return us to his time served: "Sir, all this service, / Have I done since I went" (5.1).

To have the well-known lines about the "silly bees" in mind is to have a lens through which to read Ariel's pleas to Prospero. For, when the spirit brings up the matter of his release, in act 1, the magician can only remind him:

> Prospero: How now? Moody?
>   What is't thou canst demand?
> Ariel: My liberty.
> Prospero: Before the time be out? No more. (1.2.245–48)

Prospero comes off like the bee-king, chiding his peevish subject and reminding him of time's bondage.

At stake in both Ariel's and Dowland's lyrics is the idea of servitude and bondage. We should not see Ariel's poem as a paean to Nature or as imbued solely with fantasies of woodland spirits. He is no Puck. His master is no fairy king, but an all-too-human duke, displaced, exiled, and gifted with new powers, but a human nonetheless. There is no magical transformation in *The Tempest* in the way that there are transformations in *Midsummer*

Night's Dream. Nobody gets an ass's ears here. Instead, we have the magic of lyric language itself, and the ways in which poetry and music can create in the mind of the listener the sense of being changed. *Liquescat anima*.

No souls are truly turned to liquid. It is a metaphor, a figure, and it is precisely in this sense of being a figure that it has power. Campion's praise of Dowland, like Dowland's own poetry and like Ariel's place in *The Tempest*, lives in the world of "as if." These are impersonations, actings-as, performances. It is, Campion would say, as if my soul were liquefied. It is as if Ariel is a harpy; it is as if strange phantoms come in masque and music; it is as if all of this had been a dream; it is as if there were a time when bees could speak.

These plays of mythic lyricism create worlds of like and as, and if Ariel's freedom is a fantasy, or Dowland's recognition unrequited desire, then so too is our own. For in the world of court, as in the world of Ovid's *Metamorphoses*, all acts of artifice are mediated. Creatures perform because they are commanded to. Ceyx and Alcyone is as much a fable of artistic commission as it is a story of love, loss, and transformation. Ariel's poem creates a discourse of artistic independence. The image of the bee becomes an image of self-generating artistry—a move from sleep and water to new flight and nectar. Where the bee sucks, there suck I. Now, we are far from salt seas that crust the lips or from the deluding inspirations of the bottle. Take not a drunkard for a god. But then again, what does it mean to have drunk up, or spilled the liquid of one's life in playing? What would it mean, to go back to Dowland's Epistle, to imagine a world in which "incouragement" needs no "applause"?

> Release me from my bands
> With the help of your good hands. (5.1.327–28)

Prospero's claim upon the audience returns us, too, to Dowland, as if now he is the supplicant before the King of Bees, seeking release from service to the bonds of time. Prospero seems to call for applause, but he calls, too, for a power of the hand. *Siste divi-*

nas manus, stay your divine hands, Campion had pleaded. Do not tap my now-liquid soul, not just yet. These are concluding fables of, quite literally, manumission: a release through hands.

But as we look back through the play, we see the hand as both release and bondage. Caliban is a creature of his hands: those long fingers that would pluck the berries, fish, and point out secrets for the clowns. His fingers are not magical, but they do reveal. They do not pluck the strings, but they do, in their own way, open up an Orphic scope of all creation. Springs and berries, crabs and nuts, birds, marmosets—all fall as food beneath his fingertips. His fantasy of freedom is a fantasy of what his fingers will *not* do: no more making dams for fish, no more fetching things, no more scraping of trenchers. These earthy hands seek their release not just from tasks but from poetry itself. Caliban's celebration at the end of act 2 has all the feel of verse unmoored. His "Freedom, high-day! High-day, freedom!" may recall, as Douglas Bruster has suggested, Will Kempe's shouts and jigs, as well as the ill-mannered exclamations of the rioters and holidaymakers who had threatened London's civic stasis in the late Elizabethan years. It may be, in Bruster's words, less a shout of enslaved native than a "rite expression of a folk id."[30]

By contrast, Ariel is carefully controlled. His song is high art for the Jacobean listener, and Prospero commends its courtliness: "Why, that's my dainty Ariel." Ariel, now, remains refined, carefully poised, even a bit girlish. The play's last movements take us out of phantasms and airy flights and place us squarely in the world that Prospero must enter once again: a world not of seeming but of being. "I drink the air before me," Ariel announces on his way—one final gesture to this world of water before the Italians enter, one last time, fully awake, dry, clear-eyed, and forgiving. "Was't well done?" Ariel's last words in the play take us back to the artist as an actor, and to Morpheus himself, impersonating the dead Ceyx in a dream. Recall Colin Burrow's interpretation of this Ovidian moment: "these are the . . . lines of an uneasy actor who is not quite sure that he lives up to the part he is playing."[31] Dowland and Ariel have spent their time anxious about living up to parts they played. Both live in a paradox of early modern artistry: a need for institutionalized patronage, and yet a longing for artistic independence.

Lyric transforms the listener as it shapes the self. If Ariel is to be thought of as the mythic hero of this play, what of his metamorphosis? Shakespeare denies his lovers transformation into birds, and Ariel himself is left only to act the avian aggressor when commanded to appear "like a harpy, clap[ping] his wings upon the table," and disrupting Alonso's banquet. But he was always Prospero's bird. "This was well done, my bird," he commends Ariel after he leaves the drunkards with Caliban (4.1.184), and when Prospero at last releases him, he verbally transforms him into flight:

> My Ariel, chick,
> That is thy charge. Then to the elements
> Be free, and fare thou well. (5.1.316–18)[32]

Prospero must return to mundane things, but Ariel is now released to air, and what makes this play not just so comically but so mythically restorative at its conclusion is this final, Ovidian metamorphosis. For when Prospero casts himself upon the mercy of his audience, he too pleads now not for water but for air: a "gentle breath" to fill his sails, as elevating as the air that lifts Alcyone and Ceyx's new-grown wings.

3

Poetry and Performance in *The Winter's Tale*

The Tempest opens the First Folio, and with it, the Comedies. There is much both archetypally and sensually comic about the play: its restoration of the seeming dead, its restitution of political and social order with a ritual of betrothal, its farcical clowns, its puns and wordplay. The Comedies end with *The Winter's Tale*, and there is a good deal that is both funny and restorative in it as well. The ballad-monger Autolycus practically takes over the fourth act, and his flamboyant wit, his arch disguises, and his joyous song have seduced the play's audiences from its first performance. Simon Foreman saw it at the Globe on May 15, 1611, and he spent a full third of his journal entry on this "rogue," clearly taken by the character he called a "colt-pixie." Autolycus may be as much a comic sprite as anybody in *The Tempest*, or *A Midsummer Night's Dream* for that matter, and the restoration of Hermione, the resolutions of its characters' myriad disguises, and its powerful acts of forgiveness and remorse make this play as richly comic as the one that opens the First Folio's first section.[1]

Some think the play's inclusion may have been more afterthought than argument, however. Its text has its own set of signature marks. There is a blank page between its opening and the end of the play before, *Twelfth Night*. Modern scholars have supposed that the copy of the play came late, perhaps due to a lag in transcribing or to some difficulties in obtaining rights. Stephen Orgel has averred that "the fact that the play was placed last has as little significance as the fact that *The Tempest* was placed first."[2]

Or as much. Both texts were carefully prepared by the scribe Ralph Crane, and both bear the hallmarks of his work.[3] Both plays represent the central features of Shakespearean late theater: the elaborate syntax that, at times, breaks boundaries of meaning; the heightened use of music to create a theater of sonic impression; the plotlines of great sea travel, displacement, reconciliation, and remorse; the fascination with the daughter as the intersection of aesthetic and political reflection; and the broader questions of legitimacy, inheritance, and power, all expressed in terms of metamorphosis.[4]

It is tempting to juxtapose the two plays. King Leontes appears, at times, a madder (in both senses of the word) Prospero. Queen Hermione's return fulfills, in a displaced but no less satisfying way, the wished-for resurrection of a mother gone before *The Tempest* even starts. There is a powerful Ovidian undercurrent to both. The tale of Ceyx and Alcyone haunts their narratives of sea voyage, death by water, and the dead coming back in dreams. The Orphic sense of musical performance, too, shadows both plays, and together with the stories of Persephone and Pygmalion, it weaves together in *The Winter's Tale* (in the words of A. D. Nuttall) "a complex sequence of unrivaled power." Nuttall finds the play's "ironizing lyric celebrations of nature" a culmination of a process working through the comedies as a whole.[5] Certainly the character of Autolycus inhabits an ironic Ovidian mythography: "My father named me Autolycus, who, being as I am littered under Mercury, was likewise a snapper-up of unconsidered trifles" (4.3.23–26). His mythic genealogy—a child of a shape-shifting god, grandfather of wily Odysseus—made him, for Ovid, a figure for false poetic imagining: "He could make white black and black white."[6] The twin of Philammon (Apollo's child), Autolycus is something of a false musician, and he comes off as a kind of bad brother to Ariel: a songster without patronage, left to hawk ballads for money, whose metamorphic skills have now decayed from godly shapes and avian threats into false beards.[7]

At least one early reader of the First Folio seems to have twigged to some of these echoes. A copy now in the Mesei University Library in Japan contains extensive annotations by an early owner, in a hand and spelling datable to the first third of the seventeenth century.[8] Most of these annotations reflect prompts and provocations. They reproduce key phrasings of the plays, note certain plot developments, attend to characters, and by and large provide a basic précis of the actions and the subject matter of the text. Occasionally, the annotator comes up with something striking. At the close of *The Tempest*, he has written:

> sorrows turned to joy
> unexpected preservation
> extraordinary[y] operation
> strange things not to be admired
> fortune witches

Such responses may not slake our thirst for contemporary literary criticism. But they do feed our imagination. They make clear, as many of this annotator's marks do, that he is a reader fascinated by the spectacle of theater, by the unexpected and the unbelievable, by strangeness, fortune, witchcraft, and the resolutions of the stage.

His annotations to *The Winter's Tale* return explicitly to these concerns. On the play's first page, he attends right away to its opening discussion of the "entertainment" in Bohemia, a word that appears but once in the first scene but that shows up repeatedly in his marginal comments at the top of the play's opening: "nobler enterteanment . . . princes bred young together enterteane their friendship . . . Great thanks for royall enterteanment." Clearly, the annotator sees something in this word, and it shows up again when he records the "entertainment at a shepeards feast" much later in the play. It is, in fact, one of his favorite words of approbation, noting scenes in other plays where various performances take on a pleasant quality. In reading through his annotations, we can see he has an eye for spectacle and, with that eye, a sensitivity to things strange and amazing. Another of his frequently repeated words is "incredible." In *The Winter's Tale*, he comments on Autolycus's "incredible knaueries" and Perdita's "incredible discouery to be leontes daughter." His last annotations to the play clearly reflect a personal response and not simply an abstract of what has been happening:

> picture equaling life
> things so incredible as may make the beholders to beleeue they are done by witchcraft
> the Queene Hermione liues and speakes

What Shakespeare's play has done for this particular reader is to spark a sense of wonder and amazement. There are no comments on the difficulty of Leontes's speeches, no remarks on the famous cruces of the play (the stage direction, "exit, pursued by a bear," and the association of the statue-like Hermione with the work of "Guliano Romano"). There are, however, comments that chime with the kinds of things that Simon Foreman had found memorable in performance. Like Foreman, this annotator draws a maxim from its actions. Compare his comment, "a true gentleman may sweare a lye for his friend," with Foreman's, "Beware of trusting feigned beggars or fawning fellows." And while the annotator pays careful attention to Hermione's revival (something Foreman either missed or had forgotten), both he and the diarist take note, immediately, of Leontes: for Foreman, he is "overcome with jealousy of his wife"; for the First Folio annotator, he "becomes Impatientlie Iealous," and beset with "Incurable height of Intolerable Iealousie."

I think this annotator got *The Winter's Tale* (much as he got *The Tempest*) as something truly strange, testing the boundaries of believability. Nobody in the play attributes Hermione's resurrection to "witchcraft." Nobody calls anything "incredible." Yes, they stare and are baffled. But it is this annotator who reflects what generations of readers and audiences have felt about it: that its plot simply cannot be believed, and that there must be something witchy or magical about its ending. It inhabits the sorceric world more of *The Tempest* than of *Twelfth Night*, a grammar of stunned negations: incredible, impatient, incurable, intolerable.

The Winter's Tale pairs with *The Tempest* as a play about the force of theater and the poetics of metamorphosis. "Picture equaling life" is as good an aphorism about acting as about myth. To live and speak returned from the (seeming) dead may be a theme for Ovid. But it is part of both plays' actions, and a haunted quality behind their lyric voicings.

It is, as well, an aphorism for the theater, and the notion of living pictures or the dead returning enhances *The Winter's Tale*'s verbal and visionary relationship with the First Folio's opening feints: its claims for literary texts as orphans to be guarded; its fascinations with accurate copy and representation; its imagery of a dead playwright brought to life. "My Shakespeare, rise." Ben Jonson's half-line chimes in the ear, whether we hear it in Prospero's commands or in the music that brings Hermione back to movement. What better phrase than "picture equaling life" could be the distillation of Jonson's own sonnet that opens the Folio itself? That sonnet, paired with the picture of the playwright, asks us to compare the likeness and the life, the word and the will. And what better phrase could be invoked for Jonson's charge, later in his couplets, "To the Memory of My Beloved author, Mr William Shakespeare":

> Look how the father's face
> Liues in his issue, euen so, the race
> Of Shakespeare's mind, and manners brightly shines
> In his well torned, and true filed lines.

This is the point of praise as much as it will be the problem of a play whose father figure constantly questions whether his face lives in his issue. This is the point, too, of the relationships between the actor and arts of playing. "The Queene Hermione lives and speaks": what better comment could return us to the final poem of the Folio's commendations? There, John Mabbe had averred: "An actor's art / Can die, and live to act second part." In *The Winter's Tale*, Paulina becomes the stage manager of Hermione's rebirth, as she announces, "Do not shun her / Until you see her die again, for then / You kill her double."

There is a powerful association in these idioms of likeness, reproduction, and performance in the First Folio and in *The Winter's Tale*, and they represent a broader problem in the Jacobean aesthetic—a problem about showing and displaying truth through artifice, a problem about how we can believe our eyes, especially (as in the case of James's own performed spectatorship) when other eyes may do the seeing for us. The Jacobean aesthetic raised questions about not just eyes but ears, for what was changing, too, in the first decades of the century were modes of musical and poetic performance. The old Elizabethan tropes of private melancholy, lyric pastoral, and queenly service were giving way to new idioms of public entertainment. John Dowland, upon his return to England after a decade away, found "strange entertainment," and performers who would only "shroude themselues vnder the title of Musitians." Dowland comes home to a new court, full of new practices and "strangers from beyond the seas."[9]

So, too, we move from *The Tempest* to *The Winter's Tale*. In *The Tempest*, music is an agent of metamorphosis. The landscape's sounds are sweet and ravishing. The carefully planned entertainments on the island represent a courtly blend of song and spectacle designed to call attention to the planners: to their imagination, artistry, and execution. Lyrics express fear and desire. They contribute to the restitution of the long-thought dead and the redemption of the exiled.

In *The Winter's Tale*, however, Autolycus sings his songs and hawks his ballads not to bring his listeners into harmony but to make them pay, and pay attention.[10] The undercurrents of desire in *The Tempest* float along the surface of Bohemia here. The ballads of act 4 suggest illicit sex and cuckoldry. They mock the metamorphoses of Orphic song. The music of *The Winter's Tale* is, but for its last call, a music of terrors and transgressions turned to foolishness, of awful things told and sold for a bit of entertainment. Only at the play's end, when the statue of Hermione will be revived, does music play its Orpheus-like, transforming role. "Music; awake her—strike!"

Music, too, throughout *The Winter's Tale* raises not only aesthetic but social and commercial questions about print and publication in the making of performative authority. "I love a ballad in print," says Mopsa in act 4. The social drama of performance in Bohemia goes on in a world of texts. Autolycus trades in printed objects. His authority comes from the sheets themselves, for even though the content of his ballads may be strange or unbelievable, the simple fact that these are printed ballads renders them, at least for audiences such as the rustic Mopsa, "true." Relationships of print to music were in flux during the early Jacobean years, and part of what *The Winter's Tale* explores is just what Dowland himself was exploring in his songbooks: how does an author establish authority in print; what does it mean to take the sounds of plucked strings and tuned voices and fix them on notes and staves; and, finally, how does the publication of refined and courtly art song compare with the running off of broadsides for the street?[11]

There is much that is true and false in print throughout *The Winter's Tale*. Paulina, as I have already noted, sees the matter of legitimacy to be one of facial proofreading. Leontes, at the play's end, acknowledges his daughter as having been "printed off." And in the scenes with Hermione on trial, Leontes will call for an indictment to be read (whose accusations he will follow) and an oracle to be unscrolled (whose affirmations he will not).[12]

Leontes lives as much in worlds of sheets as Autolycus, and part of my argument is that these characters share more than we might expect. The former struggles with the old tropes of the lyric and the pastoral, while the latter mocks the courtly power plays of rule. Leontes's jealous fantasies seem spun out of a dirty ballad hawked on city streets, and when Autolycus appears in act 4 it is not, I think, out of nowhere, but as a comic echo of the angry King. We hear the echoes of the first acts in the later ones. The music of the balladeer is but a breath away from courtly airs.

In my account, *The Winter's Tale* takes representation and replication as its theme. It talks about inheritance in terms of print and copy; it questions what is real and what is imaginary; it shows us figures who read and misread the bodies and acts of others; it questions relationships of past and present, asking us to wonder whether time and memory preserve or alter; and, finally, it asks its actors to perform in ways almost unprecedented on the stage—to convince us that Leontes's initial jealousy and rage has reason, and to stand stock still as a statue before music calls the performer to move.

Whatever circumstances brought *The Winter's Tale* to be the final comedy, it stands in the Folio as commendation and as commentary on the arc of humor. It plays out the implications of past music, while drawing the reader back and back again to the poetics of the Folio's opening prefaces and poems. Read and read again. Such is a command not just to the owner of the book but to the characters throughout the play.

From Pastoral to Ballad

But this was more than a play to be read. Simon Foreman, as I have already mentioned, memorably saw the play at the Globe in May 1611, and we know that it was played again at the Banqueting House in November that year, and again (along with *The Tempest*) for the celebrations surrounding James's daughter, Anne's, betrothal to Prince Frederick. It was performed again at court in 1618, 1619, and 1624.[13] What was it that made the play so appropriate for royal audiences? The text we have—with its arresting ambiguities and textual conundrums—seems hard fare for an audience that, as we know from other sources, often greeted its celebratory masques and plays with less than sober attention. And in its story of a jealous king, a dead boy, and a manic balladeer, it may seem an odd play before a court that, after 1613, had lost its Prince of Wales and had apparently relegated one of the greatest musicians of the age, John Dowland, to a subordinate accompanist. What must have appealed to the Jacobean audience was what must have appealed to the First Folio's annotator: the play's opening attention to royal entertainments and its incredible turns worthy of witchcraft.

The Winter's Tale begins, as many do, with minor characters reviewing history and plot. Archidamus (whom we will never see again) and Camillo (whom we will) reflect on differences between the two courts of Sicilia and Bohemia. Camillo notes that the King of Sicilia will visit Bohemia the coming summer, and Archidamus responds (interrupted):

> Wherein our entertainment shall shame us; we shall be justified in our loves . . . Verily I speak it in the freedom of my knowledge. We cannot with such magnificence—in so rare—I know not what to say. We will give you sleepy drinks, that your senses, unintelligent of our insufficience, may, though they cannot praise us, as little accuse us. (1.1.8–15)

This opening exchange lays out the template, not just for the actions of the play, but for the actions of the Jacobean court. Invited entertainment was the currency of diplomatic value for the age. Visiting dignitaries, families, and relatives would come and go, but they would certainly be entertained. King James loved acts of lavish hospitality. Drink flowed for him, for example, at the home of Oliver Cromwell in 1603, when the new king was en route to London to be crowned. In the words of the chronicler Thomas Fuller, "All the pipes of the house expressed themselves in no other language than several sorts of the choicest wines," and James is recorded as having cheered: "Morry mon, thou hast treated me better than anyone since I left Edinburgh."[14] On a later occasion in 1606, hosting James's sister and her husband, King Christian of Denmark, wines flowed to such an extent that, as John Harrington put it, the court players in the mask so "abandon[ed] their sobriety" that the whole affair ended in a drunken slapstick:

> The Lady who did play the Queens part did carry most precious gifts to both their Majesties; but, forgetting the steppes arising to the canopy, overset her caskets into his Danish Majesties lap, and

> fell at his feet, tho I rather think it was in his face. Much was the hurry and confusion; . . . The entertainment and shew went forward and most of the presenters went backward, or fell down, wine did so occupy their upper chambers. Now did appear in rich dress, Hope, Faith, and Charity: . . . Hope and Faith . . . were both sick and spewing in the lower hall . . . I have much marveled at these strange pageantries . . . ; I neer did see such lack of good order, discretion, and sobriety, as I have now done.[15]

It is easy to imagine Archidamus thinking of such scenes: we will get you so intoxicated that you will not care whether or not the shows are any good. And it is easy to imagine James's court, seeing the play in something of a night before the morning after, loudly approving the imagined reception in Bohemia. Archidamus may think that their entertainments may shame them; but, if Harrington's account is anything to go by, there was plenty of self-shaming going on in courtly entertainments.

If Harrington "marveled," so, too, would any audience, for after this brief exchange in its first scene, *The Winter's Tale* moves directly to Leontes's court and the imminent departure of Polixenes. To tell the story of this scene in bare plot seems incredible: failing to convince his childhood friend to stay more than the nine months he has already stayed, Leontes turns to his wife, Hermione, who does convince the friend to stay, and in that convincing, Leontes sees an infidelity. He works himself into a jealous rage, imagining Hermione and Polixenes in love, in bed, and ultimately, parenting the child with whom Hermione is pregnant.

Strange pageantries indeed, for there is little in Sicilia to suggest a quality of entertainment to be matched by rival courts. For all the music that will fill the play once it emerges in Bohemia, there is little song here. No fanfares announce the characters; there are no entertainments at the feast; nobody sings or listens. And yet, there is much in this first act that evokes both the lyricality of older songs and pastorals and, too, the undercurrents of the street ballads that will emerge in full force in act 4.[16]

If the first scenes of the play are all about remembering events, they are also about remembering poetry. Polixenes's memory of childhood is a memory of an earlier poetic language. He expresses past events in terms of the pastoral lyricism of the age of Spenser and Sidney. From the beginning, he frames time in terms of pastorality. "Nine changes of the watery star hath been / The shepherd's note since we have left our throne / Without a burden" (1.2.1–3). These are the opening lines of scene 2, and they define the double worlds of past and poetry for Polixenes. Read literally, he simply states that nine months have passed according to the observation of the shepherds since Polixenes left his throne without worrying about it. And yet, in the play's lyric world, these words take on the resonances of the musical and the mysterious. That "shepherd's note" and "burden" evoke song and story, musical performance among rustics that, as we will see by the play's end, inform the joyous singing of the sheepshearing scene in Bohemia. Polixenes has pastoral forever on his mind. When Hermione persuades him to recall his childhood with Leontes, he does so in terms of a poetic time.

> We were, fair Queen,
> Two lads that thought there was no more behind
> But such a day tomorrow as today,
> And to be boy eternal.
> . . .
> We were as twinned lambs that did frisk i'th'sun,
> And bleat the one at th'other;

And he goes on,

> In those unfledged days was my wife a girl;
> Your precious self had then not crossed the eyes
> Of my young playfellow. (1.2.62–78)

Polixenes speaks like an old Elizabethan courtier-poet. Compare his language with the verse of Thomas Weelkes, whose *Ballets and Madrigals* appeared in 1598:

> Vnto our flocks, sweet Corolus,
> Our bagpipe song now caroll thus,
> Whilst flocks & heards bee grazing,
> Let vs our rest bee praizing,

To teach our flocks their wonted bounds,
On Bagpipes play the Shepherds grounds:
The tender Lambs with bleting,
Will help our ioyfull meting.[17]

Compare his language, too, with the verses in Thomas Nashe's play, printed in 1600, *Summer's Last Will and Testament*:

Lambs frisk and play, the Shepherds pype all day
And we heare aye, birds tune this merry day.[18]

Those lambs are everywhere in the Elizabethan imaginary. They fill Sidney's *Arcadias*, Old and New, for example at this moment early in the *New Arcadia*: "each pasture stored with sheep feeding with sober security, while the pretty lambs with bleating oratory craved the dams' comfort."[19] Even in his address to Hermione herself, "Your precious self," Polixenes returns to an old idiom—a phrase used in the sixteenth century for Christ, now turned to adoration of a living woman rather than a savior.[20]

These forays into lexicography reveal Polixenes to be a man who makes his childhood out of the Elizabethan pastorals and play.[21] His presence, too, prompts courtesies of older courts as well. Hermione pleads, Polixenes relents, she gives him her hand. These are performances of graciousness. She uses the word "grace" three times in less than thirty lines here, much as Sidney would use it over and again in the *Defense of Poesy*, marking Polixenes as courtier of coded courtesy. "Tis grace indeed."[22]

But in the courtesies of older courts, Leontes sees treason. He misreads the codes of lyric graciousness as unfeigned passion. "Too hot, too hot!" he breaks in. He sees not the pastorals of memory but "entertainment," a word he uses repeatedly to condemn the politeness of his wife and friend. His heart dances, his syntax breaks, and he sees not courtly hands but "paddling palms and pinching fingers." He sees not Sidney-like feigning but "practiced smiles / As in a looking-glass."

He loses it, and what he loses himself in is not the older poetry of court but the contemporary rhymes of street ballads and songs. His jealous fantasies ring, horribly, with the comic ballads that emerged in the early seventeenth century—ballads about cuckoldry and sexual transgression, about women who turn into murderers and monsters. Autolycus, famously, will hawk them in act 4. But we need not go that far to hear them in the background of Leontes's anger. Trapped in his jealousy, he finds himself a figure of ballad cuckoldry lost at court. His fantasies spin out—Hermione and Polixenes have touched illicitly, he has made her pregnant, they have been carrying on without his knowledge. He works himself into a hot rage over this imagined infidelity, a heat that we will feel, again and again, in Bohemia: in the "hot service" of the Clown, in Autolycus's joke that the Clown's purse "is not hot enough to purchase your spice," and in his call for a "hot infusion." Indeed, Leontes's iterative anger has its comic answer in act 4, when Autolycus explains his own daring skill at picking pockets.

> Aside, aside—here is more matter for a hot brain (4.4.679)

Even though Autolycus speaks in prose, his phrases scan as sharply as Leontes's. Hot brain or *tremor cordis*—both figure forth a bad anatomy of understanding, and to compare these two men's speeches is to watch the stabs of verbal repetition twist them into near incomprehension.

> Tȯ mingle friendship far is mingling bloods.
> I have *tremor cordis* on me; my heart dances,
> But not for joy, not joy. (1.2.108–10)

> What an exchange had this been, without boot! What boot is here, with this exchange! (4.4.670–72)

Both speakers focus on repeated words, phrases that break the flow of syntax and of sense. They show us just how limited language can be when faced with fear or fancy. Autolycus replays Leontes's anger as a farce, shows us the comic behind his exaggerations, and in retrospect, points to how the King had linguistically and socially lowered himself away from old courtly feignings into blunt colloquialisms. Leontes's speech grows increasingly colloquial here: words for sexual congress, apostrophes of anger, brusque calls to the boy Mamillius. *I'fecks, bawcock, smutch.* This is the language of street brought home to court. It is the wordplay of the balladeer brought to where lyricality should rule.

"Play, play," Leontes commands the young boy (1.2.184). Again, Leontes repeats, as if saying a word over and over again would somehow rope its meaning into hold. This is the syntax of a debased or a devalued character, the syntax of such an incessant iterater as Shylock in *The Merchant of Venice*.

> Why, there, there, there, there! (3.1.77)
> What, what, what? Ill luck, ill luck? (3.1.92)
> Good news, good news! Ha, ha, heard in Genoa! (3.1.98)[23]

Every word seems to come, here, with a finger thrust into the air, much as Leontes, a theatrical generation later, will repeat his words. And with each repetition, Shylock's suspicious ghost seems to return, haunting the Sicilia as he haunted Venice.

But Leontes outdoes Shylock in his syntactic breaks and his semantic innuendos. His words increasingly smack of double entendre, perhaps no more explicitly than in the idioms of sluicing and fishing for sexuality (an idiom of fishing that Autolycus will take up, too). And when Leontes whips himself into a rage of his imagined sights, he practically yells to Camillo.

> Ha' you not seen, Camillo–
> But that's past doubt; you have, or your eyeglass
> Is thicker than a cuckold's horn—or heard–
> For to a vision so apparent Rumour
> Cannot be mute—or thought—for cogitation
> Resides not in that man who does not think—
> My wife is slippery? If thou wilt confess,
> Or else be impudently negative,
> To have nor eyes, nor ears, nor thought, then say
> My wife's a hobby-horse, deserves a name
> As rank as any flax-wench that puts to
> Before her troth-plight—say't, and justify't. (1.2.264–75)

Leontes's concatenating of broken phrases here holds together not through common syntax but through comic repetition.[24] He will go on and offer up a string of questions, opening with "Is whispering nothing?" and concluding with that "nothing" seven times in four-and-a-half lines. Now, he is a jealous Shylock channeling Lear: "Nothing will come of nothing," said that old king. Leontes gives us a mad ruler not in the wilderness but in the street. Lear may find beasts upon the heath, but now Leontes conjures a menagerie of the illicit: the cuckold with his horns, a hobby-horse, and a "slippery" wife. That latter figure resonates with all the slippery fish of sixteenth-century comic verse and, in its own weird way, looks forward to the tales of Autolycus and his ballad of a woman who had turned into a "cold fish." This is the language of what Hamlet punningly would label "country matters." "Hobby-horse" is an editorial emendation for the Folio's "Holy-Horse," but it seems right when read against such lyrics as those of Thomas Weelkes.[25]

> Ovr cuntry swains, in the morris daunce,
> Thus wooe & win their brides,
> Will for our towne, the hobby horse
> At pleasure, frolike rides.[26]

And Leontes's strange coinage "flax-wench" (the only appearance of the term, according to the *OED*) recalls "flax-wife," the subject of a tale included in Robert Greene's *A Notable Discovery of Cozenage*: "How a flax-wife and her neighbours used a cozening collier."[27]

Leontes, in short, descends. His broken sentences, his repetitions, his colloquialism all take him out of the pastoral lyricism of his childhood friend and set him as the comic cuckold in a street song. Howard Felperin had noticed something of this quality when he asserted that "Autolycus's ballads re-enact in a grotesque or surrealist form . . . Leontes' opening fantasies of illicit pregnancy and condign punishment."[28] But Felperin, I think, has it backwards. It is not so much that the balladeer's later appearance makes the King's earlier paranoia seem harmless. It is that the King has already anticipated the strange sexuality of ballad cuckoldry: its weird ability to transform women into monsters.

"My wife is slippery." Readers since Samuel Johnson have found this phrase to connote instability or sexual infidelity. But "slippery" is a palpable word for the early modern reader. It connoted sliminess and fishy feel as early as the mid-sixteenth century, and the phrase "slippery as an eel" was well in circulation by the 1550s. "All that be long and slipperie as Yeels and Congres" was the phrase found in Holland's translation of Pliny from 1601. It is, I think, a short step from Leontes's slippery wife to Autolycus's tale of a woman "turned into a cold fish."[29]

And in that short step lies the metamorphic nature of Leontes's jealousy. Everyone knows he is a bad reader of people, a spectator not of what is there but of what his hot brain imagines him to see. But what that bad reader becomes is, in his own way, a crazed Ovid. Leontes's spasm to Camillo offers up a mock-Orphic menagerie. Horned cuckolds, a slippery wife, a hobby-horse, a flax-wench, a personified Rumor, and eyes and ears that seem to hover disembodied from their heads—this is the landscape of Leontes's anger. *The Winter's Tale* needs no Caliban in the flesh. It has its monsters ever present before the eyes of a jealous king. Young Mamillius's memories of stories full of "sprites and goblins" cannot hold a candle to Leontes's visions of his sullied sheets: "goads, thorns, nettles, tails of wasps." And all around him, people change accordingly. Camillo, fresh from this encounter, seems to Polixenes "changed" in "complexions." Polixenes himself is changed as well: "A party in this alteration, finding myself altered with't" (1.2.376ff).

Kings Set Onstage

And as we read or watch, we witness alterations of its characters. Hermione grows visibly pregnant ("She is spread of late / Into a goodly bulk," 2.1.19–20), and Leontes becomes not only verbally and viscerally unhinged but works himself into a bodily transformation. "I am a feather for each wind that blows" (2.3.153).

Throughout these middle acts, *The Winter's Tale* becomes a play of alterations, and a reader schooled on Shakespeare's most familiar lines could not but hear in Polixenes's avowal an echo of a Sonnet's famous phrase.

> Love is not love
> Which alters when it alteration finds,
> Or bears with the remover to remove. (116.3–4)

Love, in that Sonnet, is an "ever-fixed mark." And yet, throughout *The Winter's Tale*, the marks of love and power shift and shade. "Mark my counsel," "mark her well," "mark and perform it"—the word "mark" shows up ten times in the play, each time signaling a chance to notice, obey, and record. But as we mark Leontes, we see him increasingly off his performance, and his theatrical status has a political force as well.[30]

James I and his court would have found much in the first movements of the play to please their sense of entertainment. Would they have found as much in Leontes himself?

Poetry was politics and politics was poetry for the king. Throughout his many published works, he equated rulership with verbal self-control. Ben Jonson praised him as a master of poetic form and public oratory: "How, best of Poets, do'st thou laurel weare!"[31] This is precisely what Leontes is not, and part of the appeal—and part of the terror—of *The Winter's Tale* lies in its challenge to Jamesean rule. His broken verses would have jarred against a royal poetics, and his audiences would have heard much that he argued long before.

Leontes's family provides a stark contrast to a royal court now confident in establishment of family ties, of spousal troth, of children's legitimacy, and of a mastery of documents that gave the king (in the words of Jonathan Goldberg) "a relationship to language [that] provided a primary identity."[32] Earlier English monarchs had, of course, prided themselves on their creative skills. Henry VIII took credit as a lyricist and a composer. Elizabeth translated major works of Latin literature and composed poetry of wit and subtlety, such that George Puttenham could dub her a writer of poems "passing sweete and harmonicall . . . gorgeous and bewtifull."[33] But James was different. Long before taking on the joint throne, he had associated royal rule with literary and linguistic instruction. He articulated an ideal of parental prowess centered on the mastery of verbal form. Goldberg brings out this ideal in a subtle reading of James's "Trew Law of Free Monarchies" of 1597, where the then King of Scotland figured his relationship to God, the "sharpest schoolemaster." His "Schort Treatise on Scots Poesie" (1584) adumbrated a vision (in Goldberg's words) that "Royal power expresses itself by giving others words . . . the ideal of regularity in verse is also a version of social decorum, all things in their place."[34]

This relationship between the social and the prosodic sets James's treatise apart from his many sources (Cicero and Quintilian, Puttenham and Gascoigne).[35] He is concerned less with the questions of invention and inspiration that motivated classical theorists than with the technical matters of rhythm and rhyme. He wants regularity in verse, and he wants that regularity to be easily perceived. "Your eare man be the onely iudge and discerner thairof." He contrasts, then, the regularly scanning line, "Into the Sea then Lucifer upsprang," with the awkward one: "In the Sea then Lucifer to upsprang."[36]

Such distinctions may seem simplistic to the scholar, but they speak directly to James's own developing conception of verbal regularity and political control. They speak directly, too, to many of the difficulties that the speeches in *The Winter's Tale* have posed to editors. Leontes, in particular, verges on indecipherable obscurity. Listen to him free-associate before Mamillius:

> Thou want'st a rough pash, and the shoots that I have
> To be full like me; yet they say we are
> Almost as like as eggs—women say so,
> That will say anything. (1.2.127–30)

He goes on, lines hardly making syntactic sense, interrupting himself, barely scanning the pentameters. The passage in the First Folio breaks up the lines with parentheses, and modern editors have struggled to repunctuate. Like Polixenes, we may well respond, "What means Sicilia?" and like Hermione we may judge, "He something seems unsettled."[37]

To be unsettled is precisely to be out of prosodic and political control, and James returns to these themes in his great *Basilikon Doron*, the manual for royal rule he prepared for his son, Henry, in 1599. Repeatedly, he stresses relationships among political and verbal prowess, recognizing that the king is always, as it were, onstage before an audience of judges.

> It is a trew old saying, That a King is as one set on a stage, whose smallest actions and gestures, all the people gazingly doe behold.

As such a performer, the future king should bear "speaking and language" in mind.

> I iyone your gesture, since action is one of the chiefest qualities, that is required in an oratour; for as the tongue speaketh to the eares, so doeth the gesture speake to the eyes of the auditour. In both your speaking and your gesture, use a natural and plaine form, not fairded with artifice.[38]

James here provides a template against which we, and he, assess Leontes. It is not simply that the Duke acts and speaks irrationally, or that we cannot discern the motives for his jealousy. It is that the disjunction between speech and action represents him as a bad actor, as a ruler on a stage ill speaking and ill reading. He undermines the fundamental Jacobean unity of word and power. His speech and gesture come off far from natural and plain. And in his increasing emotion, Leontes strides as a man "fairded with artifice"—to translate James's Scots, embellished, adorned, made fake.

"Forget not," James counseled, "to digest euer your passion, before ye determine vpon anything."[39] But Leontes is an actor ruled by passion, a bad Hamlet overcome by emotion.

> What would he do,
> Had he the motive and the cue for passion
> That I have? (*Hamlet*, 2.2.561–63)

That is the point that Hamlet does not understand—that acting is impersonation, that it does not demand the unbridled display of feeling but, instead, requires the masked imitation of emotion.

James clearly understood this, too, as both a player and a king. For while he recognized that a king must act upon a stage, he condemns rulers who would consort with

> Comoedians or Balladines, for the Tyrans delighted most in them, glorying to bee both authors and actors of Comoedies and Trageies themselves. . . . And all the ruse that Nero made of himselfe when he died was *Qualis artifex pereo*? Meaning of his skill in menstrally, and playing of Tragoedies; as indeed his whole life and death, was all but one Tragoedie.[40]

Throughout acts 2 and 3, Leontes seems more and more a tragic tyrant, author and actor of his own self-theatrical display. And this point, it seems to me, reveals the larger political and social point about the shift for Sicilia to Bohemia. Most critics have seen Autolycus's entrance as a break in action, as an unanticipated comic shift, or as a welcome relief from the anger and disturbance of the first three acts. But all of this has been anticipated. Leontes has already cast himself as a cuckold in a ballad comedy of errors. He has scripted out for himself a bad tragedy of betrayal and revenge. He calls for texts to be read—the indictment against Hermione, the oracle that exonerates her—only to rewrite the scripts as he sees fit. And so, when Autolycus appears, it is not as some strange creature out of nowhere. It is as the comically restorative version of the duke we have already seen. He is explicitly and self-confessedly the author and the actor of his own comedy. He is the *artifex*, a comic king constantly inviting us to hear him preen. He enters, in a sense, as Leontes transformed. To adapt James's words, he is a tyrant turned into a "balladine."

That word defines better than any other—better than Foreman's "rogue" or "colt-pixie"—the character of Autolycus. James may have been the first to use the word in a British vernacular, at least according to the *OED*, and it records two subsequent appearances that nuance the word's effect: one, from Hearon's *Preacher's Plea* of 1604, "Meeting with our common adversary . . . in the fashion of a Rimer or Balladine"; the other, from Bacon's

Advancement of Learning of 1605, "Trickes of Tumblers Funambuloes, Baladynes." This is the world of self-conscious performance, of dance, acrobatics, and display. This is the world, too, of the European stage and street, for "balladine" comes clearly from the French, while Bacon's "Funambuloes" comes from Spanish or Italian, literally meaning tightrope walkers.

And yet, for all of his descent, Leontes never shows up on the stage with Autolycus. He is absent from these scenes in act 4, as if no town were big enough for the two of them. Some have suggested that the two characters could be doubled in performance: that the same actor could play King and clown and, in the process, bring out the mirrorings of both. Such an idea, provocative for modern theater, would have been completely unhistorical. Leontes would clearly have been performed by a tragedian of Burbage's stature, while Autolycus appears tailor-made for great clowns such as Robert Lowin or John Armin. But the point remains well taken. Leontes and Autolycus are the flip sides of each other, and when the King will return—composed, complete, and cautious—the clown will have been long gone.[41]

The Songs of Autolycus

And if we miss him, we have become parties to the alteration he has worked upon the landscape. Music is the force that moves him—Autolycus enters singing, and his songs take up the coarseness of Leontes's anger, cooling them to streetwise sass. They evoke a popular, a broadside, and an increasingly printed practice of tale-telling through sung verse. They are far different from Ariel's courtly lyrics in *The Tempest*, or the Orphic strains of Queen Katherine's lutenist in *Henry VIII*, or "Hark, hark the lark" of *Cymbeline*. They are more akin to the rough verses of the clowns on Prospero's island. Trinculo and Stephano sing not according to the strains of court but to the lines of ballad. Their songs seem much more like those of Autolycus—but the comparison, it seems to me, is not just one of form or genre but of time and place.

Prospero's is an island trapped in time. For a dozen years he has lived there, and the music of his island still chimes with the ravishments of an Elizabethan Dowland. Its native soundtrack is the set of "sweet airs" Caliban will hear. Stephano and Trincolo bring ashore a kind of music not heard there before, a music of the Jacobean street. Trincolo announces, "this is the tune of our catch," and that last word was, by the early seventeenth century, taking on a new and specific meaning. The "catch" was a short bit of music set for voices. The *OED* cites its appearance first in 1601, and Shakespeare was already using it in *Twelfth Night* (whose first recorded performance was February 2, 1602): "Let's have our catch"; "Let our catch be."[42] This is the music of the Belches and the Aguecheeks of the world, and it is the tune to which Cleopatra imagines her literary afterlife will be sung.

> Saucy lictors
> Will catch at us, like strumpets; and scald rymers
> Ballad us out o' tune. (*Antony and Cleopatra*, 5.2.210–12)

This is the music that was newly emerging in English streets, and new publications brought them together in popular prints. This is the world of Autolycus. He trades in broadside prints, in catches, and in ballads. For all the pastoralism of the landscape, his voice rings out as urban, familiar, and knowing.

Autolycus enters sixteen years past the opening acts. Whatever strangeness lies on Bohemian shores, we are, here, in the present of the Jacobean world, where pastoral becomes an arch performance. Autolycus's opening song rings with these ironies:

> When daffodils begin to peer,
> With hey, the doxy over the dale,
> Why then comes in the sweet o'the year,
> For the red blood reigns in the winter's pale.
>
> The white sheet bleaching on the hedge,
> With hey, the sweet birds O how they sing!
> Doth set my pugging tooth on edge,
> For a quart of ale is a dish for a king.

The lark that tirra lira chants,
  With hey, with hey, the thrush and the jay,
Are summer songs for me and my aunts
  While we lie tumbling in the hay. (4.3.1–22)

This is much less a song than a soliloquy: a personalized, highly mediated version of a popular expression, now turned to the purposes of character development. Samuel Bethell thought these lines "*not* an Elizabethan 'nature' lyric but a product of Jacobean wit which incidentally parodies Elizabethan simplicities," and I agree completely.[43] The daffodils may open, but they do so not before the ladies of the court but before the doxy over the dale. The *OED* defines "doxy" as a term of "Vagabond's cant," for a rogue's mistress or a beggar's wench. The word shows up in Middleton and Dekker's *Roaring Girl*, as well as in a nearly incomprehensible "canting song" by Dekker.[44] The niceties of pastoral morph into vulgarities. So, too, in Autolycus's second stanza, the sweet birds sing over a hedge that has been laid with drying laundry. And their song does not rouse a courtier's tongue but rather sets his "pugging tooth on edge"—a phrase that not even the *OED* can gloss but which, I believe, jibes with the early seventeenth-century word "pug," meaning a whore or courtesan. The *OED* is more assured here, citing Cotgrave's 1611 *Dictionary*: "A Pug . . . a Whore that follows the Camp."[45] And at the end, these are songs for "me and my Aunts," another Jacobean term for prostitutes.[46]

At every chance, Autolycus shifts pastoral desire into whoredom.[47] His song returns us to the tensions of act 1, where Polixenes and Leontes offered competing literary versions of their pasts and presents, where older courtesies butted up against charged cant. And yet, sixteen years and hundreds of miles past Sicilia, this song jars in the ear. A rogue tune, a bit of knavery, a set of stanzas resonant of street ballads—all true. Its sound, its swing, its nonce-words all evoke what theatergoers would have heard outside the confines of the Globe or Blackfriars.

But Autolycus is no real-life rogue plucked from the street. He is a literary construct, a figure of and for performance in itself. "His real association," Anne Barton put it, "is with fictions rather than with genuine evil."[48] He is a fabricator, but he also is a fabrication.

In his subtle reasoning about *The Tempest*, Orgel makes an important point about Prospero's stagecraft. "The masque in *The Tempest* is not a court masque, it is a dramatic allusion to one, and it functions in the structure of the drama not as a separable interlude but as an integral part of the action."[49] The ballads in *The Winter's Tale* function similarly, and to pore through works of scholarship such as Natalia Würzbach's *Rise of the English Street Ballad*, or to scan through the sites collected for the online English Broadside Ballads Archive, is to be struck by differences, as well as similarities, between songs of Bohemia and England.

The broadside ballad, as a social and literary act, merged the old oral traditions of storytelling with the new commercial possibilities of print.[50] While many of the subjects of the ballads would have been familiar, popular, and unattributable to any single author, the physical object of the ballad had become increasingly associated with the printer and the seller. The social function of the ballad may have been to circulate familiar narrative, to entertain through stories of the unseen and the bizarre, and to reinforce the norms of sexual and personal behavior. But the commercial function of the ballad was, increasingly, to make money. Throughout the later sixteenth century, the ballad texts become increasingly self-referential—they call attention to themselves as objects to be sold, as things in print that have a price. In turn, the balladeer becomes a self-conscious performer, someone advertising not only his wares but his own skill at hawking them.

By the 1580s, social commentators noted the widespread presence of the balladeer in towns and cities and the ways in which their performances were becoming increasingly commercialized. "What a frye of such wooden rythmours doth swarme in stationers shops," complained Richard Stanyurst in his prefatory letter to his translation of the *Aeneid* (1582).[51] Every critic, pedagogue, and commentator—from William Webbe through Thomas Nashe through Robert Greene—had something to say about the "base trade" of these balladeers.[52] By the close of the sixteenth century, the balladeers were taking on the status not just of performers of familiar songs or peddlers of paper, but as authors themselves. "Every red-nose rhymester is an author," complained Joseph Hall in 1592, and once again, in 1597: "Some drunken rhymer thinks his time well spent, / If he can live to see his name in print." By 1612, W. Turner could lament that "the world is ful of thredbare poets, / that liue vpon their pen."[53]

Ben Jonson's *Bartholomew Fair* of 1614 has long been appreciated for its detailed illustration of the balladeer's art and artifice. His songster-seller is not named from myth or metamorphosis, but from the commonplace. Nightingale enters singing, and his avian name compels his audience to see him "flutter . . . till he have ne'er a feather left." Nightingale sings "A caveat against cutpurses," and his lines have the patter of the popular.[54]

> My masters, and friends, and good people, draw near.
> And look to your purses, for that I do say.
> And tho' little money in them you do bear,
> It cost more to get than to lose in a day.

Jonson's goal is social satire. His characters ventriloquize the sound and sensibility of everyday experience.[55] This completely differs from the scenes with Autolycus, and it would be a mistake, I think, to take his prancing and pronouncing as straightforwardly as Jonson's Nightingale. The lyrics in *The Winter's Tale* are far more complex, strange, ambiguous, and resonant with the dramatic problems of performance and impersonation building through the play. Autolycus is far more a self-conscious and self-theatricalizing figure than Nightingale—someone more in tune with the idea of the balladeer as author. He uses lyric to present himself. He casts himself—by name, by lineage, by social status—as the true subject of his singing. Whatever the origins of his songs, they are, in performance, about him.

And that is the point. Musicians, high and low, had come to print to authorize their works and claim authority for them. Elizabethan composers such as William Byrd and Thomas Tallis were overseeing publication of their compositions. But it was John Dowland who articulated, in the prefaces to his songbooks, a clear and self-conscious sense of authorship in print. Dowland made clear, from the appearance of his *First Book of Songs* of 1597 through his final volumes, that he was engaged in a "hard enterprise" of committing "our priuate labours to publike view." By the publication of his *Lachrimae* in 1604, he could complain about the unauthorized dissemination of his work in print ("publisht by strangers without my name or approbation"). By 1612, in his last volume, *The Pilgrimes Solace*, he could announce his return to English audiences by affirming the places where his music had appeared in print: "some part of my poore labours haue found favour in the greatest part of Europes, and have been printed in eight most famous Cities beyond the Seas."[56]

Dowland affirms his reputation on the printed page, and such an affirmation makes him both the author and the actor of his own script. He seeks his ownership of printed pages—something that the balladeers increasingly were trying to address as well. If "every red-nosed rhymster is an author," so, too, could be courtly players, and as someone self-exiled from courtly life, Autolycus stands at this nexus of the popular and polished publication. "I love a ballad in print," said Mopsa. It is not simply that the printed text makes things seem "true." It is that printed music could, now in the first years of the seventeenth century, become something to buy and sell, to affirm fame, to be the object of desire.[57]

The modern theatergoer, though, will be disappointed that, for all of Autolycus's claims, we have no prints surviving of his songs. The music to *The Winter's Tale* eludes us. Of Autolycus's seven songs in act 4, only one of them, "Jog-on, jog-on," can be assigned to a contemporary tune with some assurance. All the other songs have no surviving settings. There are later seventeenth- and eighteenth-century scores for the rest, and there is a possible version of the three-part performance of "Get you hence" attributed to Robert Johnson. But there is nothing of the absolute historical assurance of, say, Johnson's music for Ariel's "Where the bee sucks." Even a cursory examination of editions of *The Winter's Tale* will offer different settings for its songs. Orgel, for example, includes music drawn from a songbook and a manuscript of half a century past the play's first production, as well as from a collection of Stuart masques. The editors of the *New Variorum* print completely different settings, some based on conjecture, some on comparison with practices contemporary with the play. Even "Jog-on" differs in key, tone, tune, and arrangement in these two editions.[58]

All of this rumination takes me back to Orgel's point about *The Tempest*'s masque: that it is not a masque itself, but "a dramatic allusion to one." Autolycus's songs, whatever their original settings, should not be confused with the run of ballads sung on city streets or with their miming in *Bartholomew Fair*. Autolycus remains, to return to King James's word, a *balladine*—a self-conscious, self-theatricalizing escapee from court. His lyrics call attention to himself: his skills, his ruses, his persona. There remains something artificial about him, as if he were a court singer now impersonating the low cant of street song: as if a Dowland were to find himself playing the part of one of Jonson's rogues.

Dowland's song, "Fine knacks for ladies," does exactly that. It shows us how the courtier can adopt the voice of balladeer. It shows us what the popular would look like as an art song.

> Fine knacks for ladies, cheap choice brave and new,
> Good pennyworths but money cannot moue,
> I keepe a fair but for the fair to view,
> A beggar may be liberal of love,
> Though all my wares bee trash the heart is true.
>
> Great gifts are guiles and looke for gifts again,
> My trifles come, as treasures from my minde,
> It is a precious jewel to be plain,
> Sometimes in shell th'Orient's pearle we find,
> Of others take a sheaf, of me a grain.
>
> Within this pack pinnes points laces and gloues,
> And divers toyes fitting a country fair,
> But my hart where duty serves and loves,
> Turtels and twins, Court's brood, a heav'nly pair,
> Happy the heart that thinks of no removes. (*Second Book*, 12)

The song first appeared in the *Second Book of Songs and Ayres* of 1600, and Diana Poulton voices a critical consensus when she states, "The song inevitably calls to mind the pedlar's songs that Shakespeare gave to Autolycus."[59] Like "Lawn as white as driven snow" and "Will you buy any tape," this song sets out to sell. They offer overlapping inventories: Autolycus's "lace" and "toys" and "gloves" are here, along with echoes of his "pins and poking-sticks of steel." But more than simply offering another version of the peddler song, "Fine knacks" offers a commentary on it, a reflection on relationships of value between things and feelings. It argues for fidelity beneath the surface, for a true heart behind the trashy wares, for an Orient pearl under the shell. It is a song about performance in itself, a song about the ways in which the old conventions of the street, the proverb, and the commonplace can be invigorated into new sincerities.

Autolycus may not explicitly go this far, but Polixenes does, and his commentary on the entertainments in Bohemia bears reading against Dowland's stanzas. After Autolycus sings and leaves, the servant, shepherd, and the disguised Polixenes show up, and they stand as audience before a dance of satyrs. Polixenes then turns to Florizel. He recognizes that the young man is in love, that his "heart is full of something." He goes on:

> Sooth, when I was young,
> And handed love, as you do, I was wont
> To load my she with knacks. I would have ransacked
> The pedlar's silken treasury and have poured it
> To her acceptance—you have let him go,
> And nothing marted with him. If your lass
> Interpretation should abuse, and call this
> Your lack of love or bounty, you were striated
> For a reply, at least if you make a care
> Of happy holding her. (4.4.342–50)

Polixenes sounds as much like a balladeer as Dowland here. Much as he looked back on a pastoral and lyric youth with Leontes, now he recalls a boyhood out of ballad. The strange grammar of his reminiscence—calling his old beloved "my she"—together with the assonances ("knacks . . . ransacked"), double-edged colloquialisms (the verb "marted" meaning to make a bargain, but rippling with sexual innuendo), and alliterations ("happy holding her") all give his speech the feel of popular song.[60] Like Dowland in "Fine knacks," he makes the point that knacks are only superficial signs of fancy. True love lives deeper, and if any girl would take that "silken treasury" for truth, it would be an abuse of interpretation. But Florizel assures him that she cares less for the "trifles" of the peddler: "The gifts she looks from me are packed and locked / Up in my heart." And the he turns to Perdita, takes her hand, and finds it "soft as dove's down and white as it, / Or Ethiopian's tooth" (4.4.352–58).

"Fine knacks for ladies" seems to hover over this exchange. Its knacks, trifles, gifts, and heart all reappear among the courtiers in Bohemia, as if they were remembering bits of song. And if Dowland would find an Orient pearl beneath his shell, so too will Florizel seek out the exotic and see Perdita's hand as white as an Ethiopian's tooth.

Bohemia is not so far from the Sicily as we might think. It refracts the histrionics of Leontes into comedy. It takes the language of the careful, courtly lutenist and dresses it in country clothes. It shows us characters performing, disguised, and impersonating others. It raises, in short, the central question of this play: what does it mean to act a part? What does it mean to speak as someone else, to wear the beard, or take on the attire of the swain? Autolycus performs. But so does Polixenes, and they both do so in ways that make us ask: how do they do that?

Exits

Such questioning of character and of performer is a common response to the theater, and the critic Michael Goldman long ago posed it in terms of our experience of *King Lear*.

> The play's interest in suffering and endurance is plainly echoed in the problem of playing Lear and in our reaction to the performance of the role. How much more can the actor take? We ask—and the

question implies, how much more can we take? A good production of *Lear* is not easy on its audience.[61]

A good production of *anything* is not easy on its audience, but a good production of *The Winter's Tale* poses performance problems unlike anything else in Shakespeare. Leontes's irrationality and restoration must seem humanly believable. Autolycus must prance and preen in such a way that, when he leaves the stage, we truly miss him. Polixenes must be convincing to his audiences on and off the stage. And, at the play's close, Hermione must stand there, stock still, for all the world a statue. That bit of acting may be the most difficult of all. Not moving is much harder than moving. Silence is harder to convey than words. The play must reaffirm, at its conclusion, the truly transformative nature not of the artifices of the prop-room but the art of the actor.

Throughout *The Winter's Tale*, we have seen characters assess each other's authenticity. Paulina reads Leontes's little baby's face and looks for imprints of paternity.

> Behold, my lords,
> Although the print be little, the whole matter
> And copy of the father . . . (2.3.97–99)

By the play's end, Leontes will acknowledge legitimacy precisely in these terms, commending Florizel:

> Your mother was most true to wedlock, prince,
> For she did print your royal father off
> Conceiving you. (5.1.123–25)

Print is the mark of truth, validation, and inheritance. It codifies the question of "true copy" raised in the play's own text and, as I have suggested, in that text's answer to the language of the First Folio's prefaces.

But in the end, the real charge of likeness lies less in characters upon a printed page than characters onstage. *The Winter's Tale* is full of images of reproduction and impression. But it is full, too, of the questions of the theater itself. How does an actor copy a character?

At the play's close, when the statue of Hermione appears and will be brought alive, music finally plays its Orphic role. "Music; awake her—strike!" Paulina commands, and she may as well be commanding the lyricists of Hell as of Bohemia. For it was Orpheus who played before the underworld and brought Eurydice to life, Orpheus who could turn the rocks and stones to living things. "O, she is warm!" Leontes cries, and while there certainly is much to recall the story of Pygmalion, praying his cold statue into warm life, there is Orpheus as well. Music, at the play's end, serves not to entertain or titillate or satirize, but to bring stone to living flesh.

This is the music of impersonation. This is the moment of theatrical self-consciousness, when the performer of Hermione's role must stand completely still, miming stone. This is the moment when we realize that the magic of the theater lies in its ability, night after night, to make the dead come back and speak, to make those we had thought lost present again on the stage. We all are made aware that we are watching actors act, and that the play provides them, at this moment, with occasions for their virtuosity. *Picture equaling life*. The nature of artistic power is to make us believe in the unbelievable.

That is Autolycus's self-set charge. He has established himself as an ideal figure of impersonation, a charlatan proud of his ruses. He offers a set of ballads full of incredible stories, of wives giving birth to moneybags, of women turned to fish. He remains a creature of theatrical artifice, of wigs and beards and costumes that we see through all too easily.

But what we cannot see through, in the end, is the play's final call to music. "Awake her—strike!" is a command within the fiction of the play, but it is also an announcement to the listener. As Simon Smith has put it, in a recent reassessment of the dramaturgic power of *The Winter's Tale*'s music, "both playgoers and stage characters are delighted by the same music at the same time."[62] This is a different sense of emotive response, I think, than that of other moments in the play. When characters perform or sing, they are characters shaping music in their masks, giving artistic shape to action or emotion within character. Now, at the play's close, there are no onstage figures who play. Paulina's call may be to musicians who enter on the stage, but they are musicians of the theater. And their music, as far as we can tell, is purely instrumental—in both senses of that word. That is, it is music without word or human voice; but it is music as the instrument of metamorphosis itself. "Paulina's command," writes Smith, "encourages playgoers to relate their delighted responses to the statue's concurrent response."[63] Her call to awake, in other words, rouses the audience as much as it rouses the statue. All of us are called to attention here, and if we nodded throughout the performance, there is no way, now, that anyone could not awaken here. The music works on the character as it works on the playgoer. Some may have come, in the words of the Epilogue to *Henry VIII*, to "sleep an act or two" (Ep. 3). But they must come to life as much as Hermione must.

At such a moment, *The Winter's Tale* gives sound and shape not only to the power of art but to the arts of power. The Jacobean aesthetic yoked together verbal and political decorum. It was an aesthetic of performance that aspired to the feel of nature. Even though the ruler was onstage before an audience, he could not call attention to it. Kings were kings, not comedians. *The Winter's Tale* gives us a tyrant and a balladine. At the end, the former loses his theatrical histrionics; the latter disappears. We may remember Autolycus. But he has no place at court. He may be unforgettable. But what we must remember is that his was but a part. He lives in our imagination of his lost tunes. For in this play so occupied with losses and returns, Autolycus and his music remain the truly unrecoverable things about it. Scholarship cannot give us back his voice. Only Simon Foreman remembers his tatters.[64]

Leontes ends the play reminding everybody of parts they played, of life upon a royal stage. But unlike Prospero, he does not call upon the audience to wish him well. He turns the lead over to Paulina, looks forward to the leisure of their future, but for now, gets off the stage in haste.

> Good Paulina,
> Lead us from hence, where we may leisurely
> Each one demand an answer to his part
> Performed in this wide gap of time since first
> We were dissevered. Hastily lead away. (5.3.151–55)

Each one demands an answer to his part. The play has been performed over a wide gap of time. If Leontes has learned anything, it has been James I's own lessons: that "the King is as one set on a stage." Leontes's language shifts by the play's end. No longer broken in his lines, he scans with both prosodic and political assurance. His final words are true and plain, not "fairded" with the artifice of the tragedian. He has, in short, become not just a better king but a better actor, and like all good actors, he knows now, as he had not known before, when to make a good exit.

4

Pageantry, Power, and Lyricism in *Henry VIII*

If anyone knows anything about *Henry VIII*, it is that it burned down the Globe. Early in its theatrical run (most likely after only two or three performances), the play overdid its pomp and power by having its actors fire off a cannon during the scene of the masque at Wolsey's palace. Something went wrong, fabric caught fire, and the theater burned to the ground. Just about every edition of the play now begins with this tale, quoting Sir Henry Wotton's eyewitness account from June 29, 1613, and just about every editor relies upon it as a springboard for discussing the conundrums of the work.[1] The Folio had titled it *The Famous History of the Life of King Henry the Eight*, but Wotton (and other contemporaries) knew it as *All Is True*.[2] Wotton describes the show as "representing some principal pieces of the reign of Henry VIII," and critics have long questioned whether this is a complete, through-written drama with integrity of form, or a collection of episodes loosely sewn together by elaborate pageants.[3] Its "pieces" have been recognized as pendant on Raphael Holinshed's *Chronicles*, and while the play seems, at times, to repeat this source almost verbatim, there are times when it willfully departs from known chronology. Just what is "true" about *Henry VIII* has become the subject of almost everyone who dares to write about this play. And for centuries, readers and theatergoers have questioned the very quality of its lines, arguing that it must have been a shared project between Shakespeare and another writer, most likely John Fletcher. Today's consensus is that, whatever Heminge and Condell thought they were doing when they made it the last of the Histories in the First Folio, *Henry VIII* remains a work of collaboration, uneasy in its blend of the simple and the complex, the psychological and the spectacular, the read and the performed.[4]

Few have gone beyond these conundrums to get at the lyric, mythic heart of *Henry VIII*: a play that, like its other late compeers, raises questions about the place of aesthetic display in the exercise of power; that dramatizes lyrical performance through the imagery of Orpheus; and that figures forth prophetic poetry in dream and vision. *Henry VIII*, as Raphael Lyne put it, "is a history play subtly affected by the dynamics of romance," where "characters . . . encounter the strange, dreamlike reality of their happy endings," and where, as in *The Tempest*, *The Winter's Tale*, *Cymbeline*, and *Pericles*, a father-king "finds redemption in his daughter."[5] All this may well be true about the play, and there are many local points of contact with its late contemporaries. But this is a play, too, that raises questions about authorship and authority, about relationships of text to action, and about mythic ways of understanding past and present. Much like *The Tempest* and *The Winter's Tale*, it offers powerful moments of metatheater, and in the process it asks what the place of artistry may be in making sense of history and power. Its first three acts trace the fall of Cardinal Wolsey as an orchestrator of royal show. Increasingly, he comes off less as a historical than as a theatrical or even mythic figure. At times, he seems a bad Prospero whose stagy power plays get rained out. At other times, he evokes an Autolycus who remained at court, a creature of papers and prints from which he could aver (as Mopsa might) that his tales are true. And, at his end, he appears a tragic figure out of *Lear*, or *Faustus*, or *Antony and Cleopatra*, a man who lives in a Hell of his own making, who finds his fall akin to that of Lucifer, and who imagines his own afterlife in poor performance.

As the last of the history plays in the Folio, *Henry VIII* raises questions about the relationships of song to story. Is history to be found in performance: in the lyrics of old courts, the pageants of great welcome, the orations of kings and courtiers? Or is it to be found on paper: in the documents of state, the chronicles of witnesses, the records less of voices than of hands? These are the questions raised by all the history plays, but they are raised acutely by the last of them. What we see throughout *Henry VIII* are the constant juxtapositions of memory and written record. Historically, it was under Henry's aegis that the Chancery took on new powers of control, and the production of documents became the medium through which the force of law took shape. Henry's world was, increasingly as his reign went on, a world of textual production and interpretation: statutes and laws, translations of the Bible, letters among courtiers and lovers. The King's own hand and handwriting had become the marker of his royal authority. His seal was at the center of his rule. And, when it came time to create the statutes governing new forms of power and devotion, it was regulation of the written and the printed word that lay at the heart of Reformation enforcement. Printing the poetry of medieval romance (with its sacramental narratives and Catholic doctrine) was illegal. Writing the very word "pope" had become a crime.[6]

Henry's was a world of song and lyric, pageant and play, set against the rising institutionality of paper. The hand that plucked the lute could sign the writ. For Shakespeare and his contemporaries, these tensions between the spoken and the written would have been immediately clear in such collections as *Tottel's Miscellany*, where poetry of Wyatt, Surrey, and their peers continually reflected on the challenges of song and the character of writing. "Mark well this text" becomes a refrain line for Wyatt, while Surrey, Grimald, and their now-nameless heirs provided Tottel's book with eulogies and elegies that stand as graven tombstones to a passing courtly verve.[7]

The play of *Henry VIII* speaks directly to these historical relationships about the place of lyricism, myth, and books in social life. It hews closely to historical accounts of Henry's theater-state of pageantry and pomp. But it inflects those accounts with a new, Jacobean sensibility: the figure of the king nowhere more upon a stage than when he himself is observing staged performance.

Mine is a book about poetry and the past, and *Henry VIII* imagines a political past as a largely poetic one: as a condition of publicly performed verse, sometimes set to music, sometimes acted out in character, and sometimes imagined in dream or prophecy. To evoke such a past, the play returns to literary forms from the previous century to generate an awareness of that past's continued presence in the theater. I will, therefore, address the ways in which characters in the play sound like earlier Shakespearean and Marlovian figures. I will return to Dowland for the lyric resonances of Queen Katherine's laments. In the end, I will argue that this is less a history play affected by the dynamics of romance than a characteristically late Shakespeare play that frames its mythic lyricism in a documented historical story.

I called this a characteristically late Shakespeare play, and by such a statement I do not mean to elide the challenges of its collaborative origins. Nor do I wish to aver, simply, that because the play appears in the First Folio we should argue that it was read as Shakespeare's, whatever that early readership had known of making. I am not interested in statistical variations to determine just what lines are Shakespeare's and what lines are Fletcher's. What I am interested in is how the play raises authorship and individuality, collaboration and response, as themes. As I have noted, such themes had become a major part of musical, as well as literary, discourses by the first decades of the seventeenth century. Characters like Ariel and Autolycus, I have argued, dramatize the challenges of performing the scripts of others while attempting to take on an individual identity.

Henry VIII will dramatize such problems, too. Its meta-theater is always a collaborative one. The story of the Cloth of Gold, the masque at Wolsey's house, the scene between the Gentlemen in act 4 exchanging papers, the remarks in act 5 about crowds as evoking the "thunder of the playhouse," the calling by Queen Katherine for musical performance—all these, and many other moments in the play, make issues of theatrical commission and response a central theme. Whoever is responsible for each of its lines, the play in the aggregate presents as much a reading of the Shakespearean tradition as an example of it. It collocates allusions, idioms, and verbal feints that we have heard and read before. Its musicality and pageantry seem old and at times old-fashioned, as if its purpose is to evoke in the minds of its audience the sounds and songs that they would barely have remembered. In the end, the play asks everyone what roles we play in making meaning, whether truth is historical or poetic, and what happens when we are called on to participate as spectators in the creation of political art.

Vertuous Fabric

Would that it were so simple. Part of the power of Henry Wotton's tale of theatrical misadventure is precisely the way in which it draws on the themes and motifs of the play itself to write about the moment of its failure. Wotton's story, whatever its absolute accuracy, compels *as a story* because it works to dramatize a moment of failed masquery. It is so self-aware of its imaginative power that we can take it not just as chronicle but as a critical response to the theatrical imagination. It is as much a work of verbal artifice as anything in the play itself. As we reflect on the relationship between the documentary and the dramatic, it can help us understand, as well, the play's own uneasy relationship to history.

Wotton's letter has been frequently reprinted, but rarely in its entirety, and to read it in full is to see its arc of politics and humor.[8]

July 2. 1613.

Sir,

Whereas I wrote unto you, that I would be at Cambridge as on Saturday next, I am now cast off again till the King's return to London, which will be about the middle of the week following. The delay grows from a desire of seeing Albertus his business settled before we come unto you, where we mean to forget all the world besides. Of this we shall bring you the account.

Now, to let matters of state sleep, I will entertain you at the present with what hath happened this week at the Bank's side. The Kings players had a new play, called All is true, representing some principal pieces of the reign of Henry VIII. which was set forth with many extraordinary circumstances of pomp and majesty, even to the matting of the stage; the Knights of the Order with their Georges and garters, the Guards with their embroidered coats, and the like: sufficient in truth within a while to make greatness very familiar, if not ridiculous. Now, King Henry making a masque at the Cardinal Wolsey's house, and certain chambers being shot off at his entry, some of the paper, or other stuff wherewith one of them was stopped, did light on the thatch, where being thought at first but an idle smoke, and their eyes more attentive to the show, it kindled inwardly, and ran round like a train, consuming within less then an hour the whole house to the very grounds.

This was the fatal period of that vertuous fabric, wherein yet nothing did perish, but wood and straw, and a few forsaken cloaks; only one man had his breeches set on fire, that would perhaps have broiled him, if he had not by the benefit of a provident wit put it out with bottle ale. The rest when we meet: till when, I protest every minute is the siege of Troy. God's dear blessings till then and ever be with you.

Your poor Uncle and faithful servant.
HENRY WOTTON.
I have this week received your last of
the 27th of June, wherein I see my steps
lovingly calculated, and in truth too much
expectation of so unworthy a guest.

There is much information in this letter, but there is much imagination, too. Scholars have relied upon it to confirm the contemporary title of the play as *All Is True*. They have affirmed that it was, at the time of this performance, a "new play," probably acted only a few times by the King's Men. They have argued from its narrative that the accident happened toward the play's beginning, at the scene of the great masque, rather than (as another eyewitness seems to have it) "as the play was almost ended."[9] But for a tale of *All Is True*, Wotton's account seems almost too good to be true. It has a drama of its own that moves from the grand to the ridiculous, as it attends to the key vocabulary of the play and of the theater itself.

Wotton begins by offering an entertainment. Matters of state may sleep before this story. Yet this is a play, and a tale, as much about matters of state as any of the gossip he had offered earlier. From pomp and majesty, the story moves to foolishness—from Henry and his court, it ends with the farcical image of a man's breeches catching fire and dousing them with a lucky bottle of ale. There is a literary feel to Wotton's prose, too, a feel a reader would expect from someone largely regarded as one of the most educated men of his day, who had himself published a poetry well crafted, if not now well read. The phrasing, "Knights of the Order, with their Georges and garters," has the anapests and alliteration of a ballad. "Kindled inwardly" has the internal rhyming of a lyric, while the simile "ran round like a train" conjures the vivid image of a line of gunpowder lit in anticipation of effect.[10] Wotton lives in a world in which anticipation of a friend can seem as protracted as the siege of Troy, a brilliant act of self-allegorization, transforming everyday desire into epic, or (to reverse his own terms in the letter) making the very familiar into greatness.

"The fatal period of that virtuous fabric." It is a memorable phrase, but one that also conjures up another memory. For the modern reader, as much as for the playgoer of the early 1610s, it recalls Prospero's magical evaporation of the theater's ruses:

Our revels now are ended. These our actors,
As I foretold you, were all spirits, and
Are melted into air, into thin air,
And like the baseless fabric of this vision,
The cloud-capped towers, the gorgeous palaces,
The solemn temples, the great globe itself,
Yea, all which it inherit, shall dissolve,
And, like this insubstantial pageant faded,
Leave not a rack behind. We are such stuff
As dreams are made on, and our little life
Is rounded with a sleep. (*Tempest*, 4.1.148–58)

Prospero ended with a sleep. But Wotton began with one, and as we read his letter against these lines from *The Tempest* we can see how it does something very similar. It reveals pomp and majesty to be a world of prop and costume. Whatever pageantry the stage had held becomes insubstantial before a flame that melts it into air, and much like the bare ground before Prospero's staff, the great Globe now is left burned with not a rack behind.

Wotton's letter becomes as much a piece of magic storytelling as anything in *The Tempest*. It is, in itself, a great entertainment, and it offers up a point of entry into a play that juxtaposes truths of history and theater. Much like that play, Wotton's tale is a tale of cloth and paper—the stuff, in the historical sense, on which all dreams are made. Prospero's "stuff" recalls its range of sixteenth- and early seventeenth-century connotations: the quilting under armor, the furnishings of a house, the textiles of a courtier. "Stuff" meaning paper is attested only in the eighteenth century, but its resonances are there long before: in 1555 in an association of papyrus with stuff and paper; and in Bacon's *New Atlantis* of 1626, where the stuff made by "diuerse Mechanicall Arts" includes "Papers, Linens, Silks, Tissues."[11] *Henry VIII* is full of stuff in all these terms, and it is that palpable quality to all that stuff (things to write on, to embroider, to mark, to wear) that marks the play's pageantry. And yet, along with all that stuff is song and performance, story and oral lore.

Modern critics have found "truth" to be at the play's heart, and Anston Bosman summarizes the consensus: "the play [is] negotiating between the truths of history and romance."[12] But Bosman recognizes this as something of a false dichotomy. Both history and romance intertwine throughout the play, and I see their tension within the story and in Wotton's letter—a world in which paper, fabric, and material take on new political purposes in the Tudor court; a play in which its characters are asked to rely at times on the documentary and at times on the performed. Let matters of state sleep. I will entertain you.

I do pronounce him in that very shape

Wotton's is a tale of expectations raised and dashed. It is a story told in the first person of how to be entertained. For modern readers, to come to the play's own Prologue after Wotton's letter is to see just how these two texts interpret what we are about to read ourselves. From its first words in the Folio, *Henry VIII* raises specters of theater, power, and possibility, only to dismiss them. "I come no more to make you laugh." The Prologue's opening avowal sets it far apart from Shakespeare's other choral beginnings: the plot summary and moral judgments of *Romeo and Juliet*; the brilliant vauntings of *Henry V*; the antiquarian necromancy of *Pericles*. *Henry VIII*'s is a Prologue designed not to prepare audiences for what happens but to guard them against what will not. This is no comedy. Those expecting

> a merry, bawdy play,
> A noise of targets, or to see a fellow
> In a long motley coat guarded with yellow,
> Will be deceived. (Prologue, 13–17)

Some think these lines evoke the memory of another play about Henry VIII, Samuel Rowley's *When You See Me You Know Me*, almost a decade old by 1613 and possibly revived in that year.[13] That play showed the king's court as a world of jesters and bombast. This play avoids such "show," giving its "chosen truth" stripped of "fool and fight." But for a King's Men's audience of Henry Wotton's contemporaries, fresh in their minds would have been plays of recent seasons—plays such as *The Tempest* and *The Winter's Tale*. No bawdy play, no fellow in motley. We now are far from Leontes's claim of a "bawdy planet," of Autolycus's ironic "I am a poor fellow," or the Clown's iterative banter about the "tall fellow."[14]

Even without the modern editorial assistance of Wotton's letter, this Prologue would impress a reader of the First Folio with its shift of tone and form. After the collection of Comedies and Histories, these lines may say as much about the subject of the play as about the subjects of what will follow. By showing how "mightiness meets misery," by making audiences "sad" (not sorrowful, but serious, reflective, and thoughtful), the Prologue announces less a historical pageant than an old-fashioned *de casibus* tragedy: a tale of greatness brought down. Read on its own, the Prologue has the feel far more of tragic impetus than of history, and it helps shape *Henry VIII* not only as the culmination of the arc of British history ranged in the Folio but also as the pivot point for the next section of Tragedies. In short, this is a play of truth, not show, and though the text is full of pageantry and masque, its readers have now been prepared to see those shows as increasingly empty things.

That sense of disappointment governs the first scene, a long exchange between the Dukes of Norfolk and Buckingham describing France and England's meeting at the Cloth of Gold ceremony in 1520—a ceremony staged by Wolsey and, by the first decade of the seventeenth century, familiar to an audience reared on Holinshed's history.[15] But this is more than a cribbed chronicle. It takes us back to *Julius Caesar*, where the Romans recall the staged ceremony of Caesar's refusal of the crown. It reminds us of the first speeches of *The Winter's Tale*, with its stories of "entertainments" and its promises of play. Each of these episodes, and many more in Shakespeare, describe a great spectacle and, in the process, reflect on the social and political function of display. Their purpose is not only to prepare the plot; it is to define rulership in terms of show.

Buckingham had been in prison when the ceremony took place, and so Norfolk must describe it to him and, in turn, to us. He brings the great field into the small chamber. The "glory" and the "pomp" of kings is now the matter for the actor's skill. But in that skill, we hear the playwright's voice. Recall, for example, Enobarbus on the river pageantry of Cleopatra. Her burnished throne, her golden boat, and her purple sail all ride the winds, with boats stroked to the "tune of flutes."[16] It is a play with musical accompaniment, as much a speech about the "stuff" that we are made of as Prospero's. Cleopatra lies in her "cloth-of-gold tissue." It is a scene, Enobarbus says, that "beggar'd all description," far more glorious than he could tell, but also far more glorious than any Jacobean theater could put on. Cleopatra's barge lives only in the actor's lines, and we must see it as the spectacle of oratory rather than of stagecraft.

So, too, Norfolk's story of that other Cloth of Gold rings out like Enobarbus's.

> Men might say
> Till this time pomp was single, but now married
> To one above itself. Each following day
> Became the next day's master, till the last
> Made former wonders its. Today the French,
> All clinquant, all in gold, like heathen gods
> Shone down the English; and tomorrow they
> Made Britain India. Every man that stood
> Showed like a mine. Their dwarfish pages were
> As cherubins all gilt; the madams, too,
> Not used to toil, did almost sweat to bear
> The pride upon them, that their very labour
> Was to them as a painting. Now this masque
> Was cried incomparable, and th'ensuing night
> Made it a fool and beggar. The two kings
> Equal in lustre, were now best, now worst,
> As presence did present them. Him in eye
> Still him in praise, and being present both,
> 'Twas said they saw but one, and no discerner
> Durst wag his tongue in censure. When these suns–

For so they phrase 'em—by their heralds challenged
The noble spirits to arms, they did perform
Beyond thought's compass, that former fabulous story
Being now seen possible enough, got credit
That *Bevis* was believed. (1.1.14–38)

To read the speech aloud or hear it is to hear the cadences of Enobarbus. Norfolk's enjambment,

like heathen gods
Shone down the English,

echoes Enobarbus's half-lines about his queen:

like a burnished throne
Burned on the water. (*Antony and Cleopatra*, 2.2.198–99)

In both speeches the senses come alive. There is sound, shape, feel. But unlike Enobarbus, Norfolk makes explicit just how artificial all this is, how much a work of craft is the display of power. This is a world of *like* and *as*, not one of Cleopatra's Orient majesty, but of the local European trying to impersonate the exotic. There is a difference between Enobarbus's comparison of barge to throne and Norfolk's comparison of the French to heathen gods. And Norfolk goes on. They were so full of gold and gems that every man "stood like a mine," and would "make Britain India." The "dwarfish pages were / As cherubins." The ladies wore such ostentatious ornaments as to almost sweat under their weight, and their work "was to them as a painting." This is not just a pageant; it is, in Norfolk's own word, a "masque," and "cried incomparable."

Norfolk's speech is an essay in the power of the simile. If Enobarbus is attempting to describe things as they were, Norfolk is attempting to describe things as they aspired to be. Everyone in this show is a performer, everyone is costumed like or as something else. It is a show designed to make the viewer see things that are not there. The English and French kings, Norfolk notes, were so glittering in their luster that spectators saw them side by side *as if* there was but one of them. And rather than simply describe the kings as suns, Norfolk makes clear that the kings were *seen as* suns and described so by the viewers: "When these suns / —For so they phrase 'em—." Finally, the only way that Norfolk can evoke the grandeur of this moment is to see it in terms of fantasy and romance. It is a "fabulous story," so remarkable that even the old tale of Bevis of Hampton could be believed.

This is as much a speech about the power of the theater as any Prologue could have offered, and it strikes Buckingham as just too much: "O you go far!" Norfolk quickly replies that all was as he said, and even a great storyteller could not do it justice.

> All was royal.
> To the disposing of it naught rebelled.
> Order gave each thing view. The office did
> Distinctly his full function. (1.1.42–45)

Norfolk's is the vocabulary of a literary critic: disposition, order, office, function. These are the terms of schoolroom rhetoric and the textbooks of forensic oratory. They are the ideals of verbal arrangement, now transferred to things and shapes. Even in his response, protesting the reality of the event, Norfolk rephrases it as literary artifice.

And behind every artifice must be an author. Buckingham asks precisely in these terms who was responsible:

> Who did guide—
> I mean, who set the body and the limbs
> Of this great sport together, as you guess? (1.1.45–47)

Who was, he asks, the mage behind this pageant, as if this "great sport" were really nothing more (or less) than a giant puppet show? Norfolk answers that it was the Cardinal of York, Lord Thomas Wolsey, who had put the show together, and yet who had no business doing so. Mention of Wolsey raises Buckingham to mockery: he has his finger in every pie; he is a "keech," a bit of suet left out in the butcher's shop. Such anger brings out Wolsey's background, that of a butcher's boy who had no business to rise so high in the kingdom. Norfolk responds that there must have been something meritorious in him to overcome his ancestry and justify his rise to power. But Lord Abergavenny (who has to this point been a silent witness to this dialogue) chimes in: "I cannot tell / What heaven hath given him." For Abergavenny, all Wolsey has is pride, and that pride gives him little but life in Hell. The Folio's original punctuation of this moment brings out something in this scene that, I think, Shakespeare's audiences would have recognized:

> Whence has he that
> If not from hell? The devil is a niggard,
> Or has given all before, and he begins
> A new hell in himself.[17]

Wolsey begins to emerge from this conversation as stage phantasm, something like a poor man's Mephistopheles, more a creature out of Marlowe than of malice. "Why this is hell, nor am I out of it," the devil says in *Dr. Faustus*, and he defines himself as always in Hell, a state of mind, a condition of moral life. Little wonder then that Buckingham should rise to the bait, asking why Wolsey had planned the expedition in the first place: "Why the devil, / Upon this French going-out, took he upon him . . . ?" (1.1.72–73). Why the devil, indeed? Wolsey now carries with him lists and documents, "the file of all the gentry," who will attend and who will not. Much like old Mephistopheles, Wolsey becomes a creature of accounts. He sets down those who will live and who will die, and we will soon see Wolsey's minion, like some lesser demon, come for Buckingham himself. But Buckingham and Norfolk are not done yet. The meeting of France and England, for all of Wolsey's machinations, was no great success. The weather undermined it. A "hideous storm" broke up the proceedings, and Buckingham finds it a bad omen for the peace: "this tempest, / Dashing the garment of this peace . . ." (1.1.90–93).

It is an amazing moment: power undermined by nature. Wolsey cannot shape a tempest to his purposes. Like an angry lesser

Prospero, Wolsey walks in for a brief moment here, "the purse . . . borne before him," his secretaries "with papers" (s.d., after 1.1.114). He shows up to mock the Duke, to find him guilty, and to see in his examination proof of his guilt. We see them, but obviously Norfolk and Buckingham do not. Wolsey is onstage for a few lines, then exits. And Buckingham and Norfolk continue as if nothing had happened: the former talks about him and his "beggar's book"; he "reads in's looks / Matter against me." The two call him cunning, commenting on his treaties and his articles and combination. Buckingham avers that "The Cardinal / Does buy and sell his honour as he pleases," and Norfolk is sorry to hear this. "I . . . wish ye were / Something mistaken in't" (1.1.122, 125–26, 192–93). To which Buckingham replies:

> No, not a syllable.
> I do pronounce him in that very shape
> He shall appear in proof. (1.1.195–97)

By this point in the first act, we must ask not *who* is Wolsey but *what* is he. The language of the two Dukes increasingly turns the Cardinal into some strange creature, and Buckingham's lines have the feel of sorcery itself. He "pronounces" Wolsey "in that very shape." In the utterance of the description lies the truth. This is the language of the Prospero-like magus, who can make new shapes appear, whose own syllables may carry with them power to mask and to reveal.

But for now, it is Wolsey who is in control. Wolsey is the one who charges Brandon and the Sergeant to appear with warrants to arrest Buckingham on high treason. "I shall perish / Under device and practice" (1.1.203–4). Buckingham finds himself the victim of an almost magical manipulation. "Device" recalls that moment from *The Tempest* when Ariel makes the banquet vanish "with a quaint device." And "practice" had connoted, throughout its appearance in other plays, a ruse, a stratagem, a trick. Buckingham finds himself transformed from loyal servant into traitor, and it is a metamorphosis worthy of Ovid.

> It will help me nothing
> To plead mine innocence, for that dye is on me
> Which makes my whit'st part black. (1.1.207–9)

I hear in these lines the genealogy of Autolycus, in Golding's translation of the *Metamorphoses*:

> He could mennes eyes so bleere,
> As for to make y black things whyght, and whyght things black appeare. (11.362–63)

Buckingham leaves the stage, "the shadow" of his old self, his "clear sun" now "dark'ning" (1.1.225–27).

This is the language of Ovidian metamorphosis transformed into political control. It caps the imagery of Wolsey building throughout the play's first scene. Wolsey emerges as an aspirant Prospero, a stage manager of pomp. His great pageant of the Cloth of Gold, however, gets washed out in a tempest. He is a man of papers, but his "beggar's book" pales in comparison to Prospero's magic tome. He has the power, still, to blacken reputation and blear men's eyes. But as the play progresses, we will see his tragic fall precisely in these terms of stagecraft and illusion.

The Tragedy of Wolsey

Wolsey emerges in the arc of his three acts as something of a failed Faust or a weaker Prospero, whose spells and ciphers cannot lift him from his fall. He had begun as orchestrator of the pageant: first the Cloth of Gold, which Norfolk had retold. Then, there is the masque itself at his own house, the scene in act 1, scene 4, where he presides as a stage manager of state.

Wolsey directs his players in their acting and their language, but there is a difference here, and throughout *Henry VIII*, from the masques of *The Tempest*. In the earlier play, the performances had been dramatic simulacra—staged literary versions of a masque. But here, in *Henry VIII*, all may be true. What if we took these shows to be true masques? John D. Cox, in a prescient interpretation of the play, had suggested as much: "*Henry VIII* . . . is an experiment in adapting the principles of the court masque to the tradition of the public theaters."[18] Cox argued that the Jacobean masque contributed to the idea of spectacle within the play: that the thematics of performance finds itself in Wolsey's staged illusions and in the affirmations, after his fall, of the King's present power. More recently, critics have argued that the staging of royal power is essential to the play. Pageantry, in the words of Roderick McKeown, "offers the play more than its theme—it gives the play its structure, and this dramaturgical choice is determined by the particular form of pageantry that influences the play: . . . the royal entry."[19]

Henry VIII does not evoke masque. It incorporates it. The masque is not just spectacle. It is the occasion to observe the King himself as both participant and spectator. It is the artistic device for reifying power. To return to James I's own phrasing from the *Basilikon Doron*, "a King is as one set on a stage, whose smallest actions and gestures, all the people gazingly doe behold." Such beholding, however, needs to be taught, and part of the job of the court masque was to instruct an audience in new ways of gazing. The audience must learn to see both depth and surface, to appreciate the costume, gesture, mask, and movement of an actor and, at the same time, to see behind them to affirm that it is always the King playing.

Wolsey stages Henry's masque largely for the purpose of displaying his own skill at seeing beneath the surface. To the Lord Chamberlain, he enjoins: "Go give 'em welcome; you can speak the French tongue. / And pray receive 'em nobly, and conduct 'em / Into our presence" (1.4.58–60). Act, move, and speak, Wolsey commands, and at this moment he appears more like the Hamlet of Elsinore, welcoming the players and providing them with lines. But here, it would appear that such speech will go on not in the King's English but in French. "They speak no English," the Lord Chamberlain avers, after the King and others enter "as masquers, habited like shepherds, ushered by the Lord

Chamberlain" (s.d., and 1.4.66). Now, the Chamberlain seems to play Ariel to Wolsey's Prospero, moving everyone around in dance. He functions as interpreter to the performers, conveying (obviously in French) Wolsey's implication that the King dances among them. Then Wolsey breaks the illusion:

> Let me see then.
> By all your good leaves, gentlemen; here I'll make
> My royal choice. (1.4.87–89)

He points to the masked Henry, who reveals himself: "Ye have found him, Cardinal."

The force of this moment must be read against its source in Holinshed. There, Wolsey tried to find the King, but chose wrongly.

> The cardinall taking good aduisement among them, at the last (quoth he) me seemeth the gentleman with the blacke beard, should be euen he: and with that he arose out of his chaire, and offered the same to the gentleman in the blacke beard with the cap in his hand. The person to whom he offered the chaire was sir Edward Neuill, a comelie knight, that much resembled the kings person in that maske than anie other.
>
> The king perceiuing the cardinall so deceiued, could not forbeare laughing, but pulled downe his visar and master Neuils also, and dash out of such a pleasant countenance and cheere, that all the noble estastes there assembled, perceiuing the king to be there among them, reioised verie much.[20]

Holinshed makes this a comedy of error, with Wolsey wrongly choosing a mere knight for the King and, in the process, generating laughter and rejoicing. The masque, historically, becomes the occasion for the King to unmask, rule, and shape an audience response.

The masque in *Henry VIII*, however, illustrates how Wolsey can see past the royal disguise. It is essential, in the play, for him to choose correctly because it marks him as the true controller of the moment. But his revelation has a payoff that remains the play's own invention. For just when Henry has been found, the

King asks for another to be unmasked: "What fair lady's that?" The Chamberlain identifies her as Sir Thomas Bullen's daughter, and the King chooses her for a kiss.

Unmasking now becomes a central motif of the play. It is not so much that everyone is a performer. It is that we must see the personages behind those performers. The question "Who is that?" emerges as the question of these first scenes. "Who am I?" is the move of the Shakespearean theater. "Who is that?" is the move of the Jacobean pageant. As Isabel Karremann has argued, the first years of James's rule saw plays keyed to presenting the old, Tudor narratives in ways designed to highlight audience identification. Plays such as Rowley's *When You See Me You Know Me* (1604) and Thomas Heywood's *If You Know Not Me, You Know Nobody* (1604–1605), in Karremann's words, "alert the audience to use their knowledge of current political figures and discover who is behind the mask of the persona."[21] The critical pressure of *Henry VIII* is thus to recognize something both about court life then and public life now. It was, and remains, a life of recognizing *others*. Seeing through the masks of power generates a deep unease about the place of artifice in the exercise of rule.

And so it is that Norfolk and the Chamberlain blame Wolsey for the King's infatuation with Anne Boleyn and hope that, one day, Henry will see through Wolsey's ruses: "The king will know him one day" (2.2.20). Just as Wolsey would unmask a disguised Henry or the Chamberlain would pick out Anne among the masquers, so Norfolk imagines a future when Henry will unmask Wolsey for what he may truly be. For now, however, he is a shaper and shape-shifter.

> He dives into the King's soul and there scatters
> Dangers, doubts, wringing of the conscience,
> Fears and despairs— (2.2.25–27)

Norfolk's language grows mythic in accretion, and the image of Wolsey scattering the King's emotional innards recalls Ovid's vision of the hideous Gorgon landscape in book 4 of the *Metamorphoses* (in Arthur Golding's translation):

> The shapes as well of men as beasts lie scattered everie where
> In open fields and common ways, the which transformed were
> From living things to stones . . . (4.951–53).

Norfolk continues in sustained Ovidian echoes. Wolsey, he says, counsels divorce from Katherine, who "like a jewel has hung twenty years / About his neck." Recall the vision in book 11 of the *Metamorphoses* of King Pluto to whom Orpheus would sing and beg release of his dead wife, Eurydice: "And downe his brest hung from his necke a cheyne with jewels fyne." The scene gets stranger, with the Chamberlain protesting, "heaven keep me from such counsel," and praying that "Heaven will one day open / The king's eyes." For Norfolk, such prayers should work quickly, otherwise they all will be transformed.

> We had need pray,
> And heartily, for our deliverance,
> Or this imperious man will work us all
> From princes into pages. All men's honours
> Lie like one lump before him to be fashioned
> Into what pitch he please. (2.2.44–49)

Now, the language of metamorphosis comes filtered through St. Paul's famous analogy to God: "Hath not the potter power of the clay to make of the same lump one vessel to honour . . ." (Romans 9:21). Golding relied on these idioms to translate Ovid's first lines of the *Metamorphoses*. "Of shapes transformed to bodies straunge, I purpose to entreate," and the world emerges from Chaos, "a heavie lump and clottred clod of seedes." To be transformed from prince to page is to be metamorphosed backwards—a kind of reverse apotheosis. Suffolk, however, will not stand for such manipulation. "As I am made without him, so I'll stand" (2.2.51). He prides himself on his own status. He will not define his identity as made by others. He is, at this moment, the assertive Renaissance self-fashioner, a figure who places himself outside the realms of acting, who makes himself author of his own form.

Henry, however, remains pliable at Wolsey's hands. We see

him next when the Lord Chamberlain exits and the King "draws the curtain" to be seen sitting "reading pensively." Prospero-like, he pulls aside the curtain. At this moment, we see Henry much as we had seen Ferdinand and Miranda—as actors in another person's play. And yet, unlike those two young lovers of *The Tempest*, Henry here seems curiously self-aware:

> Who's there, I say? How dare you thrust yourselves
> Into my private meditations?
> Who am I? Ha? (2.2.64–66)

What are we looking at? An actor playing a king, a king playing a performer, a character unsure of his own self? We must hear these words against the other question of the play: "Who is that?" Henry turns the inquiry upon himself. Am I an actor or a person? Am I made by others or myself? The King finds himself the object of spectatorship when he least wants it. What Henry fails to know here, as character and king, is that there are no private meditations for the ruler. Everything is always seen by others. "The king," as James I had written, "is as one set on a stage, whose smallest actions and gestures, all the people gazingly doe behold." Henry's question brings its Jacobean audience back in time. It pulls aside a curtain of the past, revealing an earlier monarch who had created chambers of privacy, who had sought to maintain an inner, private world through whisper and through correspondence, who had created circles of influence to shield himself from public censure. It is as if we have walked in upon a king who does not realize that his kind of kingship is now over.

Act 2, scene 4: the king enters again, and the elaborate stage direction shows us, one more time, how Wolsey stages politics. Now, it is the trial of Queen Katherine, and the scene develops between the Queen and Cardinal less as law court than as theater. The stage direction is an elaborate piece of prose indebted to Holinshed. Each character enters with costume and prop: short silver wands, habit of doctors, the purse with the great seal and cardinal's hat, silver crosses, silver mace, silver pillars, sword and mace, cloth of state. This is a list not just of things of power but things of the stage, an inventory of the artifacts required for the show. It tells the reader where each character will sit and stand, and Wolsey begins like a Prologue entering onstage:

> Whilst our commission from Rome is read
> Let silence be commanded. (2.4.1–2)

He enters with a script, ready to read another paper, but the King rejects it:

> What's the need?
> It hath already publicly been read . . . (2.4.3–4)

What has more force, text or spectacle? Wolsey would hold to documents, but Henry wants the scene. And so when Katherine kneels before him, she speaks less as a pleader in the law court than as a soliloquist. Her questions may be offered to the King—"In what have I offended you? What cause / Hath my behavior given to your displeasure?" As she continues, her questions become increasingly rhetorical, as if she were a character alone onstage arguing with herself:

> What friend of mine
> That had to him derived your anger did I
> Continue in my liking—nay, gave notice
> He was from thence discharged? (2.4.29–32)

Her questions are unanswerable, and Wolsey thinks it "bootless" to go on. The dialogue, as it develops, does not go on with the King; it goes on between Wolsey and Katherine. Henry says nothing, as if watching a performance between two actors vying for his judgment. For when Katherine announces that she rejects Wolsey as a judge ("I utterly abhor, yea, from my soul, / Refuse you for my judge"), Wolsey replies as to an actor poorly scripted: "I do profess / You speak not like yourself." Katherine responds as to an actor who has come to believe his own fictions of performance:

> and your words—
> Domestics to you—serve your will as't please
> Yourself pronounce their office. (2.4.111–13)

She moves to leave, Henry utters but three words ("Call her again"), and she responds only to reject the whole proceeding. "I will not tarry." And then she exits.

This whole scene has more the feel of an audition than a trial. It is as masque-like in its spectacle and staginess as Henry's dance with Anne. Behind all of these scenes lie questions of performance and identity—Katherine announcing who she is and what she finds Wolsey to be, Wolsey responding that the Queen does not speak like herself. And when the actor leaves the stage, when Katherine makes her exit, only then can Henry speak. The fiction is broken, the King as beheld spectator is no more, and he turns to his Cardinal as a playgoer would turn to a companion at a change of scene. Even then, there is a consciousness of being a performer. Henry goes on for over fifty lines explaining why he seeks divorce. "I have spoke long," he says to the Bishop of Lincoln. He becomes a character who has said too much, an actor who has tarried too long on the stage.

In the arc of Wolsey's rise and fall, it is this legalistic theater that increasingly exposes him for who he is. Unlike *Hamlet*, where the performance of a play is made to work on the conscience of the royal spectator, here the performance of trial is made to work on the conscience of the performers.

And then in act 3, when Wolsey comes to see the Queen, he seeks an audience in private. She, by contrast, resists. Nothing in her conscience "deserves a corner . . . truth loves open dealing." Wolsey, however, cannot seem to drop the masque of his magic, and his answer comes in Latin. *Tanta est erga te mentis integritas, Regina serenissima.* "O, my good lord, no Latin," says the queen. "A strange tongue makes my cause more strange." Let me, she says, "be absolved in English" (3.1.32, 39, 40, 48). Wolsey, always scripted, always the mage, intones in a language that comes off more as an incantation than an act of learning. All is true: truth for the Queen is truth of the vernacular, the unstaged, and the everyday. For Wolsey, though, it is this world of learning that makes him the fashioner of others.

This sense of Wolsey as increasingly sorceric comes up clearly in the next scene, when the Chamberlain complains: "for he hath a witchcraft / Over the King in's tongue" (3.2.18–19). And yet, Norfolk sees him unmasked: "O fear him not. / His spell in that is out" (3.2.19–20). In the masquery of court, the King has stripped his Cardinal of his spells. The honey of his language now has soured. Believe it, this is true. This is the pivotal moment of the play, the moment when illusion moves to truth, when masque and pageantry will give way to the documents of statecraft.

"The Cardinal's letters to the Pope miscarried" (3.2.30), Suffolk narrates Wolsey's undoing as the interception of letters. Documents pass into unintended hands, as if a script had come to the wrong actor. Now, the reading King becomes a figure of interpretation—not a man alone behind a curtain, but a public judge who can see past honeyed tongues and cardinals' masques and get to the heart of things.

Pageantry and illusion move to written texts. Wolsey and Cromwell talk of packets and papers. The King reenters "reading a schedule," and he speaks of "papers of state." Norfolk echoes: "It's heaven's will. / Some spirit put this paper in the packet / To bless your eye withal" (3.2.129–31). Paper replaces pageant in the play, and the word "paper" comes up again and again to give the sense that now power will be that of the literate. The job of eyes will be less to watch pageants than to read words. Wolsey comes in for accusation: "Heaven forgive me." But heaven has little to do with this. Henry has his own book of life, the "inventory of your best graces." Henry performs "this earthly audit." Henry moves to the documentary, a world of paper that makes all things true. Wolsey may speak well but, as Henry avows, "Words are no deeds." Now we see the dramatic split at the heart of the play, and we see Wolsey's tragic fall as the fall of the actor who has believed his own script. Now, instead of talking about Wolsey making people out of courtly clay, it is the King who affirms his own creative role:

> Have I not made you
> The prime man of the state? I pray you tell me
> If what I now pronounce you have found true . . . (3.2.162–64)

The King, not Wolsey, is the maker here. Henry is the creator. This is not a world of Ovidian metamorphosis. It is a world of divine order articulated through a divinely appointed king. And when that king gives Wolsey documents, "Read o'er this," he is left alone to offer a soliloquy as rich in self-inspection as anything out of an Elizabethan tragedy:

> What should this mean? . . . (204)
> I must read this paper (209)
> This paper has undone me (211)
>   What cross devil
> Made me put this main secret in the packet
> I sent the King? (215–17)
> The letter, as I live, with all the business
> I wrot to's holiness (222–23)
>   I shall fall
> Like a bright exhalation in the evening (226–27)

Wolsey iterates the textual condition of his downfall, as if—like a foolish Faustus—he has committed things to paper that he wishes to retract. Each character has searched for meaning, whether such a meaning may be found in staged performance or in lyric listening, or in documentary sheets. Wolsey's is a tragedy of paper. As he repeats his questions, he makes his own self the object of his eye. He reads and rereads his own past. And in that reading, he recounts his fall. His is the language of the fallen angel, the morning star turned into evening darkness. If we had any doubts, we then will see, in Wolsey's next soliloquy, his explicit association: "And when he falls, he falls like Lucifer" (3.2.372).

Wolsey's soliloquies take us back to an earlier dramatic time. "This is the state of man," he offers, in a move redolent of Hamlet's meditations. "I have ventured, / Like little wanton boys that swim on bladders" (3.2.353, 359–60). His words bring back the desperation of blind Gloucester.

> As flies to wanton boys are we to th' gods,
> They kill us for their sport. (*King Lear*, 4.1.37–38)

This is a tale of Wolsey's "high-blown pride" (3.2.362) brought down, and in this scene he rises to the eloquence of old tragedians. It must take a great deal to pull this histrionics off, to make it seem sincere, to be an actor on a stage of fallen pride. The character of Wolsey now becomes unmasked for what he always was, an actor who believed himself a playwright, and Cromwell comes in now to provide that actor with one final audience for his performance. "I have no power to speak, sir" (3.2.373). Cromwell's near silence makes him the observer in this scene, an actor out of character, increasingly moved by the arts of his compeer.

Wolsey can address his fellow actor on the stage, confessing his awareness. "I know myself now." From the unmaskings of the actor-king, Wolsey unmasks himself. This is the language of those other plays of early Jacobean Tudor history now transferred to the actor's self-awareness, as if Wolsey says to Cromwell: When I see *you*, I know *me*. And, rising to the opportunity, Wolsey gives up a last performance worthy of any tragic royal.

> Cromwell, I did not think to shed a tear
> In all my miseries, but thou hast forced me,
> Out of thy honest truth, to play the woman.
> Let's dry our eyes, and thus far hear me, Cromwell;
> And when I am forgotten, as I shall be,
> And sleep in dull cold marble, where no mention
> Of me more must be heard of, say I taught thee—
> Say Wolsey, that once trod the ways of glory
> And sounded all the depths and shoals of honour,
> Found thee a way, out of his wreck, to rise in—
> A sure and safe one, though my master missed it. (3.2.429–39)

If Norfolk's story of the Cloth of Gold brought back Enobarbus's account of Cleopatra on her barge, now Wolsey's farewell takes us back to the African Queen herself. Like Cleopatra, he imagines a debased future in performance. He is forced to play the woman, much as Cleopatra will predict herself played by a squeaking boy. And much like Cleopatra to Octavius, Wolsey will tell him what to say:

> Say, good Caesar,
> That I some lady trifles have reserved . . . (*Antony and Cleopatra*, 5.2.160–61)
> And say,
> Some nobler token I have kept apart . . . (*Antony and Cleopatra*, 5.2.163–64)

Like Cleopatra, Wolsey falls in spectacle:

> Mark but my fall, and that that ruined me. (*Henry VIII*, 3.2.439)
> It smites me
> Beneath the fall I have. (*Antony and Cleopatra*, 5.2.167–68)

Both Queen and Cardinal become increasingly histrionic, increasingly possessed by rhetorical questions and exclamatory apostrophes. "O Cromwell," and again, "O Cromwell, Cromwell." Repetition is the mark of the unmanned, and if Wolsey is called to play the woman, it is to evoke the calls of the dying queen: "O Antony!"

I can no more

Wolsey's plot presents a template for assessing Queen Katherine, as her own queenship comes to be defined through her aesthetic choices and response. In her call for song, her invitation to musicians, and her choreographed vision, she marks her political decline through increasing artistic command. If Wolsey moved through public masque to self-display, Katherine moves to private audience, dream, and imagination. Hers is an ambiance of sleep and tears, of ravishment and inspiration. She is the site of a new lyricism for the play, but of an old lyricism for its audience.

Act 3 opens with "the queen and her women at work." The phrase "at work" implies acts of female aesthetic and crafted performance: needlework, embroidery, or tatting. This is a scene of women's hands, and Katherine's call for music enjoins a shift in the work of women's fingers.

> Take thy lute, wench. My soul grows sad with troubles.
> Sing, and disperse 'em if thou canst. Leave working. (3.1.1–2)

Shakespeare's plays are full of musical performances before an onstage audience, but this moment in *Henry VIII* remains unique. In almost all the other plays, singers are males: fools, clowns, young boys, or spirits who are called upon to entertain or, at times, who sing at their own will for themselves or others.[22] *Henry VIII* remains the only play in which a female character sings at the command of another female character. It shifts dramatically its site of aesthetic making, moving the audience away from masculine displays of masque and pageant to feminine displays of handiwork. It takes us inside private chambers, rather than to public halls or fields of battle. It shows us Katherine as commissioner of the imagination, and her aesthetic aegis moves progressively inward, culminating in the vision that, while we may see it on the stage, we must imagine as transpiring in her own head.

Recent scholarship has revealed how the figure of the singing woman stood at the nexus of threat and desire for Early Modern Europe.[23] On the one hand, singing women could be seen as temptresses or sirens. Linda Austern argues that "the bewitching exquisite music of the learned courtesan of continental Europe, a type seemingly absent from native English society, exerted a special and somewhat repulsive fascination for English observers."[24] On the other hand, women's song could "serve as a purely spiritual salve for all earthly travail when played for themselves alone, or as an intentional or accidental invitation to the pleasures and dangers of love when played to men. . . . Occasionally, noble ladies request music from their serving-maids or gentle lady companions when they have need for solace."[25]

Katherine's call for music may seem simply like the second of these cases, but the text of her wench's song takes us back to the first and far more challenging scenario.[26]

Song

Orpheus with his lute made trees
And the mountain tops that freeze
    Bow themselves when he did sing.
To his music plants and flowers

Ever sprung, as sun and showers
    There had made a lasting spring

Every thing that heard him play,
Even the billows of the sea,
    Hung their heads and then lay by.
In sweet music is such art,
Killing care and grief of heart
    Fall asleep, or hearing, die. (3.1.3–14)

What does it mean for a woman to sing of Orpheus? Austern quotes a scene from Robert Greene's *Greene's Never Too Late* of 1590 where a young man, Francesco, is seduced by a woman, Insida, with a lute.

> While thus Insida sung her song, Francesco sate, as if with Orpheus melodie he had been inchaunted, having his eyes fixed on her face, and his ears attendant on her Musicke, so that he yielded to that Syren which after forst him to a fatall shipwrack.[27]

A female Orpheus can be a dangerous thing, and it seems clear, in *Henry VIII*, that such a performance must be contained within a woman's chamber. But there is more, I think, than affect or seduction here. By singing about Orpheus, the wench presents the power of aesthetic metamorphosis. In a play so much concerned with pageantry, illusion, and the masque, this scene illustrates how commissioned performance can transform the listener. It reimagines Orpheus before King Pluto as a female lutenist before a deposed Queen. It presages not the return of a beloved to the world above, but the release of a rejected woman into sleep.

These lyrics may be full of cliché, but they take on new dramatic force as female. Orpheus calling trees and mountains into audience had become a familiar trope of late sixteenth- and early seventeenth-century lyric. His halting of the seasons would have been a commonplace for Jacobean audiences, while the final phrasing of the lyric would have seemed an all-too-familiar maxim for an audience reared on sixteenth-century song.

In sweet music is such art,
Killing care and grief of heart
Fall asleep, or hearing, die.

When Caliban had heard the "sweet airs" and had longed to sleep and dream again, I sought to illustrate how his was the vocabulary of an old Elizabethan, and now, *Henry VIII* looks back to an old courtly melancholy sweetness. The Orphic landscape brings us back to Dowland's "sweet woods," where his solitary singer sang "To birds, to trees, to earth." Much as this Orpheus could make the earth sit still, so Dowland voiced his commands in his *Third Book*.

Flow not so fast ye fountains,
What needeth all this haste?
Swell not above your mountains,
Nor spend your time in waste.
Gentle springs, freshly your salt tears
Must still fall dropping from their spheres. (*Third Book*, 8)

"Sleep," Dowland sang elsewhere, "is a reconciling," and throughout the lyrics that he set to music there is this continual association of sleep with imaginative freedom. Katherine's theater of sorrow has Dowland's script behind it. The line she hears, "in sweet music is such art," has the feel, now, of a maxim invoked to signal not just mere delight but ravishment itself. As Dowland put it, in one of his songs from the *Pilgrimes Solace*: "Music, all thy sweetness lend."[28]

But what makes this scene of musical ravishment now so poignant is its interruption. It cannot have its full effect. This moment of sublime, lyric privacy has to be broken here, and broken by a man, quite literally to dis-spell the magic of this chamber of affect.

Henry VIII is a play full of broken pageants. From the rained-out Cloth of Gold, to Wolsey's truncated masque, to the elaborate failure of Katherine's trial, the play raises scenes of showy display only to disperse them. So, too, at this moment in act 3, the characters onstage together with the audience find themselves ripped from ravishment. We barely have the time to feel the enchantment of the woman with the lute. We barely have the time to imagine Orpheus working his art upon the landscape, much as the musician works his or her art upon our ears. "Enter a Gentleman," and Katherine questions, "How now?" and it is over.

The power of this scene lies in the ways in which it sets up and then quickly dispels the concords of performance and politics. The Gentleman's interruption breaks the spell of the performer, and it breaks the spell of Katherine's last command. Such are the broken pageants of this play, and when Katherine reemerges in act 4, scene 2, it is as someone almost literally broken, "sick," and held up by her last, true servants.[29]

Now, Wolsey is dead, and Katherine offers up a eulogy that sees through his old ruses to reveal him as a man more of flesh than of fantasy.

> He was a man
> Of an unbounded stomach. (4.2.33–34)
> I' th' presence
> He would say untruths and be ever double
> Both in his words and meaning. (37–39)
> His promises were, as he then was, mighty;
> But his performance, as he is now, nothing.
> Of his own body he was ill . . . (41–43)

Katherine demystifies Wolsey into a man of body parts. She reveals him the poor performer, as if Autolycus had stayed on at court and worked his lies. The doubleness of words and meaning, the performance for its own sake—this is the language of the shifty balladeer.

And now, he is gone. Only at this point can Katherine recall the musical artistry of her private chamber; only now, having affirmed that Wolsey is both dead and demeaned, can she call for a truly ravishing music.

> Good Griffith,
> Cause the musicians play me that sad note
> I named my knell, whilst I sit meditating
> On that celestial harmony I go to. (4.2.77–80)

Then stage directions, "Sad and solemn music," and she sleeps.

"Solemn music" marks the visionary in the late plays: that intersection of imagination and aesthetic response that gives to these works the feel of what I have been calling mythic lyricism. Posthumus's final vision at the close of *Cymbeline*, much like Queen Katherine's here, will appear with "solemn music," while *The Tempest* calls three times for "solemn music," and Prospero will invoke a "solemn curfew" and spell forth his magic with a "solemn air."

Katherine's life onstage ends with a performance as arresting, mythical, and musical as any of the late plays. The stage direction is as complex as anything in *The Tempest*—less, I think, a direction for performance than a description of the imagination. But unlike *The Tempest*, or the *Winter's Tale* (but, perhaps, somewhat like that final vision in *Cymbeline*), this moment in *Henry VIII* offers up not a masque or marvel before others but, instead, a dream.

> Enter, solemnly tripping one after another, six personages, clad in white robes, wearing on their heads garlands of bays, and golden vizards on their faces, branches of bays or palms in their hands. They first congee unto her, then dance; and at certain changes, the first two hold a spare garland over her head, at which the other four make reverend curtsies. Then the two that held the garland deliver the same to the other next two, who observe the same order in their changes, and holding the garland over her head. Which done, they deliver the same garland to the last two, who likewise observe the same order. At which, as it were by inspiration, she makes in her sleep signs of rejoicing, and holdeth up her hands to heaven. And so, in their dancing vanish, carrying the garland with them. The music continues. (4.2.SD 82)[30]

Solemnity controls the moment, and we see now how that notion prepares us for something otherworldly. The vision's personages enter "tripping one after another." Elsewhere in Shakespeare, nymphs trip in; "tripping" is the word of visionary dance for Ariel and Feste; Ulysses has his Greekish girls sing "tripping." This is a specific word of delicate, largely female, performance. The figures "congee" to the dreaming Katherine—a rare word in Shakespeare, meaning to bow or curtsey in leaving. But here, it implies curtseying in greeting (in *All's Well That Ends Well*, Bertram announces, with great affectation, "I have congied with the duke, done my adieu with his dearest . . ."). The language of this stage direction grows increasingly rarified, a language of heightened courtliness, and the repetition of the word "garland" affirms its staginess. Is this a scene of pastoral crowning, a dumb show of obeisance, an allegory of politics, or an affair of beauty? Whatever it is, it is a tale of art.

"As if by inspiration." *Inspire* and *inspiring* appear throughout Shakespeare, but the noun "inspiration" shows up only in the earliest of plays and then, again, here. There is a sense, as we read and reread this stage direction, that we are exploring a deep past of Shakespeare's lexicon, a past of courtly dream and vision. Listen to Joan of Arc in *Henry VI, Part 1*:

> First, let me tell you whom you have condemned:
> Not one begotten of a shepherd swain,
> But issued from the progeny of kings;
> Virtuous and holy, chosen from above,
> By inspiration of celestial grace
> To work exceeding miracles on earth. (5.6.36–41)

Joan's voice, for all its prowess and its prophecy, is lyrical here: shepherd swains and inspiration and celestial grace take us back to the pastorals of Shakespeare's literary youth. I hear in Katherine's own farewell to this earth toward a celestial harmony, and in the language of her vision, an echo of this earliest of Shakespeare's condemned women. Like Joan, too, Katherine from this moment on will speak increasingly in lyric terms. Her long exit is a tale of metaphors and mimes, hearkening back to songs and soliloquies of a past generation.

"Spirits of peace, where are ye?" she calls, and Griffith, still with her, simply says, "Madam, we are here." But she is not assuaged. "It is not you I call for." She explains that she had seen "a blessed troop / Invite me to a banquet," and she bids her imaginary musicians to depart (4.2.83–88). Her handmaid, Patience, now announces: "Do you note / How much her grace is altered on the sudden?" (4.2.96–97), and this sense of alteration comes back when Katherine avows to Capuchius, "O, my lord, / The times and titles now are altered strangely / With me since you first knew me" (4.2.112–14). "Alteration" is, again, the key term of the play, as if the metamorphic impulse now were not to grant eternal life but move the body into death. "When I shall dwell with worms, and my poor name / Banished the kingdom." Katherine now speaks like a lyric lover, almost (if it were not so anachronistic) operatic in her final speeches, arias of farewell.

> Remember me
> In all humility unto his highness.
> Say his long trouble now is passing
> Out of this world. Tell him in death I blessed him, (4.2.161–64)
> When I am dead, good wench,
> Let me be used with honor. Strew me over
> With maiden flowers that all the world may know
> I was a chaste wife to my grave. (167–71)

She goes on, ending with the half-line: "I can no more" (174).

A history of Shakespeare's farewells comes back in her character: Othello ("And say besides . . ."), Cleopatra ("Say, good Caesar . . . and say . . ."), Antony on Brutus ("And say to all the world . . ."). The old laments of Dowland come back as well, the dolor of a future to dwelling with the worms, the lyric sorrows of a speaker imagining death, the floral imagery of the grave. "In darkness learn to dwell," enjoins one of those lyrics. If Katherine imagines herself dwelling with the worms, it is in a farewell to life as ariose and aching as Dowland's own assay in Italian from the *Pilgrimes Solace*:

> Lasso vita mia, mi fa morire,
> Crudel' amor mio cor consume,
> Da mille ferrite, che mi fa morir.
> Ahi me, Deh, che non mi fa morire,
> Crudel' amor, mi fa sofrir mille martire.

> Let go my life, you are making me die.
> Cruel love eats up my heart,
> Gives me a thousand wounds, which kill me.

Oh, alas, do not let me die,
Cruel Love makes me suffer a thousand martyrdoms.[31]

The interjections, the apostrophes, the outbursts here echo against Katherine's farewells. And if she imagines herself strewn (weirdly Ophelia-like) with maiden flowers, it is to remind us, too, of Dowland's singer in the "trembling shadow": "As I sing, sweet flowers I'll strew."

"I can no more." These four words had become a touchstone of a mythic, lyrical departure. Songsters, lyricists, and playwrights evoking classical antiquity have characters give up in silence with the phrase. Lovers died for a century with these words on their lips, from Surrey's bereft swain, "Now knowest thou all: I can no more," to Mary Sidney's Cleopatra, "I can no more, I die," to Shakespeare's Suffolk of *Henry VI, Part 2*, "I can no more; live thou to joy thy life," and his Queen Margaret of the same play, "Ay me, I can no more! die Margaret!" Katherine's exit line embeds a literary and dramatic history of departure, of figures of loss and power saying farewell in the most emotive ways.

Speak to the business

After Katherine's music, her vision, and her lyric outbursts, we are left with verities of clock time and the documents of office. "It's one o'clock," Gardiner announces at the opening of act 5, as if to take actors, audience, and readers out of the imagination and put them back, squarely, in the measurable time of court. Now, there is Cromwell, "the king's hand and tongue," in Lovell's memorable phrase—as if the new man was far less a creature of the masque and pageant than an extension of the physical, lived body of the King himself. The play increasingly moves away from theatricality to business. "Charles," says the King to Suffolk, "I will play no more tonight," as if Henry has at last realized that kingship can no longer be the site of fiction (5.1.56). Like James I, who recognized that a king was always onstage, yet who needed to separate himself from the comedians and balladines, Henry affirms his rule in this all-too-present world. Everything, now, is hand and tongue.

> Give me your hand (5.1.95)
> Calumnious tongues (5.1.113)
> Give me thy hand (5.1.116)

The final act becomes the place not of great stages of performance, but a "council-table," with its "chairs and stools," where Cromwell will hold court. "Speak to the business," the Lord Chancellor states, and we are now all business (5.2.35). Cranmer is summarily tried and convicted—convicted not just of heresy but of a duplicity worthy of Wolsey himself. "That's the plain truth," says Gardiner. "Your painted gloss discovers, / To men that understand you, words and weakness" (5.2.105–7). Now we are in the worlds of plain truth; painted glosses are dismissed. And all that Cranmer has in his defense is but a thing. He shows the King's ring to the men, and they all recognize it to be real: "Tis no counterfeit," and soon Henry will enter, things will be set right, and Cranmer will be exonerated (5.2.136).

The theater, by this point, is left not for statesmen but for clowns. The Porter and his Man offer a statement about how the crowd responds to public celebration. There will be christening, Elizabeth has been born, and all will become spectacle again. Court becomes, in the Porter's phrasing, noisily transformed into the "Parish Garden," that center for bear-baiting and boisterous display. Spectacle becomes the subject for their banter: Moorfields and its archers; "some strange Indian with the great tool come to court"; an allusion to a "Haberdasher's wife of small wit"; and finally the "youths that thunder at a playhouse." The scenic world of the Porter and his Man is the world far removed from cloths of gold and courtly masque. It is the world of rough display, of balladeering calls, of sex and violence, of the groundlings in the pit (5.3.1–63).

The play grows, toward its close, increasingly uncomfortable with such audiences. "Mercy o'me," cries the Lord Chamberlain, "what a multitude are here!" (5.3.64), and as the scene draws to its chaotic climax, we are unsure of just where lines are drawn between the actors and the audience. The Porter shouts, "Make way there for the princess," his Man threatens, "You great fellow, / Stand close up, or I'll make your head ache," and the Porter points, "You i'th'chamblet, get up o'th'rail, I'll peck you o'er the pales else" (5.2.84–87). Are they speaking to actors on the stage, massed as a crowd, or are they breaking down the fiction of this fanfare and yelling at people in the audience itself? We are as much as anybody on the stage brought into fictions of performance. The play breaks down, its lords asserting business and fact, its fools asserting sights and spectacle. It is as if Jonsonian urban comedy is banging up against courtly decorum, and all the play can do at the end is try to stage one more trumpeted, canopied display.

Baby Elizabeth comes in, with King and Cranmer, and it is the latter character who names her and who begs leave to speak the last great orations of the play. He offers up the prophecy of what she shall become, a golden age of what the audience would have recalled as the Elizabethan age of "truth," and "good" and "safety." And at the end, Cranmer foresees from this "maiden phoenix" a new heir, the unnamed James here: "He shall flourish" (5.4.24–54).

Henry remarks that Cranmer speaks "wonders," and "Thou hast made me now a man" (5.4.55, 64). He answers his own question of four acts before, "Who am I?," and in this answer he gives up the persona to become the person. Now, we must leave the ruses of the theater for the business of rule. As at the close of *The Tempest* or *The Winter's Tale*, there is a sense here that spectacle, masque, song, and even poetry can only take us so far in the world. The Epilogue, whomever it is by, recognizes these limits of theatricality. Some will be pleased, some not; some have come to the theater but to sleep; some are expecting witty city jokes. The play, the Epilogue announces, is only about "the merciful construction of good women," and the men in the audience should be expected to clap as their ladies urge them on. The late plays, all in their own ways, explore the staging of renunciation. They give us displays of spectacle or song or tripping dance only to make us realize that the clap of hands does not set actors free but frees ourselves. We wake from the ruses of the theater, from the dreams or fantasies of island lyrics, Bohemian ballads, and old Tudor pageantry and Orphic stanzas.

It is fitting, then, that Henry Wotton should have been our guide to the play's history. His is a tale of noise and paper, of an interrupted pageant as strange as the storm that breaks the Cloth of Gold or the brusque Gentleman that stanches Orphic reveries in Katherine's chamber. The burning man who puts his breeches out with ale is as much comic commentary on the scene as the Porter in act 5. As Wotton reminds us, nothing, in the end, "did perish but wood and straw, and a few forsaken cloaks." Even in its explosive interruption, nothing really disappears but stuff and stage prop. The fabric of the theater—whether virtuous or baseless—is just that, a fabric.

There is much in this play that feels Shakespearean, and there is much that does not. But we need not pinpoint the words of one or any other author. Taken as a whole, *Henry VIII* stands as a powerful Jacobean commentary on the whole Shakespearean tradition: on its emotions of wronged or wronging women, on its claims for lyric artistry as stanching social chaos, on its insistent meta-theatrics of the court. It is as much a "reading" of the Shakespearean theater as it is a text within it. To watch Wolsey fall or Katherine lament or Cranmer prophesy is to watch bits and pieces of the old art come back for an audience that may remember such things well, but may also realize that theater is a thing that some will like and some will sleep through, some will smile at and some will applaud.

5

Aesthetic Judgment and the Audience in *Cymbeline*

Almost from its first performance, *Cymbeline* was an enigma. Simon Foreman saw it, probably in spring or summer 1611, and he struggled with its complicated plot and confusing disguises. Foreman remembered much, but he remembered things in order and in emphasis far different from what we might recall upon reading or seeing the play.

> Remember also the story of Cymbelin, king of England in Lucius's time, how Lucius came from Octavius Caesar for tribute and being denied, after sent Lucius with a great army of soldiers who landed at Milford Haven, and after were vanquished by Cymbelin, and Lucius taken prisoner, and all by means of 3 outlaws of the which 2 of them were the sons of Cymbelin stolen from him when they were but 2 years old by an old man whom Cymbelin banished, and he kept them as his own sons 20 years with him in a cave. And how one of them slew Clotan that was the Queen's son going to Milford Haven to seek the love of Innogen, the King's daughter, whom he had banished also for loving his daughter. And how the Italian, that came from her love, conveyed himself into a chest and said it was a chest of plate sent from her love and others to be presented to the King; and in the deepest of the night she being asleep, he opened

> the chest and came forth of it, and viewed her in her bed, and the marks of her body, and took away her bracelet, and after accused her of adultery to her love, etc. And in the end how he came with the Romans into England, and was taken prisoner and after revealed to Innogen, who had turned herself into man's apparel and fled to meet her love at Milford Haven, and chanced to fall on the cave in the woods where her 2 brothers were, and how by eating a sleeping dram they thought she had been dead, and laid her in the woods and the body of Cloten by her in her love's apparel that he left behind him and how she was found by Lucius, etc.[1]

Everything seems out of place. Cymbeline's war with Lucius, the revelation of his banished sons, and Cloten's death do not take place until act 4. Iachimo (called simply "the Italian" here) and his bedroom ruse fill part of act 2.[2] Innogen's transformation to the boy Fidele is the stuff of the middle of the play, and she wakes up beside Cloten's body in act 4, scene 2—long after Foreman had recalled that one of the King's sons had killed him, and apparently unnoticed, here, that he is headless.

As we know, Foreman is hardly a precise guide to the plays he saw. But even by his own associative logic, this one seems to elude him. He can barely finish up the story, twice breaking into an *et cetera*. His garbling may be a matter less of his own inattention than of the difficulties of the play itself. *Cymbeline* intertwines its story lines in ways almost inexplicable until the end. It offers set pieces of soliloquy and song, only to undermine their aesthetic effect. Much like the other late plays, it stretches English verse almost beyond the limits of grammaticality.[3] Its major characters disappear for scenes on end, and its political resolution—peace between Britons and Romans—wraps up with little preparation. "Cymbeline's audiences," in Martin Butler's words, "often find themselves unsure about what kind of play they are witnessing, and spend much of the action trying to intuit the underlying direction of events"—a statement that may say as much about Simon Foreman as ourselves.[4]

Cymbeline is long, difficult, and messy.[5] Reading the play in its First Folio appearance makes things little easier: stretches of speech seem ill set and confusingly punctuated. For all the ministrations of Ralph Crane (largely believed to be the scribe behind its text), the stage directions remain much less informative and evocative than those of other plays he oversaw. Occasionally, characters show up and say nothing in their scenes. Perhaps most confusing (or manipulative) of all, when Innogen, disguised as Fidele, drinks the potion that puts her to sleep, the direction does not say that she seems or appears dead. It simply says she *is* dead (4.2.194), making her revival a few scenes later even more striking for the reader.[6]

The annotator of the Misei copy of the First Folio similarly struggled with these puzzles. From the start, he recognized confusions and impersonations. "Courtiers counterfeit outward sorrow" stands at the top of his first page of the play, and his further remarks sustain this sense of feigning from the start: "dissembled Queene promises vtmost kindness to whom she Intends all mischief"; "Certainties are either past remedies"; "diuelish deuices"; "false and falselie purchased proofes"; "falsehood and lying becomes not great men"; "dreames made of the fumes of the braines"; "damnable wickedness of a dissembled Queene"; and finally, "Infinit questions of the circumstances of strange chances."

The play emerges, from these marginalia, as an essay on dissimulation. It is not simply, as Samuel Johnson would put it a century and a half later, that the play was full of "folly . . . absurdity . . . confusion, and . . . impossibility."[7] It is that such impossibilities are the subject of the play. This is a story of strange chances, of counterfeit characters changing clothes, mistaking others, and trying to find proof of self in dress. Little wonder that one of its most frequently repeated words is "garment."[8] Clothes and clothing, takings and mistakings fill the play, and if its devilish devices challenge a first-time playgoer or reader, they seduce the literary critic. Shakespeareans of the late twentieth and early twenty-first century have found its contradictions and its distances central to Shakespeare's own redemptive theater. As Butler summarizes it, "Such fractures appeal to post-modern tastes for fictions that reveal their engineering and question the terms of their own mimesis."[9]

I want to open up this compressed, and somewhat coded, critical assessment by exploring how the play reveals its engineering—how its characters reflect on theatrical and lyrical performance and, in the process, how they interrogate the place of beauty in the exercise of power. There is an arc to lyricism in the play, a clear line from the challenged to the challenging, traced through allusions to the classics. These resonances ask us to consider what it means to be human and inhuman, speaking and listening. They ask us, too, to consider the play's status as performance and as text, as something we may hear or read. Allusions to classical materials (or back to Shakespeare's own, earlier works) provoke the play's personae and its audience to make, in Colin Burrow's words, "certainties out of tiny pieces of material evidence." The play lives in a world of "fictive extrapolation . . . turning allusions into illusions, creating alternative moods" both for characters and for us.[10] For in addition to its many verbal echoes of Ovidian characters, *Cymbeline* shares most broadly in that Morpheus-like handling of persona and illusion that had formed the core of book II of the *Metamorphoses*. Its play of bodies is a play of impersonations. The visions of its characters are those that come in sleep.

Cymbeline raises questions about how to describe the experience of art or theater. Like Simon Foreman, we are challenged by its twists and counterfeits. Like the two minor characters that open many of the plays, we struggle to retell a complex story in convincing ways. Such recitations take on a new challenge in the late plays. As they become increasingly less linear, more episodic, and more markedly meta-theatrical, these plays challenge not only the audience but also those inside their fictions to report clearly. Iachimo is the Simon Foreman of *Cymbeline*. He enters Innogen's bedchamber surreptitiously, hidden in a trunk of props and costumes. He sees everything, and yet, because his charge is to retell as accurately as he can the scene he witnesses, he does what many of the spectators of Shakespeare's theater had been doing—he takes notes. He writes down what the sleeping girl has read, lists all the aspects of her room, and even marks the mole beneath her breast. When, later in the play, Posthumus challenges him to report, he gives account. Each item comes for challenge: someone may have told you this; you may have heard it secondhand. Iachimo's job is to present the scene of Innogen's bedroom in such a way as to convince his audience that he was there.

In this action, he shares with Simon Foreman, Henry Wotton, and the many courtiers at masque and pageant in the Jacobean world the responsibility of writing as if he were there. The story of the Jacobean theater increasingly becomes a story not just of performance (let me convince you of my skills at impersonation) but of critical description. Let me convince you of my skills of sight, remembrance, and narrative organization.

Cymbeline becomes a play of how to tell a story and how to respond to artistic performance. It is a play less of making than reception, and Cloten will function as an audience of the inept. Music and poetry come forth not just to amaze or to delight. They come forth to enjoin an audience to feel, respond, and tell. *Cymbeline* embodies, in my view, an idea and ideal of criticism. Iachimo, Cloten, Innogen, Posthumus, the rustic brothers, Pisanio—all face the music and are asked to judge. The mythic lyricism of this play sets the stage not for commissioning but for listening. Art, here, is something not just commanded but seen and heard. What matters more and more in this play is how characters (and audience) feel when confronted with a lyric. *Cymbeline* shows how rule breaks down in the face of art; how, in the end, it is not so simple to equate the harmonies of strings and polities.

What does it mean to listen as a fool? What does it mean to try, and fail, to sing? What does it mean to speak the language of old lyrics in the voice of a vulgarian? These are the questions that surround the characters, and Cloten becomes the touchstone for these failings. I look closely at the ways in which he engages with lyric voices, and I argue that he brings to the fore one, new lyric voice for Shakespeare's audience. That voice is Catullus, the Roman poet who had become increasingly the template for desire in the late sixteenth and early seventeenth century.[11] Catullan idioms and ideologies were shaping lyric and dramatic presentations in such writers as Thomas Campion and Ben Jonson, and there is, by the beginning of the seventeenth century, a new fascination with the Roman poet as the site of lyric art.[12] Catullus spoke directly to the urban, and urbane, eroticism of the London poets.[13] "Vivamus mea Lesbia atque amemus" became a touchstone for the celebration of desire for a new generation.[14] Throughout *Cymbeline*, characters will evoke or echo a Catullan line, a phrase, a sensibility, in order to enable us to measure their aesthetic skills. For a play of Britons confronting Romans, the legacy of Catullus stands as an example of how legacies of Roman art and power may provide examples for an English lyric sensibility.

It may provide, as well, an example for our own. Much recent criticism has turned anew to *Cymbeline*'s confusions, fascinated with its dramatic self-consciousness and allusive evasions, finding meaning in the gaps and wrinkles of performance and print. The play constantly looks back to earlier Shakespearean material, and whatever led the printers of the Folio to place it last, it functions as a map to readerly remembrance. Telling its own story is difficult: for us, for its history of audiences, and for its own characters.

"What's the matter?"

Two Gentlemen have trouble with the plot. "What's the matter?" asks the Second, much as spectators from Foreman to the present seem to ask. The First, charged with outlining the biographies of characters and motives for their actions, cannot appear to get that matter out. His speech continually interrupts itself. Brief, expository sentences fight against long parenthetical clauses.

He that hath missed the Princess is a thing
Too bad for bad report; and he that hath her–
I mean, that married her, alack, good man,
And therefore banished—is a creature such
As seek through the regions of the earth
For one his like, there would be something failing
In him that should compare. (1.1.16–22)

Again and again, to simple questions of the Second Gentleman, the First runs on, interrupting with assessments, trying to keep all the names straight. His lines still baffle editors. Even to a simple question—whether Innogen is the "sole child to the King"—the First Gentleman cannot give a straight answer.

His only child.
He had two sons—if this be worth your hearing,
Mark it: the eldest of them at three years old,
I'th' swathing clothes the other, from their nursery
Were stol'n, and to this hour no guess in knowledge
Which way they went. (1.1.57–61)

The center point of what will be the play's later resolution—the King's sons revealed—stands as a strange aside here, if it be worth hearing.

At the heart of the play's opening is the question of what is worth hearing. How do we distinguish between the central facts of story and the peripheries of subplot? How do we keep it all straight? What are the signposts for recognizing what is and is not important? How do we judge, admire, or value the tellings and retellings of what we have, or have not, seen ourselves?

Innogen sees these questions, at the start, as matters of imagination. She stands on the shore, missing Posthumus's farewell, and turns to Pisanio to transform him into something mythic:

I would thou grew'st unto the shores o'th' haven
And question'st every sail. (1.3.1–2)

Pisanio becomes an Ovidian tree, grown out of human flesh and interweaved into the shore—a tree interrogating every sail, like some strange creature, doomed to speak. For every simple statement of the servant, Innogen provides a mythic over-reading. Pisanio sees ordinary objects: Posthumus's "eye or ear," his "glove or hat or handkerchief," diminishing as his ship draws to the horizon. Innogen turns them into rich poetic figures:

> Thou shouldst have made him
> As little as a crow, or less, ere left
> To after-eye him. (1.3.14–16)

Innogen does not merely say that Pisanio should have stayed until his master had shrunk down in size. She affirms that he should have "made" him into something, as if in the watching Posthumus would be transformed into one of those haunting birds of the *Metamorphoses*. Her verb here, "after-eye," must be a Shakespearean coinage—or, more pointedly, must be her coinage, and she spins out an imaginative blend of new anatomy and old myth to imagine how she would have seen the ship depart.

> I would have broke mine eye-strings, cracked them, but
> To look upon him till the diminution
> Of space had pointed him sharp as my needle;
> Nay, followed him till he had melted from
> The smallness of a gnat to air, and then
> Have turned mine eye and wept. (1.3.17–23)

The eye now takes on a life of its own, following after, stretching its nerves until they crack. Those eyes witness a change, and Innogen's speech offers up a set piece of schemes and tropes, figuratively transforming her love into a needle, then a gnat. Editors of the play have noticed that this scene evokes King Ceyx's farewell, his waving from the ship, and Alcyone's weeping on the shore as he evanesces beyond the horizon. In Arthur Golding's version of the *Metamorphoses*, it reads:

> Shee lifting up her watrye eyes behilld her husband stand
> Uppon the hatches making signes by beckening with his hand:
> And shee made signes to him ageine. And after that the land
> Was farre removed from the shippe, and that the sight began

> To bee unable to discerne the face of any man,
> As long as ere shee could shee lookt uppon the rowing keele.
> And when shee could no longer tyme for distance ken it weele,
> Shee looked still uppon the sayles that flasked with the wynd
> Uppon the maast. (11.537–45)

Alcyone is living her farewell; Innogen is imagining it. And what she is imagining is what we might call a proleptic metamorphosis—her lover is, in her own eyes, already transformed into something else. Long before King and Queen fly off as birds, Innogen reimagines the present landscape and its populace as creatures out of myth: writhing half-human trees, eyes stretching out of heads, and a diminished sailor vanishing into an insect.

Here, and throughout the play, Innogen is a mythographer of the imagination, someone who cannot tell a tale without imbuing it with figuration, someone who turns the commonplace into the mythic. In this, she seems to have far more in common with Iachimo than with Posthumus—the latter, always literal; the former, always full of figure.

Iachimo is a brilliant narrator, transforming things into aesthetic objects, making his language into something so well wrought that it, at times, almost abandons its transparency for art. He speaks a prose, in 1.4, barely comprehensible by others on the stage, its syntax twisted, its references so opaque that they beg for emendation. Agreeing with Posthumus to bet ten thousand ducats that he could become intimate with Innogen, Iachimo then says:

> You are afraid, and therein the wiser. If you buy ladies' flesh at a million a dram, you cannot preserve it from tainting; but I see you have some religion in you, that you fear. (1.4.129–32)

Editors since the early eighteenth century have emended his first words in the Folio, "You are a friend," to give a clarity to what has seemed oblique or even obscene.[15] "You are a friend" connotes a shared bond between the men—not modern friendship as such, but rather the experience of women. Roger Warren makes a weak case for the Folio, only to pull it back: "'You are her friend, her lover, and know her, so you know she will yield, and wisely won't accept the wager'—but surely no audience would pick all this up."[16]

But that is, I think, the point. No audience would pick all this up, and neither does Posthumus: "This is but a custom in your tongue; you bear a graver purpose, I hope." He seems confused by Iachimo's turn of phrase, finds it, perhaps, too glib or light. He hopes there is a "graver purpose" here, something behind the ornaments of rhetoric. Iachimo replies: "I am the master of my speeches, and would undergo what's spoken, I swear."

Such an exchange does not, on its own, justify restoring the First Folio's words, nor does it justify a modern editor's search for "clear sense." The speeches are confusing, and deliberately so. They remain of a piece with all that has been going on in *Cymbeline* to this point—a set of speakers who retell the past (the Gentlemen), imagine what they have not seen (Innogen), or script out a future (Iachimo). They urge an audience, inside as well as outside the play's fiction, to let loose a sense of meaning—if not jettisoning completely a faith in words, then at the very least permitting it to stretch a bit, much like the eye-strings of Innogen's fantasy.

"Who's there?"

Innogen opens act 2, scene 2, with this question more for us than for her handmaid. Like *Hamlet*'s sentinels, she wonders if a friend or enemy approaches, and that resonance creates an ominous, foreboding aura to her bedroom. "What hour is it?" Once again, she asks the kind of question of a sentry, and as in *Hamlet* it is midnight. We are prepared for an unwished-for entry—an invader, or a ghost—and Innogen prays to the gods to "guard" her from the "fairies and the tempters of the night." No phantasm appears. Instead, the earthly Iachimo emerges from the trunk, all full of myth and lyric voice. He speaks of Tarquin and Cytherea, rushes, lilies, rubies, windows white and azure. It is the language of old Shakespeare here, of the poet of *Venus and*

Adonis and the *Rape of Lucrece*, the language of Ovidian allusion. He enters much less like an actor than a spectator, reared on old poetry and ready for a scene out of the *Metamorphoses*. He may well be a ghost—but here, a ghost of older sensibilities, of lyric voice pressed into service of physical threat. And then, he catches himself ("But my design"), takes out a notebook, and prepares to "write all down" that he has seen.

He offers up a catalogue of the stage, a set of props and costumes, scenery and makeup, that is as much an "inventory" (his own word) of what may be there as a record of what should be there. In scene 4, he changes what he has said here, and the difference between the two descriptions is a matter less of what things were than of what effect Iachimo wishes to convey. In scene 2, he writes down for his remembrance what he sees, giving an inventory of the things as his eye moves across the stage. There are the pictures, the adornments of the bed, the figures in the tapestry, the mole underneath her breast, and then the book of Ovid's *Metamorphoses*, the page turned down at the story of Tereus and Philomel.

It is a very literate and literary inventory, the very kind that playgoers were making of the theater they had seen. Watching a play, as Tiffany Stern has shown, was an active (if not interactive) process in the early modern theater, and what Stern calls "literate playgoers" often arrived with their table-books and notebooks, ready to transcribe a good phrase or a memorable interchange. Compilation texts proliferated, in part to provide those who had not seen plays with access to their highlights, in part to provide text pirates with material to print. The acts of watching and transcribing were, for Shakespeare's audiences, interwoven practices, and Iachimo enacts that practice in the theater of Innogen's bedroom.[17]

We watch him take his notes, but when he reports back to Posthumus, we hear something very different. Whatever privately he noted, when he publicly performs the inventory, it is not a tale of little objects but of grand displays.

it was hanged
With tapestry of silk and silver; the story
Proud Cleopatra when she met her Roman,
And Cydnus swelled above the banks, or for
The press of boats or pride: a piece of work
So bravely done, so rich, that it did strive
In workmanship and value; which I wondered
Could be so rarely and exactly wrought,
Such the true life on't was. (2.4.68–76)
. . .

The roof o'th'chamber
With golden cherubins is fretted. Her andirons—
I had forgotten them—were two winking Cupids
Of silver, each on one foot standing, nicely
Depending on their brands. (2.4.87–91)

We sit and listen or we read and we see and we get less and less Innogen's bedroom than, say, Cleopatra's barge. The "tapestry of silk and silver" brings to mind the "cloth-of-gold of tissue" hanging on the Queen's pavilion in *Antony and Cleopatra*. Iachimo's claims for "workmanship and value" take us back to Enobarbus's description of the artifice that could "outwork nature." Cleopatra's "pretty dimpled boys, like smiling Cupids," come back, now, as the "golden cherubins" and "winking Cupids" that adorn Innogen's walls and fireplace. And Posthumus, affirming everything—"This is true"—comes off as something of a choral interrupter, much like Agrippa and Maecenas in Enobarbus's performance.

Much has been said about Iachimo's stagy claims here, his manipulations and his Ovidian veneer.[18] There is a feeling that he gives Posthumus less a vision of what he has seen than what he has read, a pastiche of allusions out of the *Metamorphoses*. But, given Iachimo's explicit presentation as a note-taker and memoirist, his recitation takes on more the flavor of a commonplacer's memory of *Antony and Cleopatra*, chunked together out of scribblings at the play.

He sees a small scene through the eyes of a great playgoer, and his lyric skill in reportage transforms the local to the royal. It offers up a metamorphosis of rhetoric, a transformation of a space of dark anxiety ("who's there") to one of brilliant splendor. Read side by side with Innogen's imagined farewell, these scenes illustrate how characters take Ovidian matter as the template for imagining a metamorphic world. They take the ordinary and rephrase it as the stunning.

"Who's there?" becomes the question for the audience, and Simon Foreman's précis of the play invites us to ask that of him. He offers only a few names, gives us a skeleton of the play's actions, and makes us ask of him: were you really there? We can only take Foreman (and his contemporaries) so far. What they are offering are not so much attempts at accurate accountancy than narratives of interest and imagination. Wotton's story of the burning of the Globe was as much a crafted literary narrative as anything onstage. And, if Foreman does not quite measure up to Wotton, we can see him try. His interrupting *et ceteras* evoke Iachimo himself, calling himself back to his "design," bringing memory to bear on memoir: "I had forgotten them." Order is everything in telling a story or describing a scene, and Iachimo's performance in scene 4 is a performance of a very high order.

"Gross Handling"

Cymbeline bristles with performances of a high order, from the famously beautiful "Hark, hark the lark," through the poignant trio of the rustic brothers, to the visionary verse of Posthumus's dream. Such moments have been long appreciated for their lyricism, and "Hark, hark" remains one of the great anthology set pieces out of Shakespeare's songbook.[19]

And yet, in the moment of performance, these lyric beauties are misunderstood, mistaken, and appropriated not for delectation but desire. If Innogen and Iachimo set the stage for witnessing, it is Cloten who answers them. He offers lyric prowess against bluster, introspection against rash behavior, and speech that hovers on the edge of beauty and ugliness. In David Armitage's words, Cloten presents a "masquerade" of poetry, where his decapitation by the rustic exiles echoes Orpheus's by the Maenads.[20] He figures forth the displacement of the human body for its voice: classical allusion pressed into the service of social satire or political critique. And in his violent entries and his final exit, he exposes the place of mythic violence in a play possessed by bodies clothed and reclothed, dead and revived, lost and found. For me, he stands as a fulcrum on which lyricism and power balance. He is a creature of the earth, but when he seeks revenge, he asks for wings. Cloten's performances and his response to performance show the ways in which the play presents poetry and music to question the social function of wrought language.

What is the place of beauty for the powerful? Cloten seems not to know. He enters the play as a human body in all its odorous materiality. "Sir," his obsequious First Lord asks, "I would advise you to shift a shirt" (1.2.1), and he continues, "The violence of action hath made you reek as a sacrifice" (12.1–2). "Where air comes out, air comes in" (1.2.3). The First Lord's jibe may seem to poke at Cloten's body, but it gets to the heart of the spoken word itself. Cloten's exchanges with his courtiers in act 1, scene 2, rip through all of the familiar polysemies of Shakespearean wordplay. They conjure up the back-and-forth of the boys in *Romeo and Juliet*; they evoke Hamlet's sparring with Polonius; they resonate with Hal and Falstaff punning through the pain. "His body's a passable carcass if he be not hurt" (1.2.8–9). When is the body but a carcass and when does it hold the human? Such are the claims of the play. And if the play asks just what happens to a body vented of its air, what of the torso released of its head?

Decapitation threatens everywhere, long before Cloten himself loses his head. Here, the flattering First Lord plays down Innogen's prowess. "Sir, as I told you always, her beauty and her brain go not together. She's a good sign, but I have seen small reflection of her wit" (1.2.25–26). Right from the start, the courtier rhetorically severs head from body. But we, and the Second

Lord, know better. "She shines not upon fools lest the reflection hurt her" (1.2.28–29).

Why should she spread her wit before an idiot? Throughout the play, characters measure up against the artistry before them. To see and hear is to be judged as someone worthy of the show, and Cloten's cloddish antics take us back to the original bad audience of myth, King Midas. Midas had chosen poorly, preferring Pan's pipes to Apollo's lyre, and in punishment for his critical judgment Apollo gave him ass's ears. This image of the King deformed for bad aesthetic taste filled early modern social and political satire.[21] John Lyly's play, *Midas*, of 1592 layered the moral allegory of the myth into a new political critique of colonial prowess.[22] Shakespeare's *Midsummer Night's Dream* plants the story into an extended comedy of action and allusion, as the ass's ears sprout out of Bottom's head. "I have a reasonable good ear in music," he announces, in a moment of Midas-like taste. "Let's have the tongs and bones" (4.1.27–29).[23] For George Sandys, synthesizing a century of social, literary, and political interpretations of the myth, Midas is a "fool," "sottish," and "an ignorant prince, vnable to distinguish between which is vile and excellent, and therefore prefers the one before the other."[24] Midas hovers over *Cymbeline*, and the vocabulary that emerged to debase him—fool, clod, dolt, beastly, sottish—chimes with Cloten's name and nature. A tragic antitype of Bottom, he is a creature of the earth who cannot metamorphose either to rejoin his human peers or find an afterlife among the stars.

When he appears in act 2, scene 3, bantering with his courtiers about coldheartedness and coldness, the trials of winning and losing, he avows: "Winning will put any man into courage" (2.3.7). He goes on (anticipating figures of his Midas-like transformation), "If I could get this foolish Innogen, I should have gold enough" (2.3.7–8). He calls for music.

> I would this music would come. I am advised to give her music
> a-mornings, they say it will penetrate.
> *Enter Musicians*
> Come on, tune. If you can penetrate her with your fingering, so;
> we'll try with tongue too. (2.3.11–14)

His phrasing offers more than the "sexual innuendo" parenthetically identified by the modern editor. It is profoundly charged with sex. Though "come" would not be recorded until the middle of the seventeenth century in its orgasmic sense, we need not stretch the lexicon to find much here that is jejunely ribbing. Cloten may give her music, but that verb "give" carried violence with it by the 1590s, and it had a sexual edge at least as early as Beaumont and Fletcher.[25] Cloten is advised to give it to her in the morning, and the verb "penetrate" can connote nothing less than sexual incursion here. "Come on, tune." Yes, a simple command to musicians. But in Cloten's mouth, it is a mark again of power.[26]

Fingering and tongue here, too, flirt with the double edge of music and desire. They take us back to Dowland's reputation, to his famous *digitos trementes*, the trembling fingers of Campion's praise. But more than metaphor, fingering had become for Dowland and his peers the mark of true musicianship: the nexus of physical technique and aesthetic judgment. There is much in Cloten's call that chimes with Dowland's own discussions about what a true musician may be and how to measure the right audience. The skillful and the inept could stand on either side of the performance, and Joshua Sylvester brings them together in this apt description of Dowland's abilities:

> For, as an old, rude, rotten tune-less Kit
> If famous Douland daign to finger it
> Makes sweeter music than the choicest Lute
> In the grosse handling of a clownish Brute.[27]

And so, a clownish brute calls for music.

> Hark, hark, the lark at heaven's gate sings,
> And Phoebus gins arise,
> His steeds to water at those springs
> On chaliced flowers that lies,
> And winking Mary-buds begin to ope their golden eyes;
> With everything that pretty is, my lady sweet arise,
> Arise, arise! (2.3.19–25)

What makes this song so beautiful? Beyond the familiar Ovidian imagery and careful prosody, the poem explores, and exploits, a new vocabulary of aesthetic value. Phoebus's well-known steeds drink at the springs where "chaliced flowers" grow, flowers whose cuplike shapes recall the goblets of the royal or the religious. "Chaliced" is clearly a Shakespearean coinage, as is the term "Mary-buds" for marigolds. The word "winking" in the sense used here may also be original with Shakespeare (it is unattested earlier), while the form "gins" for "begins" would have been heard as the archaism modern lexicography exposes it to be.[28]

The poem is an exercise in verbal invention, a performance where convention jars against new phrasings. As in Innogen's or Iachimo's performances, this is a moment when the play revels in linguistic innovation, and Cloten's surrounding speeches take that innovation to its basest level.

> So, get you gone. If this penetrate I will consider your music the better; if it do not, it is a vice in her ears which horse hairs and calves' guts nor the voice of unpaved eunuch to boot can never amend. (2.3.26–29)

Once again, "penetrate" becomes the verbal fulcrum on which affect and violation balance. A study of its history shows how it is only in the 1610s that it had come to mean both sexual insertion and the creation of affect from music or art. Horse hairs used for viol bows were relatively new, too (the OED cites this passage from *Cymbeline*), while "guts" meaning strings from animal intestine does not appear in use until 1611. And "unpaved" meaning without stones, hence testicles (a brilliant chain of metaphorical associations), is by all accounts uniquely Shakespeare's.[29]

This is a scene of musical performance and reception full of new locutions. It gives us beauty in a song and clownish vulgarism in its hearing. Cloten's is the world of body, not of soul or spirit. He dismembers musical performance into woman's ears, horse's hair, calves' guts, and the empty scrotum of a male soprano. To reduce music to the bodily physicality of the things that make it is to turn something airy into something base. Now,

Phoebus's steeds have been flayed for their hair, and the voice of the lark cracks in the eunuch's mouth.

Cloten exemplifies contemporary social fears of the bad listener: Sylvester's "clownish brute," or more measuredly in Dowland's own words, one who does not have "the cunning to iudge and discern good Ayers from bad." In such a lack of cunning, he emerges as a modern Midas for the audience, and his name explicitly recalls the qualities of those who cannot hear the music of the lyre. In Golding's translation of Ovid's *Metamorphoses*, the golden touch only aspires to make beauty out of dross;

> . . . He towched next a clod of earth, and streight the same
> By force of towching did become a wedge of yellow gold.
> (11.123–24)

When Midas gives up and lets the waters of the River Pactolus wash him clean, his power "Infects the river," such that "even as yet the yellow gold upon the clods remains." The Maenads, too, come off as badly as the King, for they are stirred to violence by the sounds of Orpheus's lyre. They take the implements of tillers and farmers as weapons, and then besiege him with dirt itself:

> Sum cast mee clods, sum boughes of trees, and sum threw stones.
> (11.31)

Midas and Orpheus, in Golding's English, live in a world of clods, of lumps of earth that in the end cannot be alchemized to gold. And Phoebus Apollo himself, with "golden heare" and "viole made of precious stones and Ivorye intermixt," finds Midas a poor audience for his cunning and sweetness.

> Apollo could not suffer well his foolish eares to keepe
> Theyr humaine shape, but drew them wyde, and made them long and deepe.
> And filld them full of whytish heares, and made them downe to sag. (11.196–99)

In this world of gold and dross, of sweetness and cloddishness, Cloten's response to music takes us back to these bad audiences.

"Hark, hark, the lark" is an occasion for performance, but it is as well an opportunity for criticism. The lyric's beauty has its meaning in the larger frame of Cloten's brutish judgment, and he brings together the contemporary debates on good listening with the old mythologies of judgment. George Sandys would summarize generations of opinion when he glosses Midas as "an ignorant prince, vnable to distinguish between that which is vile and excellent, and therefore prefers the one before the other."[30]

Catullus, Eloquence, and Power

Cloten may not take up the kit of song, but he takes up the language of the lyric in his unexpectedly reflective soliloquy in act 3, scene 5. How does he feel about Innogen?

> I love and hate her. For she's fair and royal,
> And that she hath all courtly parts more exquisite
> Than lady, ladies, woman—from every one
> The best she hath, and she, of all compounded,
> Outsells them all—I love her therefore; but
> Disdaining me, and throwing favours on
> The low Posthumus, slanders so her judgment
> That what's else rare is choked; and in that point
> I will conclude to hate her, nay indeed,
> To be revenged upon her. For when fools shall— (3.5.70–79)

He opens with Catullus's famous words from poem 85, *odi et amo*. *Cymbeline* often juxtaposes sublime lyricism against grotesque, if not parodic, bodily action, and the movements of the characters often seem to dramatize the image of the disembodied Orpheus: a recognition of the tensions between mouth and body. Orpheus's severed head, much like the oxymoron of Catullus 85, emblematizes *Cymbeline*'s verbal ambiguities and contradictions.[31]

> Odi et amo. Quare id faciam, fortasse requires?
> Nescio, sed fieri sentio et excrucior.

> I hate and I love. You may ask, why do I do this?
> I do not know, but I feel it happening and I am tortured.

Catullus's compression has been valued ever since the poems were recovered and recopied in the early modern period. The immediacy of the statement—I hate and I love—moves to a question and answer: Why? I do not know, but this is the way it is. This is a poem of the conjugation, a poem that sustains its little drama by the voicing of its verbs. Just about every grammatical form lies in its brief compass, and different verb classes wed themselves together. *Odi et amo*: first person present active, yet different classes. *Requires*: second person present active. *Faciam*: subjunctive first person active. *Nescio*: first person present active. *Fieri sentio*: "I feel it to happen," a passive/active construction. *Excrucior*: the final verb, a passive first person. The verbal structure of the poem thus moves from active to passive in both the grammatical and the dramatic sense. It represents a loss of control, a giving up of will and knowledge. Its opening assurance loses traction in the admission of ignorance. The narrator ends feeling something happen to him; it ends having him be excruciated.

Cloten's soliloquy unfolds Catullus's compression. It develops the initial paradox by assembling a list of cases: she is beautiful, but she disdains me; even though I am attracted to her, I resent her attentions to another, and therefore I hate her; that hatred will lead me to violent acts against her. It is as if Cloten asks Catullus's imagined question and essays an answer based on what sounds like observation and decision. It is as if Cloten wishes to deny the *nescio* of Catullus's couplet: I do, in fact, know why I feel this way. In doing so, he transforms the entire essence of the Latin poem. Catullus offers up a drama of interiority, debates held in the silence of the poet's mind. The pain of hating and loving is held within, a pain only enhanced by the poet's inability to know his own condition.

Cloten, by contrast, externalizes this interior distress. *Excrucio*: torment, torture, afflict, harass, to put upon the rack or cross. Cloten may begin with a first-person announcement in the Catullan voice, but he moves on, expanding and externalizing all the resonances of excruciation. The language of physical violence permeates the scene. Metaphor becomes matter in his mouth, as the image of Innogen's disdain for him and favor of Posthumus "slanders so her judgment that what's else rare is choked." That word *choked*, with its sense of language stanched, of air unable to escape, takes us back to the earlier impression of Cloten as a wind-bag, as a carcass fit only for moving air. It takes us back to Pisanio's earlier avowal of loyalty to Posthumus: "But when to my good lord I prove untrue, / I'll choke myself: there's all I'll do for you" (1.5.86–87). It takes us back, more generally, to the imagery of rape and violence in the play: the hand against the throat, the voice of the accuser cut off, in the scene of Innogen in bed reading Ovid's story of Tereus and Philomela. It echoes, too, Shakespeare's other uses of the word (remarkably frequent in his plays and poetry, in all its various forms appearing thirty-one times in his texts). Choked with ambition, choked with the stench of battle, choked with surfeits of desire—voices on the verge of breaking off.

So Cloten would choke off Pisanio. "Close villain," he accosts the servant, "I'll have this secret from thy heart or rip / Thy heart to find it" (3.5.86–87). Excruciation is a pain to be borne together. Cloten threatens to silence Pisanio if he does not tell him right away of Innogen's whereabouts. And when, in prose isolation on the stage, Cloten reflects on Innogen and Posthumus together, he announces:

> I [will] ravish her: first kill him, and in her eyes; there shall she see my valour, which will then be a torment to her contempt. (3.5.136–39)

His rant is all about the tensions between speech and action: "my speech of insultment ended on his dead body" (3.5.139–40). That tension between word and body anticipates his Orphic end, beheaded in the flowing stream. And much like the tale of Philomela that stands behind the violence of his act, he bids Pisanio to be "a voluntary mute to my design" (3.5.151). Cloten chokes off this servant, effectively enjoining him to be a willing rather than a mutilated mute.

"My revenge is now at Milford, would I had wings to follow it" (3.5.153–54). Unlike the lovers of an Ovidian tale, Cloten's desire cannot take wing. Great flights of poetry crash in his mouth.

At the end, gifted with Posthumus's garments, ready to transform himself into a simulacrum of the lover-hero he despises, he is grounded. The only metamorphosis that he can orchestrate is one of costume. "I would these garments were come," he impatiently reflects before Pisanio returns. In his twisted logic, he recalls that Innogen had held Posthumus's garments in greater respect than Cloten's own "noble and natural person." And so, he plans, he will ravish her with those clothes on his back; but first, he will kill Posthumus, before her eyes. Then, with the dead Posthumus on the ground, he will "execute [her] in the clothes that she so praised" (3.5.129–44).

Once again, Cloten imagines a kind of negative alchemy, a transformation of gold back into dross, a revenge played in the dirt. His wish for wings gives us a crushing irony: a moment of excruciating unself-knowingness, evoking the metamorphoses of Ovidian lovers by one who thinks that all he has to do is change his clothes. "Sir, I would advise you to shift a shirt." The First Lord's opening counsel comes back to haunt us in the masquerade of Cloten as Posthumus.

Cloten's scenes lay out the central tensions of the play between the urge to lyricism and the arc of violence. And yet, for all his mockery of metamorphic beauty, for all his lack of taste, he struggles with his limitations. He may misuse classical allusion or mishear the lyre of poetry. But there remains, much as in Midas, something so unself-knowing that, by act 4, we no longer smirk but sorrow at his cloddishness.

Now, alone and in prose, he again transforms the wordplay of his wit into externalized and sexualized form.

> How fit his garments serve me! Why should his mistress, who was made by him that made the tailor, not be fit too? The rather—saving reverence of the word—for 'tis said a woman's fitness comes by fits. Therein I must play the workman. (4.1.2–6)

Dressed in Posthumus's clothes, he still is Cloten. He cannot resist the vulgar joke, translating the fit of the clothes into the sexual compatibility of the woman and then into the fits of pleasure or desire. Whatever connotations the word "workman" may have had in Shakespeare's time, it comes out of Cloten like a new obscenity. All is body here, and Cloten cannot conceive of a difference between him and Posthumus beyond the physicality of form. We look so much the same, he claims; why does she see a difference? As in his impatient criticism of the musicians in act 2, Cloten holds that anything she does not like is Innogen's fault. There, it was a problem with her ears. Here, it is a problem with senses: "this imperceiverant thing loves him in my despite" (4.1.13). And yet, it is Cloten himself who cannot see:

> Posthumus, thy head, which now is growing upon thy shoulders, shall within this hour be off, thy mistress enforced, thy garments cut to pieces before her face. (4.1.14–17)

It will be half another scene before we see that Cloten has it backwards: it is *his* head that shall be off, and Posthumus's garments on his own body that shall be cut to pieces. For all his fantasies of deformation, it is Cloten who will be deformed.

There he is, in act 4, scene 2, wearing Posthumus's clothes but unmistakably himself. Old Belarius, conjuring a memory from his pre-exiled life at court, seems to recall him.

> I partly know him, 'tis
> Cloten, the son o' th' Queen. I fear some ambush.
> I saw him not these many years, and yet
> I know 'tis he. (4.2.66–69)

Belarius leaves with Arviragus, and Cloten finds himself alone with Guiderius on the stage. Back and forth, like two bad Hamlets, they ask of each other:

> What slave art thou? (73)
>
> What art thou? (78)
>
> Knows't me not by my clothes? (83)
>
> What's thy name? (89)

We get the affirmations:

> Cloten, thou villan. (90)
> I am son to th' queen. (94)

And finally, Guiderius responds: "I am sorry for't, not seeming / So worthy as thy birth" (95–96). That word "seeming" takes us back to the passing shows of *Hamlet*, to a world in which the court is but a world of seeming, where the dress of men is but a costume for one's courtesy. And when Guiderius returns with Cloten's severed head, he finds in him as much an "empty purse" as Horatio would find in Osric. Compare the two:

> This Cloten was a fool, an empty purse,
> There was no money in't. (4.2.113–14)

> His purse is empty already. All's golden words
> Are spent. (*Hamlet* 5.2.130–31)

These are the moments of unmasking. The golden words are gone; nothing of worth remains. "Midas," wrote Sandys, "signifies a fool," and Cloten's head hangs in Guiderius's hands, as much a marker of a "brutish and ignorant life" (again in Sandys's words) as Midas's own deformed head sat upon his shoulders.

"All's golden words are spent." The same might well be said of Cloten and of Orpheus, as his head floats down to the sea. Critics have made much of the Orphic allusion in Guiderius's boast, displaying Cloten's severed head:

> I'll throw't into the creek
> Behind our rock, and let it to the sea
> And tell the fishes he's the Queen's son, Cloten. (4.2.152–54)

This is a drama, though, not just of the head, but of the river. Midas had to wash his greed out in the River Pactolus, and shards of his remaining powers littered the rocks with bits of gold. And when Apollo gave him ass's ears, he put them in a turban, letting them out only for his barber's eyes—a barber who could not keep his king's secret and so, running to the marshlands, whispered into the ground, until the reeds grew up and, blowing in the wind, rustled his condition to the world.

These are the episodes of the afterimage, stories of literary reception and reputation. Sandys had glossed the watery bier for Orpheus's head and lyre as being "borne away by the murmuring current. So the scattered reliques of learning, expulsed from one country, are transported to another." So too, he glossed the tale of Midas's barber with the rustling reeds anticipating poet's pens, both keeping afterlives of anguish alive. Guiderius's grammar clearly takes us back to these scenes of nature itself voicing reputation: the head flows out to the sea to tell the fishes of his name. Like Orpheus's still-reciting mouth, or Sandys's image of the murmuring river, or the all-too-literate reeds by Midas's marsh, it is not left for living men to tell these tales, but things of earth themselves.

If there is an aesthetics to these mythic scenes, there is a politics as well.[32] The tales of Orpheus and Midas had long been allegorized into fables of the place of poetry in power and, in turn, the ways in which the poet exercised a civilizing influence on society. If *Cymbeline* is a play about the lyric voice, then Cloten's demise brings back scenes of how power is severed from the lyric. In a world ruled by his mother, he would be both a poor poet and poor patron: mock Orpheus and Midas to the mediocre. The brilliance of these allusions pushes the play, at this point, to shift its argument away from mockery to ministry. Cloten's death opens a new place of lyric poetry, both in the play and in the court. It enables poetic voicing to create a polity in the wilderness. His headless trunk is absent, but Innogen's inert body takes its place.

This scene of Innogen and the dead Cloten has an undeniable dramatic power, echoing Juliet's drugged sleep with the dead Romeo, or even Virgil's *Aeneid*, where Priam's decapitated body, in Aeneas's retelling, lies mutilated on the Trojan shore. But, throughout *Cymbeline*, drama fractures into lyric, and the woman's body will have songs sung over it. Cloten had commanded a tune over her sleeping body in act 2. He had expressed the paradoxes of desire in Catullan terms. Now, when the rustic exiles bring her in, they mourn her in Catullus's language, far better elegists of air than of the earth.

The bird is dead
That we have made so much on. I had rather
Have skipped from sixteen years of age to sixty,
To have turned my leaping-time into a crutch,
Than have seen this. (4.2.198–202)

We do not know, at this point, that Innogen merely sleeps. Even the First Folio makes it plain that Arviragus enters with her, "dead, bearing her in his arms." The reader, and the characters, thus have the opportunity for full-fledged elegy here, and they turn, as Catullus did, to mourn a vibrant voice. In one of the best known of his poems, he laments the passing of his lover's sparrow.[33]

Lugete, o Veneres Cupidinesque,
et quantum est hominum uenustiorum.
passer mortuus est meae puellae,
passer, deliciae meae puellae,
quem plus illa oculis suis amabat.

Mourn, o you Graces and Loves,
And all of those the Graces love.
My girl's sparrow is dead,
The sparrow, pet of my girl,
Whom she loved more than her own eyes.

Much like Catullus's lover, the brothers made much on this bird, and the dark shades of sorrow fill their claims. For Catullus, it is a mythic death:

Qui nunc it per iter tenebricosum
Illuc, unde negant redire quemquam.
At vobis male sit, malae tenebrae
Orci, quae omnia bella deuoratis.

Now he goes along the dark road
From which they say no one returns.
But curses to you, cursed shades
Of Orcus, which devour all beautiful things.

This image of the dead bird in the underworld transforms itself into the image of Belarius's inner self, possessed by a melancholy so dark that it seems like Hell's slow-flowing river.

> O melancholy,
> Who ever yet could sound thy bottom, find
> The ooze to show what coast thy sluggish crare
> Might easiliest harbor in? (4.2.204–7)

These elegiac moves return us to the lyric voice of Roman verse, now eloquent in contrast to Cloten's earlier awkward assay. For golden words, placed in the mouths or ears of vulgar sons, only disable rule. But in the forest, a family of exiles can find reason and release in shared song and story. Catullus returns in a powerful allusion to remind us that real royalty comes in the skills of metered speech.[34]

It comes in both allusion and in action. With Fidele laid to rest, the brothers offer up what many have regarded as one of the great lyric performances in any Shakespeare play. Each one in sequence takes a stanza, and they then alternate each line to shape an intricate verbal web of echo and assertion.

> Guiderius: Fear no more the heat o'th'sun
> Nor the furious winter's rages.
> Thou thy worldly task hast done,
> Home art gone and ta'en thy wages.
> Golden lads and girls all must,
> As chimney sweepers, come to dust.
>
> Arviragus: Fear no more the frown o'th'great,
> Thou art past the tyrant's stroke.
> Care no more to clothe and eat,
> To thee the reed is as the oak.
> The scepter, learning, physic, must
> All follow thee and come to dust.
>
> Guiderius: Fear no more the lightning flash,
> Arviragus: Nor th'all-dreaded thunder-stone
> Guiderius: Fear not slander, censure rash.

Arviragus: Thou has finished joy and moan
Guiderius and Arviragus: All lovers young, all lovers must
Consign to thee and come to dust.

Guiderius: No exorcizer harm thee,
Arviragus: Nor no witchcraft charm thee.
Guiderius: Ghost unlaid forbear thee.
Arviragus: Nothing ill come near thee.
Guiderius and Arviragus: Quiet consummation have,
And renowned be thy grave. (4.2.259–82)

The monosyllabic rhymes (broken only by the pair, rages/wages) chime in the ear, until in the final stanza the repeated "thee" takes on an almost magical quality. The poem's imagery recalls the language of the Elizabethan *Book of Common Prayer*, that moment in the Order for the Burial of the Dead when repetition becomes rite: "earth to earth, ashes to ashes, dust to dust." It brings us back to older elegies of that age, for example to this line in the Thomas Weelkes madrigal of 1597, "For who can joy when thou in dust art laid." The opposition of the sun and winter takes us back to Dowland's overarching imagery of light and darkness, and the opening injunction will recall, too, some of Dowland's most compelling lines:

Fear not Hymen's peaceful war,
You'll conquer though you subdued are,
Goodnight, and ere the day be old,
Rise to the sun a marigold. (*Pilgrimes Solace*, 21)

But the rustics' song is not a poem celebrating marriage. The marigold does not bloom here, as it had opened as the Marybud in "Hark, hark, the lark," nor does the sun shine as a mythic god. *Cymbeline* has, to this point, been a play of gold turned into dust: of flower's "golden eyes" transformed to dirt in Cloten's sottish listening, of his bad Midas touch turning all gilding into grossness.

Care no more to clothe and eat,
To thee the reed is as the oak. (4.2.267–68)

Such lines recall the frustrated Midas, caring no more for his clothes or food, all turned to useless gold. And for the King, whose barber could not keep a secret, the murmuring reeds have been as powerful a force of defeat and humiliation as the oak.

> The scepter, learning, physic, must
> All follow this and come to dust. (4.2.269–70)

No power, no knowledge, no medicine can help Midas or Orpheus, nor can they help the local dead, as Belarius had noted just before the brothers sing, "Great griefs, I see, med'cine the less" (4.2.244). As the brothers' performance proceeds, we hear a kind of Orphic encyclopedism to their lament. Lightning, thunder-bolts, slander, censure, sorcerers, witches—a thesaurus of all the things that poetry can seem. And yet, there is no metamorphosis here. For when Belarius returns with Cloten's carcass, they lay it beside Innogen, giving them both back to the ground "that gave them first" (4.2.290).

The brothers' lyrical performance reframes the key images of earth and body of the play. It rephrases Belarius's claims on Cloten: "mean and mighty rotting / Together have one dust." It evokes idioms of the mythic tales behind its characters. But it does more. For in their shared performance, we must see these rustic exiles turned to civil selves. Poetry is a civilizing force here, bringing crack-voiced men into synchrony. These exiles find themselves a new family in shared rhyme.

That eloquence had been a civilizing force is an idea as old as literature itself. Cicero avowed, in the opening of his *De inventione*, that the arts of language brought the earliest communities together into polities—men who "were scattered in the fields and hidden in sylvan retreats" (1.ii.2). George Puttenham, in his 1589 *Arte of English Poesie*, developed these sentiments at the opening of his treatise.

> For it is written, that Poesie was th'originally cause and occasion of their first assemblies, when before the people remained in the woods and mountains, vagarant and dispersed like the wild beasts, lawless and naked, or verie ill clad, and all good and necessarie prouision

> for harbor or sustenance vtterly vnfurnished. . . . And Orpheus assembled the wilde beasts to come in heards to harken to his musicke, and by that meanes made them tame, implying thereby how by his discreete and wholesome lessons vttered in harmonie and with melodious instruments, he brought the rude and sauage people to a more ciuill and orderly life.[35]

Puttenham's summary serves as a social and a literary gloss on *Cymbeline*'s performers in the wilderness. Assembled into song, the brothers morph from the "runagates" that Cloten first had called them into a civil family. Cloten's word (which Belarius repeated, incredulously) may well be read through Puttenham's phrase: "vagarant and dispersed like the wild beasts," or, better yet, by Cicero's Latin, *feris et immanibus*. Now, joined in rhythm and in rhyme, the brothers speak in harmony, civil and orderly, their elegy revealing them, again in Cicero's words, *mites et mansuetos* (gentle and civilized).

But there is another level to their song, for it may well not be a song at all. Arviragus had hedged a bit before they spoke, addressing his brother with his rustic pseudonym:

> And let us, Polydore, though now our voices
> Have got the mannish crack, sing him to th' ground
> As once our mother; use like note and words,
> Save that Euriphile must be Fidele. (4.2.236–39)

He urges that they use the same song they had used when they had lain their own mother to rest. Funeral rites in notes and words will be the same, except now they are men, not children, and their voices have broken since their mother died. But there is more here. Guiderius replies:

> I cannot sing. I'll weep, and word it with thee,
> For notes of sorrow out of tune are worse
> Than priests and fanes that lie. (4.2.241–43)

And Arviragus responds: "We'll speak it then."

I do not hold these lines to be a relic of a problem in performance. Gary Taylor had suggested that they represent "a theatrical interpolation due to the exigencies of casting."[36] There is no evidence for such a view. Nor do I think that these words are intended to be spoken, as Roger Warren remarks, "so that there may be no risk of anything detracting from their hypnotic impact."[37]

These words are said because the singing voice is broken. The brothers' "mannish crack" echoes the play's images of straitened throats and choked-off sorrow. *Cymbeline*'s lyric stage is played along an arc of misperformance. The lovely "Hark, hark" becomes an occasion for Cloten's vulgar interpretation. Now, "Fear no more" breaks in the throat, a powerful performance, yes, but mediated by the brothers' lack of musicality. Guiderius cannot sing, but he is sharp enough to recognize that those notes out of tune would be as bad as lying priests. Old Bottom might not mind: "Let's have the tongs and bones." And Midas could not tell the difference. But these two brothers can, and in their recognition that their words must come without a tune, they move themselves away from such misjudgments and toward new lyric harmonies.

Wings of Lyric

Throughout the play, the living are incapable of pure, unmediated lyric utterance. Voices crack, songs evanesce in speech, musicians are dismissed. Only after Cloten is dead and the subplot of rustic exiles is resolved can lyric have its full effect. Only after his death can poetry reassert itself as the harmonizing device of political control. Only with his death can the family come together and recite. Only with his death can the wings of hoped-for conquest become those of an Imperial eagle. Cloten is the sacrifice that makes poetic and political harmony possible. And so, in the play's final act, it is left to the apparitional dead and deified to offer a performance as beautiful as it is beneficial, unstanched by bad voices or poor ears.

Posthumus, imprisoned and awaiting execution, falls asleep and seems to see his father, mother, and departed brothers sing to him. They come, according to the stage direction in the Folio, "as in an apparition," and they speak not in the decasyllables of blank verse or the couplets of the court, but in the old-style "fourteeners" of earlier Elizabethan drama. Such metrical affiliations place them firmly in the past: as if the ghosts of the last generation of actors and playwrights had taken the stage. Colin Burrow notes that the fourteener could have recalled, as well, the style of classical translation: "The poetic form in which these ancient Romans speak, that is, matches their antique garb: it is itself 'ancient.'"[38] After this stylized antiquity, Jupiter enters speaking in controlled iambic pentameter quatrains. He comes, as Burrow suggests, to restore not only civic but prosodic harmony, asserting in his sure decasyllables a secure sense of English verse onstage.

Shakespeare hearkens back to the poetic language of his youth. Parents come back to speak in meters of their time, a generation gone. That language is prophetic and it is Ovidian, and the play's stage directions here explicitly evoke this moment from the *Metamorphoses* when Morpheus appears.

> Enter, as in an apparition, Sicilius Leonatus, father to Posthumus, an old man attired like a warrior. (5.3.SD 123)

This is a scene of simile, of an imagined world of "like" and "as" where figures can appear in guises and attire. It is a scene of Morpheus-like appearance, and the point of the direction "as in an apparition" is to call the *reader's* attention to the effect of this scene. Like many of the stage directions in this play and in the *Tempest*, it is not so much a guide to actual performance as it is a descriptive evocation for the reader of the First Folio of what such a performance could be like. This is a moment both of reading and performance: a moment when the play's text is designed to call up in the imagination of the reader something old, something familiar, something resonant with the kinds of things that would have been read before.

Thus, when Sicilius speaks, he speaks in the meters of the old Elizabethans, like barely remembered Morpheus come back in the guise of the dead.

> I died whilst in the womb he stayed, attending nature's law,
> Whose father then—as men report thou orphans' father art—
> Thou shouldst have been, and shielded him from this earth-vexing
> smart. (5.3.131–36)[39]

That coinage in Sicilius's speech, "earth-vexing"—unique in Shakespeare, as in all of English—takes us back, in its awkward participiality, to the phrasings of earlier, high poetry (compare *Romeo and Juliet*, "Earth-treading stars, that make darke heauen light"). His syntactical twists, his asides, his rhetoricality, all make him sound like someone of at least thirty years before, a courtly translator of Golding's generation.

The politics of *Cymbeline* remains the politics of generational inheritance: whose is the right to rule? Whose is the right to marry? At the most basic level, the purpose of Posthumus's vision is to convince both him and us of his legitimacy, born after his father's death, "ripped" from his mother's womb. Sicilius affirms both his "great nature" and his "ancestry," an aegis under Jupiter's great wings. Jupiter had come and gone, borne by his eagle in Posthumus's vision, and the imagery of winged flight permeates the play as a whole.

"O for a horse with wings"! Innogen's plea for speed to meet her lover resonates throughout these later moments in the play, as she becomes a mourned bird in her boyish masquerade and images of Roman wings take on a new, political impression. The Soothsayer in act 4 sees "Jove's bird, the Roman eagle, winged / from the spongy south to this part of the west" (4.2.349–50), and at the play's end he returns to bring together the key images of music, body, and escape into an airy flight to give voice to the new peace between Rome and Britain.

> The fingers of the powers above do tune
> The harmony of this peace. The vision,
> Which I had made known to Lucius ere the stroke
> Of this yet scarce-cold battle, at this instant
> Is full accomplished. For the Roman eagle,
> From south to west on wing, soaring aloft,

> Lessened herself, and in the beams o' th' sun
> So vanished. (5.4.467–74)

Now, Cloten's inept fingerings and his discordant wordplay settle themselves into tune. The eagle, on its proper wings, rises to vanish in the sunbeams, recalling the brothers' lyric injunction to the dead: fear no more the heat o' the sun.

These images of flight are images of politics and power. But they are images, as well, of poetry. The voice rises to occasions of great prowess in the claim for wings. Recall *Henry V*'s Chorus, "O for a muse of fire that would ascend / The brightest heaven of invention" (Prologue, 1–2). Like Innogen's address, this welcome asks the auditor to leave the confines of an all-too-common earth and rise. Here, Agincourt can cram itself into the wooden O: "a crooked figure may / Attest in little place a million" (Henry V, Prologue, 15–16). So, too, Milford Haven cannot be surveyed in miles or days of travel, but it exists in simultaneous imagination on the stage. And if Innogen would wish for something of a Pegasus for her invention, so too Henry's Chorus avers how words can make things metamorphose in the mind.

> Think, when we talk of horses, that you see them,
> Printing their proud hoofs i' th' receiving earth. (*Henry V*, Prologue, 26–27)

Recall, too, Juliet, longing for Romeo's return:

> O for a falconer's voice,
> To lure this tassel-gentle back again.
> Bondage is hoarse, and may not speak aloud,
> Else would I tear the cave where Echo lies,
> And make her airy tongue more hoarse than mine
> With repetition of my Romeo's name. (*Romeo and Juliet*, 2.1.203–8)

Again, speech takes flight, now in the voice of a falconer who would bring his trained hunter back. And yet, in all her bondage, Juliet cannot speak out. Her eloquence is bound to hoarseness, and even Echo's airy tongue would grow hoarse in repeating Romeo's name.

Against the many levels of allusion and echo, Innogen's winged horse takes us back to a voice of air, a voice not rendered hoarse but soaring on the lift of pun and wordplay. Her winged horse conjures more than simply Pegasus but, rather, a symbolic system of literary language itself. Words take wing, and one thread of *Cymbeline*'s imagistic weave twists with the literal and figurative senses of this image. Wings have been everywhere in this play, and characters conjure the voices of the rustic lark or of Catullus's lover's sparrow to show what we, as an audience, must hear. Unlike Cloten or Midas, we must listen not with an ass's but with human ears.

Henry Peacham knew this well. His *Compleat Gentleman*, published the year before the First Folio and summarizing decades of advice to social aspirants, asserted the familiar case for poetry as central to a young man's cultivation. Drawing on the range of classical and contemporary writers for an argument about the social virtue of versemaking, Peacham held that poetry was "an heavenly gift," the first bearer of philosophy in human culture, and the tutor to conquerors and politicians. "Every child knoweth how deare the works of Homer were unto Alexander," he noted, and well into his own time kings and queens esteemed the poet for his teaching and his entertainment. All this would be a commonplace, were it not for the imagery that governs Peacham's opening account of poetry and prowess:[40]

> If bare saying Poetry is an heavenly gift, be too weake a proppe to uphold her credite with those buzzardly poor ones, who having their feathers moulted can creepe no farther than their own puddle, able onely to envie this Imperiall Eagle for sight and flight; let them if they can looke back to all antiquitie, and they shall find all learning by divine instinct to breathe from her bosome. . . .

There are the good and bad, the asses and the harpers, and now the buzzards and the Imperial eagles. Peacham creates a kind of avian poetic politics, an image of verse at its best in concord with the goals of rule and reason.

Such imagery returns us to the eagles of *Cymbeline* (a bird that appears more in this play than in any other of Shakespeare's). They show up from its very first scene, when Innogen affirms her love of Posthumus in the face of her father's criticism: "I chose an eagle / And did avoid a puttock" (1.1.140–41). Much like Peacham's comparison between the Imperial eagle and a buzzard, Innogen's juxtaposing of this royal bird against a scavenger looks forward to an arc of imagistic argument. Again and again, the eagle spreads its wings: in Belarius's reminiscences, in the Soothsayer's prophecies, in Posthumus's visions, and in the final harmonies of the play's last lines. That Roman eagle in the Soothsayer's last speech "forshow'd our princely eagle, / The imperial Caesar" (5.5).

Lyric poetry may bring families into harmony. It may make tame beasts and civilize the savage. But for much of *Cymbeline*, that happens only in the world of old myths. We may long to find the voice take wing, but before bedtime we are pressed to fold the page and so remind us of where we broke off our reading. Shakespeare's extolling of the poet in society had taken many forms, but here I hear it mediated, interrupted, scarcely able to break through the inabilities of human singers and their audiences. The political world of the play is its poetic world as well: a world of uneasy truces, a world where the mythic violence of old tales may all too easily come back to life, a world of clods trying to mouth the meters of the poets.

And if we hear, as Posthumus asleep had heard, we will learn that only poetry can revive the dead. His masque-like vision offers up a harmony of family performance. The final metamorphosis lies not in being turned to birds or brought to bloom or set among the stars. It lies in being turned to poetry itself. If there is an afterlife, it may be found not on wings of horses but on wings of song. "Chaste thoughts do mount," sang Dowland, "and she with swiftest wings / My love with paine, my paine with losse rewarded."

The past keeps coming back, mounted on horses or borne on wings. Brothers once thought dead are now returned. Old myths of Ovid, echoes of Catullus, shards of Dowland's verse, the fourteeners of Elizabethan translators—such allusions have a political as well as a poetic force. That Roman eagle at the play's end is as much a symbol of empire as it is of verse. "Laud we the gods," says Cymbeline in the play's final speech. This is a play that ends with an injunction to verbal performance, with a claim for "publishing" a peace that will take form in willing words. Midas and Orpheus, those emblems of disfigured eloquence, now lie as far away as Cloten's buried body or his floating head. "The fingers of the powers above do tune / The harmony of this peace." For Posthumus and Innogen, the proper listening to this harmony may be found in the dreams of sleep or staged performance. And if *Cymbeline* ends with a flourish, our challenge is to hear the harmonies of state and family in waking lives: to recognize that only in this wooden O can clods be turned to gold.

And yet, this is a play that ends a book. We now can only speculate on why *Cymbeline* closes the First Folio. Some have argued that, like those that closed the other sections, it had not appeared in print before, it was a late play, and it came from Ralph Crane's scribal hand. Others have argued for the balancing of opening and ending: *The Tempest*, with its hewing to the unities of time and space, beginning the volume; and *Cymbeline*, with its aggressive violation of those unities, closing it. *Cymbeline* is a powerfully retrospective play. A reader can find almost everything in Shakespeare somehow transformed in it. For Valerie Wayne, in a recent reassessment of the play's place in the Folio, "for those who arranged the book, its copiousness helped make it a self-reflexive tour de force."[41]

Perhaps the annotator of the Misei copy of the Folio should have the last word. Six pages before the book's end, he stops. Cymbeline, Innogen, Pisanio, and Guiderius are closing down the plot, retelling what has happened once again. "I'll speak troth," says Pisanio, narrating how Cloten came to find them, and Guiderius concludes it: "Let me end the story: I slew him there." The old man and the brothers soon reveal themselves, and King Cymbeline now knows his children. All moves toward resolution, but the annotator can only remark: "Infinit questions of the circumstances of strange chances."

This may be the best statement of the play's effect on anyone, inside or outside its dramatic fiction. Simon Foreman's account reads as a story of strange chances on the stage, and there are infinite questions that remain about how the play sits in the arc of Shakespeare's work. Its closing repetitions of the word "peace" may move the critic to imagine a political message in its placement—as if the volume's guiding hands were teaching readers of the 1620s to cease war and wash their "bloodie hands." Such hands now must lie still in deference to the "fingers of the powers above" that "tune the harmony of this peace." Whatever *Cymbeline*'s effect may have been on the Folio's first readers, it takes me back to where I began: to the fingerings of Dowland and his cohort, staying listeners with their harmony; to the sounds of Orpheus, bringing the beasts into a listenership; to the court audiences who would lay aside their arguments for entertainment. The play's conclusion may be a matter less of politics than of poetry. Infinite questions will remain. But what is worth our hearing is the pure rhyme that ends the last page, *cease* and *peace*, a lyric harmony beneath our fingers as we close the book.

Epilogue

Lyric Recognition and the Editorial Romance in *Pericles* and *The Two Noble Kinsmen*

Early on in act 4 of *The Two Noble Kinsmen*, the young Wooer tells the story of how he came upon the Jailer's Daughter, disturbed, florally bedecked, and singing by a river. She was distraught that Palamon, one of the two imprisoned suitors of Emily, had disappeared, for she had fallen in love with him. The Wooer, who had been fishing in the river, puts his angling away and listens. "Palamon is gone," she sings, and he continues in her voice:

> "His shackles will betray him, he'll be taken;
> And what shall I do then? I'll bring a bevy,
> A hundred black-eyed maids that love as I do,
> With chaplets on their heads of daffadillies,
> With cherry-lips and cheeks of damasked roses,
> And all we'll dance an antic 'fore the Duke
> And beg his pardon."
> . . .
>   Then she sung
> Nothing but "Willow, willow, willow" . . . (4.1.70–80)

The play's most recent editor, Lois Potter, calls this "an astonishing lyrical speech"—astonishing, at least in part, because it differs so dramatically from the verse of Shakespeare's named collaborator for the play, John Fletcher.[1] It is astonishing, however, not just in its contrast but its content. The Wooer takes us back to a whole history of lyric voices. The scene of listening by the river, with reeds and rustling sounds, evokes Ovid's Midas, washing out his golden touch and, later on, his barber whispering the secret of the King's deformed ears to the sedge grass. The black-eyed maids and daffodils and cherry lips and damasked cheeks recall the phrasings of a generation past: the pastorals of *England's Helicon* and the familiar tropes of lute song. The Jailer's Daughter's "willow, willow, willow" brings to mind Desdemona's famous "Willow Song" from *Othello*—a song that, in fact, predated Shakespeare and that would have been familiar to the parents and grandparents of those readers who had bought the Quarto of this play, first published in 1634.[2]

Like many of the lyric moments I have studied in this book, this is a mediated song: a memory of someone else's singing, a performance of the aesthetic consciously aware that it is a performance, distanced, emotively charged, attentive to the voice of someone who has gone. The whole scene with the Jailer's Daughter has no counterpart in the play's source. Explicitly based on Chaucer's *Knight's Tale*, *The Two Noble Kinsmen* takes the old Theban story and replays it through the courtly conventions of Jacobean spectacle.[3] In the scenes between the Jailer's Daughter and the lovers, and in the otherwise-unnamed Wooer's desires, Shakespeare (for we assume it was he, here) adds something unique to his source. Some critics have seen this addition as a response to the rising fashion for melodramatic rhetoric and the taste for newly powerful female dramatic roles. Some have seen it as a bit of classical allusion complicating a contemporary tale, as if, somehow, an abandoned Ariadne were transported from her Greek to a new English island. And some have seen it as a story of powerful, explicit sexuality in an otherwise carefully coded drama of desire. Whatever the dramatic, social, or political reasons for these episodes, they provide an occasion for another moment of lyric performance, one last shot at juxtaposing old forms with new speakers, one more charge to remind us that at the heart of character in late Shakespeare is the way in which an actor speaks, responds to, and reworks the ravishments of song onstage.[4]

"And all we'll dance an antic 'fore the Duke." All of us, she says (as quoted by the Wooer), will perform an old dance in celebration: an "antic" or, rather, an antique show, whose age and stateliness will mark the power of her memory and her respect for her noble audience. "Antic" had always been a strongly marked word in the plays. Most famously, it rears its punning head when Hamlet speaks of putting on his "antic disposition." Does it mean full of movement, charged with feeling bordering on madness; or does it mean old and artificial? How does it compare with Horatio's last declaration that he is more "an antique Roman than a Dane"? For Ben Jonson, the word carried a comparable double edge. His masque of *Oberon* (1611) has the Satyrs "leaping and making antique action" and falling "into an antique dance." As Mary Ellen Lamb puts it, in terms that may apply to Shakespeare as much as to Jonson: "This odd mixture of classical and rural English contributes an added ambiguity to the term 'antique' repeated in the stage directions, as meaning 'old' and also 'antic' or clownish. Do these 'antique' satyr dances ennoble the countryside with a sense of continuing ancient traditions? Or are the satyrs simply rendered as cloddish clowns?"[5]

Shakespeare's lyric stage had always hovered on the borderlines between the antic and the antique, and this moment with the Wooer invites a review of what I have tried to accomplish in this study. My book has argued for the lyric as the scene and source of metamorphic transport in late Shakespeare. It has shown how the late plays review strategies of lyrical performance—exemplified in Dowland's music, in his publications, and in documented reputation—in order to create a sense of temporal displacement in dramatic narrative. Such performance calls attention to the reach of art at times of loss of power or control. The lyric voices of the past come back, in the last plays, to announce visions of the dead, revivals of the suspended, and anticipations of release. Lyric performance, too, serves as a test for audiences. Cloddish clowns like Cloten jar against what we may hear as melody. Autolycus performs his ribald songs. Do we, as readers and spectators, hear the Orphic voices in the plays, ennobling the countryside? Do we sit in reverent stillness with the rivers at their song? Or do we rise up with the Maenads and dismember?

Shakespeare's last plays, I argued, share in an embodied lyricism drawing on the myths of Orpheus, but also on the practices of court and theater. They respond to and participate in the turn to interior staging, to the rising use of masque, and to the unique resources of stagecraft at the court. They resonate, thematically and socially, with changes in the Jacobean family structure and the habits of royal spectatorship. And they incorporate, as well, a new mythography of kingship, with the political allegories of harmony and touch.

Finally, I suggested that the last plays have a meaningful position in the First Folio. That meaning lay not only in the volume's placement of the texts but in how it prefaced them, scripting out instructions to a readership in language drawing on the mythic stories of dismemberment and revival. What readers have long seen as characteristic of the late plays I saw in the First Folio itself: an image of the theater's power charged with the abilities of actors to die and come back reborn, for Shakespeare, dead, to rise again, and for the scattered limbs of play and person to come back together.

For *Pericles* and *The Two Noble Kinsmen*, we do not have the aegis of the Folio to guide our readings. The plays were not included in the volume, possibly for matters of ownership or availability, possibly because the editors saw their collaborative origins as excluding them from a canon of Shakespearean drama (a matter they either elided or excused for *Henry VIII*). *Pericles* appeared in Quarto in 1609, in a form so garbled that almost everyone who has encountered it has thought it poorly printed, half-Shakespearean, and mis-transmitted.[6] When *The Two Noble Kinsmen* was printed in 1634, its title page announced it as the work of "the memorable Worthies of their time: Mr John Fletcher and Mr William Shakespeare. Gent." Both of these plays have been included—sometimes enthusiastically, sometimes grudgingly—in the late Shakespeare canon, and they participate in what we now have come to see as the characteristics of the group. They share the scenes of recognition; the displacements of families; the narratives of voyage, storm, and rescue; the complex daughterly roles; and a poetic diction increasingly experimental in its challenges to ordinary syntax. Like other late plays, they use music for celebratory and for philosophical purposes, investing in a language of performance designed to question how the harmony of public life can echo in a lyric form. They dramatize musical making and reception to ask what the place of artistry is in the exercise of power.[7]

In the process, both plays confront vernacular literary antiquity in new ways. They participate in a broader Jacobean turn to the English poetic past as an antiquarian enterprise. In this move, they balance old and new. On the one hand, masque and dumb show fill their scenes, and their stage directions elaborately describe performances as fully as anything in the First Folio *Tempest*. But on the other hand, dead authors vie with living practice for authority. The plays take us back, as the title page of *The Two Noble Kinsmen* put it, to a time of "worthies"—a word that had come to stand, in the vernacular, akin to Latin *poetae*, describing writers whose authority lay precisely in their absence.[8]

Worthy though their authors may have been, these two plays remain arrestingly uneven. Scenic form and verbal control vary markedly throughout their acts, and such unevenness has long been taken as the evidence for shared authorship. While *The Two Noble Kinsmen* identifies Fletcher along with Shakespeare on its title page, *Pericles* offers no such guide to collaboration. As in the case of *Henry VIII*, scholars have sifted through the play for evidence of word and idiom, spelling and sense, to mark the Shakespearean from the non-Shakespearean.

Modern scholarship scripts out a romance of recovery for

these two plays. The editor confronts a text of bafflement and enigma. He or she sets out to solve a riddle and, in the course of that solution, prepares a document for us to stop in awe when we find Shakespeare. For the scholar of *Pericles*, such a moment may appear at the beginning of the Quarto's scene 12 (act 3 in some editions), when Pericles emerges to speak lines of such rich tenor and controlled prosody that we must announce: Shakespeare. For *The Two Noble Kinsmen*, such a moment is the episode of the Wooer and the Jailer's Daughter, a scene that, as Douglas Bruster put it, self-awarely "embodies changes in both dramatic representation and the larger culture of early modern England."[9]

My purpose in this Epilogue, therefore, is twofold. First, I locate these two plays in the broad arc of mythic lyricism I have traced thus far. I look at episodes that strive for heightened diction and emotional effect, tracing their verbal sources in earlier texts by Shakespeare and his contemporaries. Such episodes come off less as scenes of creation than reception. They illustrate what could be done with previous material, and their literary effect depends on recognizing echoes of a literary past. Second, I want to show how the romance experience of lyric recognition has become the very means of reading and writing about the plays. There is both an internal and external tale of recognition and revival here, and we often find the truly Shakespearean in their texts not in the acts of character but in the voicings of the lyric. Shakespeare becomes, in *Pericles* and *The Two Noble Kinsmen*, our lyric poet, and modern criticism has created its own myths of ravishment to chart our uneasy feelings for these texts.

Poetry and Pericles

Pericles begins unsteadily. Gower's tetrameters step uneasily forth. His rhymes are off. The lineation, prosody, and spelling of the first scene appear insecure.[10]

To sing a Song that old was sung,
From ashes, auntient Gower is come,

> Assuming mans infirmities,
> To glad your eare, and please your eyes:
> It hath been sung at Feastiuals,
> On Ember eues, and Holydayes: (A2, scene 1)

Editors have long been unhappy with the Quarto text. Some have attributed its weakness to the work of George Wilkins, the author of an earlier prose version of the tale of Palamon and Arcite and, it has been mooted, Shakespeare's coauthor on the play. Some have found the Quarto's challenges in gaps between the authors and the printer: memorial error, compositor negligence, or the whims of actors seeking a fast publication have all been adduced (as they have been for the "bad" quarto *Hamlet*). Some have, instead, sought to see in the Prologue's verbal awkwardness—the off-rhyme of "sung" and "come" and the non-rhyme of "Feastiuals" and "Holydays"—a lame attempt to evoke the old sounds of Middle English, as if Gower had not quite brushed off the ashes of his ancient vowels.[11]

Whatever textual problems remain, there is a clear poetic hand behind these lines, as they spin out in a sibilance of renewal. Sing, song, sung. There is an arc to his announcement, a rack of vowels, a conjugation of past and present, a balance of the verb and noun. Gower's lines have an almost nursery-rhyme quality to them. Sing a song; ashes, man's infirmities. If this is not a poetry of power, it is a poetry of old familiarity, of ancient things designed to set us all at ease. Why should we listen to "an old man sing"?

Gower remains the voice of vernacular authority.[12] The play that follows retells one of his stories from the *Confessio Amantis*. But that acknowledgment means more than just a statement of the source. It shapes the text itself, and *Pericles* becomes a play full of retellings. It repeats, again and again, what someone else had sung, as if the whole play comes off in quotation marks.

Everything that could be said has already been said. In *Hamlet*, this sense of the already-quotedness of life evoked old songs and stories. Tales of Dido and Aeneas, shards of bawdy ballads, bits and pieces out of Tottel's *Miscellany*, an old man's memory of playing Caesar—all worked together in the play to show how, at least in Elsinore, everything is an allusion. Speak the speech, I pray you, as I pronounced it to you. But here, in *Pericles*, the quotedness of life is not a matter of ironic distance or of generational displacement. It is a question of pastiche.

After Gower's uneasy tetrameters, the play immediately asserts the need to phrase its antique action in the blank verse of the English stage. The characters' pentameters begin in fits and starts.

> Musicke bring in our daughter, clothed like a bride
> For embracements euen of Ioue himselfe; (A2v, scene 1)

Antiochus's call for music seems, at least to modern editors, a mistake. Perhaps it was a stage direction erroneously placed in the mouth of a character. Or perhaps it was a freestanding call, to be followed by a full metrical line. The irregularities here match the stagy invitation for Antiochus's daughter's entry. "Bring in our daughter," he announces, as if prompting both the actor and the reader to recognize an entrance. Pericles repeats this call, and his first major speech in the play describes the woman as if she were more a statue than a living being, a description that comes off more as a florilegium of Shakespearean devices than a fully fledged paean to beauty.

> See where she comes, appareled like the Spring,
> Graces her subjects, and her thoughts the King,
> Of every Vertue giues renowne to men:
> Her face the book of prayses, where is read,
> Nothing but curious pleasures as from thence,
> Sorrow were ever racte, and teastie wrath
> Could never be her milde companion.
> You Gods that made me man, and sway in loue;
> That haue enflamde desire in my breast,
> To taste the fruite of yon celestiall tree,
> (Or die in th' adventure), be my helpes,
> As I am sonne and seruant to your will,
> To compass such a bondlesse happinesse. (A2v–A3r, scene 1)

There is a difference between the speeches that look back to older forms of language and to earlier Shakespearean phrasings (such as those of *The Winter's Tale* and *Cymbeline*) and this speech, where the bits are undigested, blocked together piecemeal. For any reader of 1609, these lines would be immediately recognized as an assembly of the Shakespeare of a decade and a half before. "See where she comes." The phrase had been a trick of the early plays, a way of announcing the entry of a beauty. The Nurse, in *Romeo and Juliet*, begins act 4, scene 2: "See where she comes from shrift with merry look." In *The Taming of the Shrew*, Petrucchio finds his now-tamed Kate entering, "See where she comes and brings your froward wives" (5.2). And in the last act of the *Two Gentlemen of Verona*, Eglamour welcomes Silvia to the stage, "See where she comes" (5.1).

"Her face the book of praises." We may remember Lady Capulet to Juliet, "Look o'er the volume of Paris's face," and read his book. We may remember *The Rape of Lucrece*: "Poor women's faces are their own fault's books." The editors of the New Cambridge edition of *Pericles* recall so much they cannot find the time or space to name each instance: "eighteen instances in Shakespeare," they record.[13]

Each line seems familiar—not, here, the haunting reminiscences of old songs in new mouths, but the raw building blocks of praise, unearthed, as it were, from the 1590s and repurposed for this tale. The gods, the fruit, and then Antiochus's reference to the Hesperides in his following speech, all taste of *Venus and Adonis*, or *The Rape of Lucrece*, or the early plays, or even Marlowe. This is the feel of much of *Pericles*, and deliberately so. Its power lies in its familiarity of idiom, an old tale told in an old language, not distanced, ironized, or framed for character, but flat out.

Whatever showed up on the stage, the Quarto's pages offer up a set of old words, quoted and re-quoted, that invite the reader to familiar turf. So, too, Antiochus's Riddle is an old text, an embedded lyric brought in to be read, headed as a separate document, printed in italics, and distinguished from the surrounding pentameter by its meter, rhyme, and layout. "What makes me pale to read it?" Pericles asks, and his question may be one for us as well. The reader is half a step away from the hero. We know, if we know Gower, that this is a tale of incest, and the Riddle codes a level of transgression that could only be expressed, here, in enigma. Pericles, however, must read afresh. He must interpret this text for the first time.

How does he do it? First, he addresses Antiochus's daughter: "Fair glass of light, I loved you." From the start, he turns to metaphor, turning the living woman into a classic figure of reflection. "Look in thy glass and tell the face thou viewest." "The glass of fashion and the mold of form." "Give me the glass, and therein I will read." These lines that even I can quote from memory come back here, as if Pericles—the character and play—are summoning up all the tropes of Shakespearean self-reading. But this is not enough. From glass, Pericles turns to music, transforming the daughter from an image of reflection to an instrument of desire.

> You are a fair Violl, and your sense, the stringes,
> Who finger'd to make man his lawfull musicke,
> Would draw Heaven downe and all the Gods to hearken;
> But being playd vpon before your time,
> Hell oney daunceth at so harsh a chime. (A3v, scene 1)

Now, we are back in Dowland's world, in images of music, fingering, and sound. Remember Thomas Campion's praise:

> O qui Sonora coelites altos cheli
> Mulces, et umbras incolas astrae Stigis,
> Quam suave murmur?
> O you who on the tuneful lyre charms the dwellers of high heaven and the shades that inhabit gloomy Styx, how sweet is your sound?

Remember Joshua Sylvester's, too:

> For an old, rude, rotten, tune-less Kit,
> If famous Douland daign to finger it,
> Makes sweeter musick than the choicest Lute
> In the grosse handling of a clownish Brute.

To read Pericles's lines at the close of my study is, for me, to see the range of images come back, to hear the old metaphors and murmurs. It is to recognize, to watch Pericles pursue his line of image-making and his struggle to read the Riddle in terms of myth and power ("And if Jove stray, who dares say Jove doth ill?"). We will react much as Antiochus: "Heaven that I had thy head; he has found the meaning."

To find the meaning in late Shakespeare has been challenging his readers since Dryden and Johnson. As his career progressed, his language grew increasingly metaphorical, experimental, idiosyncratic. There is, in Stephen Orgel's words, a "poetics of incomprehensibility" in many of the late plays, and I have attempted, throughout this book, to explore some of the resonances behind this exceedingly difficult language. Shakespeare invests in new words and changes old ones; his syntax stretches grammar to the point of fraying; his extended metaphors compel us to ask whether anything in speech or song can be truly straightforward, literal, direct, or whether everything in the world of the late plays is a figure.[14]

These are the strategies that the first scenes of *Pericles* do not pursue. The language there consistently is old. These are remembered ravishments, dusted off for a new audience. Lyric poetry in the first portions of the play is the poetry of reminiscence, the familiarity of trope, the easy shoe of well-worn idiom.

These scenes that critics find to be non-Shakespearean are precisely those that feel stale, old, and trite. Raphael Lyne makes this point when he compares Pericles's speech about the storm in scene 11 with his earlier performance in scene 5. "Here the syntax and structure are nothing like as storm tossed. The language is sterile in comparison with the relentless fertility of the other."[15] Notice Lyne's language: the difference between sterility and fertility is the difference between the trite and the new, the non-Shakespearean and the authentic Shakespeare. But his is a telling image, too, for at the heart of this play is the very idea of fertility, the very notion that people can reproduce. Within the play's fiction, just as outside in its Jacobean playhouse, a once-sterile ruler had been replaced by a fertile king.

Such critical metaphors pressure us to see the late plays, and *Pericles* in particular, as somehow aligned not just with the idea of Shakespearean fecundity, but with the themes of birth, progeniture, and inheritance that possess their fictions. It is a pressure on the modern reader: just what is this strange play *like*; how does it fit in the genealogy of Shakespeare's making and, in turn, the social concerns with childbearing and child-rearing that had marked the early Jacobean years? To answer questions of this kind is to search through the literary and political landscape surrounding *Pericles*'s publication, and for many recent readers, the landmark is *King Lear*.

That there is a *Lear*-like ambiance to *Pericles* has been more felt than argued. Orgel's introduction to his Pelican edition tantalizes. He tells a story of a group of Catholic players in Yorkshire who, in 1610, were arrested for performing *Lear* along with *Pericles*, "which the authorities claimed were (or had had introduced to them) Roman Catholic propaganda."[16] "*Pericles*," Orgel summarizes, "in its concern with suffering and the extremes of experience has much in common with *King Lear*," and Lyne echoes something of this intuition: "In fearing that he is being mocked by a cruel god, Pericles resembles Lear."[17]

What is the language, though, that links these plays? Can we find something other than coincidence (the proximate publication of the Lear early Quarto and *Pericles*), the performing of both, the feel, for lack of a better term, of idiom they share? What are the differences?

In scene 5, Pericles enters immediately after Gower's Prologue, wet and troubled by the storm on shipboard. Much in these lines recalls Lear and his companions on the raw heath.

> Yet cease your ire you angry Starres of heauen,
> Wind, Raine, and Thunder, remember earthly man
> Is but a substaunce that must yeeld to you: (C1v, scene 5)

Wind, rain, and thunder collocate three times in *Lear*. Pericles's verbal fist-shaking to heaven would be easy in the King's mouth. But there is a difference. Lear rages; Pericles postures. His words evoke not so much the King himself but his play, as if he had picked and chosen what he needs. His sense of loss, for example, recalls less Lear alone than Edgar and Gloucester:

> Hadst thou been aught but goss'mer, feathers, air,
> So many fadom down precipitating

Thou'dst shiver'd like an egg. But thou dost breathe;
Hast heavy substance, bleed'st not, speak'st; art sound.
Ten masts a-length make not the altitude
Which thou hast perpendicularly fell.
Thy life is a miracle. (*History of King Lear*, scene 20, 49–55)[18]

Together on this strange, imagined cliff, Edgar speaks to his father like a man less in the air than on the sea: fathoms, breathe, substance, fell. Pericles's speech takes bits and pieces out of Edgar and makes its metaphors literal. Instead of an imaginative sea, we get the wetness of the storm. Instead of falling through the unseen air, we get the speaker thrown from a watery grave. And now, instead of affirming "thy life is a miracle," Pericles speaks of "death in peace."

The storm scene in scene 5 of *Pericles* comes off as a kind of block-book *Lear*, transposed from heath to shipboard. And even though the storm speech in scene 11 may appear more vivid, more lithe, more sophisticatedly Shakespearean, familiar bits and pieces erode out of the earlier scene's mortar.

The God of this great Vast, rebuke these surges,
Which wash both heauen and hell, and thou that hast
Vpon the Windes commaund, bind them in Brasse;
Hauing call'd them from the deepe, o still
Thy deafning dreadfull thunders, gently quench
Thy nimble sulphirous flashes. (E1v, scene 11)

Lear is here again: his own apostrophe to "nimble lightnings," and Cordelia's poignant moment with her sleeping father:

Was this a face
To be exposed against the warring winds,
To stand against the deep dread-bolted thunder
In the most terrible and nimble stroke
Of quick cross lightning . . . (*History of King Lear*, scene 21.29–33)

And Lear alone,

You cataracts and hurricanoes, spout
Till you have drenched the steeples, drown'd the cocks!

> You sulphurous and thought-executing fires,
> Vaunt-couriers to oak-cleaving thunderbolts,
> Singe my white head; (*History of King Lear*, scene 9.2–6)

Yes, Pericles in scene 11 seems more in control of verse than in scene 5. His speech chimes with alliterations ("deafning dreadful," "whistle is as a whisper," "bind them in brass") and displaced rhymes and assonances (vast / hast / brass). His sonic effects work far more powerfully than the end rhymes of scene 5. Do these differences mark authentic Shakespeare from the imitator? Or are they but better versions of ventriloquism?

I want to realign the discussion of *Pericles*'s varied quality away from limited discussions of authorial command and toward a broader sense of how the play's scenes speak, directly, to the expectations of an audience or readership familiar with the Shakespearean idiom. It is the music of *Pericles* that will differentiate it from *King Lear*, and it is in that music that I find its comically restorative response to tragic rule.

In scene 12, Ceremon, the medic on the shores of Ephesus, enters with his attendants. Someone (the Quarto is unclear here) brings in a great chest, washed up on the beach, all closed and caulked. They open it, they find a written message, and inside they see Thaisa, whom we know to be Pericles's former wife, thrown overboard and left for dead years earlier. Ceremon tries to revive her, first with ritual and medicine and then with music. The Quarto prints this scene in garbled lineation, but the sense remains:

> the rough and
> Wofull Musick that we haue, cause it to sound beseech you:
> The Violl once more; how thou stirr's thou blocke?
> The Musicke there: I pray you giue her ayre:
> Gentlemen, this Queene will liue,
> Nature awakes a warmth breath out of her; (E4, scene 12)

She stirs, Ceremon cries, "She is aliue," and his attendants comment: "Is not this strange?" "Most rare."

As in the other late plays, music comes to arouse and vivify. Playing is as much a rite as a performance, and editors, I think, have brushed away its echoes.[19] The sound of viols here (often emended to the word "vial") recalls the imagery with which Pericles had addressed Antiochus's daughter ("you are a fair viol, and your sense the strings"). The "ayre" that they will give to Thaisa may, of course, be air to breathe. But it is also melody, much like the "sweet airs" that would delight Caliban, or the "wonderful sweet air" that Cloten would command to wake up Innogen.[20] And Thaisa's warm breath emerges, giving her an almost Miranda-like thrill: "What world is this?"

There may be many resonances to the later plays, but there are also resonances to *King Lear*, and Thaisa's revival comes off as a kind of musically restorative rewriting of Cordelia's death. There, Lear had looked for signs of breath. There, he had looked for signs of stirring. He cries, he touches, he examines. But he does not sing.

To read *Pericles* against *Lear*, I suggest then, is to read it for the moments when music revives—that is, when the sounds of art make someone speak and, in that speaking, enable a new life in a lyric voice.

Turn, now, to scene 20. Gower shifts from his old tetrameters to new five-stress lines. He speaks in quatrains rather than in couplets. He invites us not just to observe, but listen, and the sonic and prosodic world of the play moves to restorative performance: "Please you sit and hark." Now, the play moves from silence into sound. Scene 21, and Pericles is revealed, not having spoken for three months, lying on a couch, inert. Lysimachus calls in Marina in the hope that she may rouse him. "Sir," she avers, "I will vse my vtmost skill in his recouerie." The Quarto does not tell us what she does. It only prints "*The Song*" among the speeches. There are no words, and we can only speculate what would have appeared in performance (an Orphic tune like that in *Henry VIII*? A call to rising as in *Cymbeline*? A Dowland-like "awake, awake"?). Something must have been sung, for when Lysimachus asks, "Marke[d] he your Musicke?" Marina replies, "No, nor lookt on vs." But then she prods a little more, and much like Gower in his last scene ("sit and hark"), she invites Pericles to "lend eare." Now, Pericles speaks; it is not in the form of words but only sounds: "hum, ha."

The purpose of this scene is to bring language back from silence. It is to evoke a cure with song, and getting Pericles to speak is like restoring voices from the dead. Marina and her father now go back and forth, goading each other into speaking and listening:

> If I should tell . . .
> Prithee, speak . . .
> Report thy parentage . . .
> Tell thy story . . .

It goes on, like a dreamt interrogation, Marina and Pericles teasing out their identities, until Pericles himself (in another moment of his riddle-solving) understands.

> Oh Hellicanus, strike me honored sir, giue me a gash, put me to present paine, least this great sea of ioyes rushing vpon me, ore-beare the shores of my mortalitie, and drowne me with their sweetnesse. (I1, scene 21)

To drown in sweetness was the powerful effect of Dowland's music. The rush of sound and the image of present pain are the hallmarks of his lyricism and his reputation. In this episode of profound self-revelation ("I am Pericles of Tyre"), the play goes back to the moment of musical ravishment, the drowning in the sweetness of performance. Pericles has indeed marked Marina's music.

What is the place of lyric in the exercise of power? *Pericles* answers that question in a powerfully meta-dramatic way. It illustrates how reconciliation comes through song. It shows how a *Lear*-like tragedy of misunderstanding can be transformed into an affirming happy ending. If only Cordelia could sing.

Pericles ends with affirmations of the seeming-dead come back to life. Now, when the King gets up, he asks for his robes, and it is as if he is looking in a mirror when he says, "I am wild in my beholding." Lear-like, he once again is calmed: "But hark what music?" Nobody else can hear it. It is, he says, "the music of the spheres," and he elaborates: "Rarest sounds, do ye not hear," and then,

> Most heauenly Musicke,
> It nips me vnto listning, and thicke slumber
> Hangs vpon mine eyes, let me rest. (I1v, scene 21)

These penultimate moments of the play take us back, once again, to Dowland and desire. These "rarest" sounds recall the "rare" music that had revived Thaisa, and that word, "rare," conjures up an emerging aesthetic world for the play's audience. "Rare" was not just unusual. It was compelling, powerful, artistically controlled. It is the word that Dowland himself would deploy to describe the sounds of the Muses themselves "yet so rare." It is the word that Henry Peacham would use to describe Dowland's own playing, "a rare lutenist." It is the word that William Webbe would use to categorize the canon of "our rare artists," Bird, Bull, Dowland, and Morely. And it is the word that listeners would increasingly rely on for that sense of ravishment that they would feel at performance: the "rare music and songs" that William Bonner heard in 1602, or the "rare consort of music" that would play in Webster's *The Devil's Last Case.*[21] *Pericles* ends in ravishment—in the display of lyric art that would recall the powers of performance to revive. Voices emerge anew to sing; ears prick to listen. The goddess Diana appears out of nowhere, like a masquer walking onstage from another show, briefly to dazzle and command the visionary to "awake and tell thy dreame."

No one awakes to tell such dreams in *Lear*. There are no goddesses to sway, no lutes or viols to arouse. There is no song to bring the dead back to the living. There is no music to wake the sleeping. Lear himself hears no melodies. Instead, it is the sound of raw, almost nonverbal pain: "Howl, howl, howl, howl!" *Lear* ends with fantasies of breath: with his rough yells, with the imagination that the feather stirs before her mouth, or that the mirror fogs. The Fool is dead, as well, "no breath at all." *Pericles* is garbled, badly printed, pastiched and patched together. But something still emerges at its close. If music does anything in this play, it shows us how little music there had been in *Lear*. If Dowland's sweetness, pain, and drowning appear at the close, it is to show not simply how song can entertain. It is to show how music can turn tragedy into comedy, how rare sounds can bring back the dead—whether they be vanished queens or buried English poets. To sing a song that once was sung.

The Two Noble Kinsmen *and the Romance of Remembered Song*

The Two Noble Kinsmen may well include Shakespeare's final writing for the stage. We open the old Quarto and find many familiarities: song and story, lovers' quarrels, mad girls, sad boys, dumb shows, rustics, nobles, fools. At times, the play reads as a retrospective of the playwright's moves. At others, it comes off as more of an impersonation, as if John Fletcher were (in the words of the critic Misha Teramura) "creating an anthology of Shakespearean moments, performing his own protean acts of appropriation and parody."[22]

This is a play that dances the antique in a host of ways. Its title page announces that it is a work of "worthies," and that word (as I have already noted) had become a signpost for the literary dead. "Worthy" had been a marker of Chaucer's reception through the fifteenth and sixteenth centuries. "Worthy Chaucer" is a phrase that fills editions, commentaries, and histories. "England's Worthies" was, by the mid-seventeenth century, a title that conveyed the scope of a literary history that explicitly began with Chaucer himself, and the title page of *The Two Noble Kinsmen* explicitly inscribes Shakespeare and Fletcher into this canon.

What makes an author worthy, in this world, is not just skill or virtue. It is death. *The Two Noble Kinsmen* opens as an elegy for past poets and traditions. Turn the Quarto's page and find the Prologue arguing precisely for the afterlives of the deceased and for the power of the past to come alive again.

> New plays and maidenheads are near akin:
> Much followed both, for both much money gi'en,

If they stand sound and well. And a good play,
Whose modest scenes blush on his marriage day
And shake to lose his honour, is like her
That after holy tie and first night's stir
Yet still in Modesty and still retains
More of the maid, to sight, than husband's pains. (Prologue, 1–8)

Old institutions and old poets remain fertile, and Raphael Lyne's critique of Pericles's speeches comes back to me, now, as the flourish of *Two Noble Kinsmen* opens up the book about legacies and lineages. "New plays and maidenheads are near akin." The challenge of theatrical invention is the challenge of the matter of the plays themselves. For all these dramas have been tales of maidenhead: what is the status of the young girl's body; how is her virginity a matter both of virtue and of value; how is the "first night's stir" of a wedded couple comparable to the opening night at the theater? One could imagine the bold similes of this Prologue in Autolycus's brash mouth, or (more coarsely) in Cloten's goads.

But then, the Prologue shifts its tone. Chaucer emerges, famous, everlasting, influential even in his death.

How will it shake the bones of that good man
And make him cry from under ground, 'O fan
Me from the witless chaff of such a writer
That blasts my bays and my famed works makes lighter
Than Robin Hood!' (Prologue, 17–21)

Chaucer complains from the grave—these later imitators are but chaff before the grain of his imagination. And if we are "too ambitious to aspire to him," at the very least the audience may help out such new writers.

Do but you hold out
Your helping hands and we shall tack about
And something do to save us. You shall hear
Scenes, though below his art, may yet appear
Worth two hours' travel. To his bones sweet sleep;
(Prologue, 25–29)

Helping hands, two hours' travel, sleeping bones. These are the tropes, now, not of Chaucer's praise but of Shakespeare's. The Prologue's lines recall much, but what they now recall is the language of another Shakespeare book, the First Folio, and in particular Ben Jonson's eulogies. His "To the Reader" frames the volume as outstripping the engraved image of Shakespeare himself on the frontispiece. The engraver tried, but:

> O, could he but have drawne his wit
> Ass well in brasse, as he hath hit
> His face, the print would then surpasse
> All, that was ever writ in brass.

That "O" comes back, I think, in Chaucer's voice in *The Two Noble Kinsmen*: we have originals and copies, past examples and new attempts to present them. We have a poet in the Prologue who complains about base writers (a complaint redolent with Jonsonian invective), and whose vision of his imitators breaks his laurel into bits of doggerel like tales of Robin Hood. Measuring up against another set of writers had been one of Jonson's classic moves, nowhere more powerful (or poignant) than in the long poem to the First Folio on Shakespeare's memory. Now, the poetic praise takes on a special resonance when read against the opening of *The Two Noble Kinsmen*. New plays may be like maidenheads, but sex and bodies are not far from critical responses to the old. How worthy, Jonson asks, are we to speak of Shakespeare?

> These are, as some infamous Baud, or Whore,
> Should praise a Matron. What could hurt her more?

Is writing whoredom? Does the dramatist present two hours' pleasure only for the cash? This, to return to the *Two Noble Kinsmen*, is the fear we bring. But Jonson moves ahead: "I, therefore will begin, Soule of the Age!" He calls upon the playwright, dead now, to return:

> The applause! Delight! The wonder of the stage!
> My Shakespeare rise, I will not lodge thee by

Chaucer, or Spenser, or bid Beaumont lye
A little further, to make thee a roome;
Thou art a Monument without a tombe,
And art aliue still, while they Book doth live
And we have wits to read, and praise to give.

Whatever the performance origins of *The Two Noble Kinsmen*, its printed Prologue resonates with printed praise of Shakespeare. Even John Mabbe's brief lines in the Folio echo in the appeal to applause and in the purpose of the play to bring the buried poet back to life.

Wee thought thee dead, but this thy printed worth,
Tels thy Spectators, that thou went'st but forth
To enter with applause.

The new play's Prologue displaces praise of the dead Shakespeare on to Chaucer. As in the First Folio's encomia, it enjoins the reader to appreciate the body behind the text, to recognize that reading and performing bring old worthies back to life. But in the end, that life lives only in imagination—between covers of a book or curtains on a stage. To his bones, sweet sleep.

We turn the Quarto's page and find the rituals of new fertility to bring back life, to break the maidenhead that separates the audience from the actors (or that keep the uncut pages of a new book from its reader). The first figure of the play is Hymen, entering with his boy and nymph, "singing and strewing flowers." Unlike *A Midsummer Night's Dream*, where the marriage of Theseus and Hippolyta played itself out through idioms of male conquest and compulsion ("I wooed thee with my sword," Theseus announced), here it becomes the occasion for ritual and song. The first words offered in the play are sung. The first text is aligned as lyric, full of roses, primrose, oxlips, and marigolds. These are the markers of old celebration. They were everywhere in Shakespeare, everywhere in lute song and in verse anthology. The poem bursts with cliché, and I think that is the point. For as in *Pericles*, this is a ritual enactment of an older form of lyricism, a dramatic move to place the action's opening in a poetic past. Just as Gower's halting tetrameters evoke an ancient worthy come back from the grave to speak anew, so Chaucer's characters emerge with all the trappings of old poesy. To sing a song that once was sung.

And in that singing, *The Two Noble Kinsmen* becomes a play of elegies. From Chaucer's passing, through the funeral of Theban warriors, to the sorrows of the Jailer's Daughter, songs emerge to mark the lyric dead and take us back to earlier performances of mourning. The dirge that closes act 1 rings against a reader's memory of the lament over Fidele's body in *Cymbeline*.

> Urns and odours bring away;
> Vapours, sighs, darken the day;
> Our dole more deadly looks than dying—
> Balms and gums and heavy cheers,
> Sacred vials fill'd with tears,
> And clamours through the wild air flying. (1.5.1–6)

The double syllables of rhyme (dying/flying) break the steadiness of the stanza, just as in Guiderius's song the rhymes' rhythm undermines our ease:

> Fear no more the heat o'th'sun
> Nor the furious winter's rages.
> Thou thy worldly task hast done,
> Home art gone, and ta'en thy wages. (*Cymbeline*, 4.2.259–62)

Such music recalls less a scene in Chaucer than in Shakespeare, but it is a Shakespeare upside-down here, as the earth and dust that would inhume Fidele are transformed into the smells, the vapors, and the sounds that lift themselves through air.

The purpose of these songs may be to motivate the drama. But it is, as well, to move us. Sad though these lines may be, sung well they elevate us along with the smoke and smells. The Jailer's Daughter tells us how to feel. She enters in act 2, scene 4, alone, reflecting on her love for Palamon, and what she says about his skill models a way of speaking about lyric poetry itself.

> To hear him
> Sing in an evening, what a heaven it is!
> And yet his songs are sad ones. (2.4.18–20)

This is as much a statement of musical ravishment as anything in Dowland's world. Recall, again, Campion's praise of how the lutenist charmed heaven's populace (*O qui sonora coelites altos cheli / Mulces*). Recall how Dowland's own name would be played on for the sadness of his songs and for the sweetness of his verse. *Semper Dowland semper dolens*, always Dowland always sad. Such was the dole of the grieving Theban women. Such is the dolor of the Jailer's Daughter.

Increasingly, the Jailer's Daughter comes off as a marker of aesthetic value—a figure of mad song, not just an Ophelia or a Desdemona, but a Queen Alcyone, watching the waves for any sign of her king's ship.

> Yonder's the sea and there's a ship; how't tumbles!
> And there's a rock lies watching under water;
> Now, now, it beats upon it; now, now, now!
> There's a leak sprung, a sound one! How they cry!
> Run her before the wind, you'll lose all else.
> Up with a course or two and tack about, boys!
> Good night, good night, you're gone. (3.4.5–11)

Like Ovid's sad queen on the beach, she sees in her mind's eye the shipwreck, hidden rocks, the sound of storms and leaks, and then the voices of the shipmates, crying in their fear. Remember Golding's Ovid:

> Anon the Mayster cryed: Strike the toppesayle, let the mayne
> Sheate flye and fardle it to the yard. Thus spake he, but in vayne,
> For why so hideous was the storme uppon the soodeine brayd,
> That not a man was able there to heere what other sayd.
> And lowd the sea with meeting waves extreemely raging rores.
> . . .
> And looke, how many surges came theyr vessell to assayle,
> So many deathes did seeme to charge and breake uppon them all.
> One weepes: another stands amazde: the third them blist dooth call
> Whom buryall dooth remayne. To God another makes his vow,
> And holding up his handes to heaven the which hee sees not now,
> Dooth pray in vayne for help. (11.557–61; 620–25)

All this, of course, is only in the Jailer's Daughter's mind. There is no shipwreck that dispatches Palamon, save in her fears. She comes off as some Alcyone in fear, or perhaps as Miranda, dreaming of the tempest that her father conjured, and the cries of the seamen. And yet, unlike Alcyone or Miranda, there is no peace in dreaming or in waking. Instead, she breaks and sings her ballads, as if she had come across a cache of Autolycus's sheets and, ranging from the bawdy to the burlesque, offers up a string of half-familiar tunes.

"For I'll cut my green coat," echoes the surviving ballad "Childe Waters." Her later song, about the "George Allow," recalls a song about a sunken ship. It goes on: "There were three fools"; "willow, willow, willow"; and a clutch of lyrics that she does not sing, but only mentions. With the exception of the song and dirge of act 1, all the stanzaic lyrics of the play belong to her, and like Autolycus, she emerges as a walking anthology.[23]

For any reader of the play's Quarto, these songs bring back an early time. The scholar works to locate their sources. But the reader would have recognized and remembered. Music brings back the past, evokes the worthies of an older stage, the boy actors and their female roles, a time when sad songs could sound like heaven. *The Two Noble Kinsmen*, in the end, remains a book of the dead. It offers a memorial to ancient writers, lost heroes, past actors, masques, and musicians. Its "Chaucer" was, by the 1630s, a writer of black letter, a poet ensconced in the editions of Thomas Speght, reprinted in archaic typeface, annotated with explanatory glosses, and framed by elaborate genealogies of his family and his patrons.[24] *Pericles* may have survived in garbled form; nonetheless, it survives as some form of a play performed by living men for living people. *The Two Noble Kinsmen* comes to us as something far more carefully curated. But it is the curatorship of the antiquarian rather than the dramatist. This is an artifact of an age gone by, a bit of Jacobean theater with Elizabethan turns, based on a Middle English poem, for the age of Charles I.

Together with *Pericles*—and as I have suggested, to some extent, *Henry VIII*—it proffers examples of creative Shakespearean reception and appropriation. What matters less to me is just who wrote each line than how those lines sound more or less Shakespearean. These are anthologies of authorship, at times deft, at times awkward, highly mediated by their printers, good and bad. I treat them less as plays than as books. They may have some attenuated relationship to earlier performances, but they come to us as products of a printer, meant for readers rather than for actors. These are not scripts. They are, in various ways, memories of scripts. They invite us to recognize and to remember.

What is the romance of our scholarship? From the beginning, we have been enjoined to read and read again. The search for an authentic Shakespeare has, since the First Folio, taken many forms, and we still wish to listen for a rhythm or a rhyme that we can assuredly say is his. Any encounter with the splay of modern editions will raise these questions, most acutely in *Pericles* and *The Two Noble Kinsmen*, where we have neither the authority of the First Folio nor the reliable accounts of performance to go on. My sense, as I complete this book, is that our search for Shakespeare remains not a search for character or class, modernity or motive. It remains a search for something lyrical. We come upon a line much as a romance king would come upon his child. What brings it back to life? What takes us to the heaven as we hear it? The romance motif of travel, shipwreck, loss, recovery, and return shapes the arc of the last plays. It shapes, too, as I have suggested, the arc of an artist's career—that of a Dowland who imagines his songs trapped on rocks of misappropriation, who returns from a decade away to find musicians in the court unworthy of their name. King Ceyx comes back only as a simulacrum and a dream. Actors die only to stand up again the next night. The late plays haunt. Like Hamlet's urgent ghost, they ask us to remember, and in that remembering we go back to read and make him rise.

Acknowledgments

My first debt is to my editors at the University of Chicago Press. Alan Thomas and Randolph Petilos welcomed the initial proposal for this book and oversaw its scrupulous refereeing and ultimate acceptance. With this, as with my previous books with the Press, I remain delighted and honored by their support and counsel.

The University of California, San Diego, has provided me with research support and sabbatical leave, as well as with the pleasure of teaching Shakespeare in its unique Department of Literature. A 2015 Keeley Fellowship at Wadham College, Oxford, offered an unparalleled place to research and write and to share portions of the book with faculty and students. Thanks are due to Jane Griffiths, Rhodri Lewis, and Daniel Wakelin, and to the Bodleian Library, the English Faculty Library, and the Wadham College Library. A term as the 2016 M. H. Abrams Visiting Professor at Cornell University presented the opportunity to teach and lecture on some of the material here, along with a wonderful library and an engaged group of colleagues to enhance the completion of the book.

Versions of this material were presented as lectures at the University of California, Berkeley, the University of Oxford, Cornell

University, Princeton University, the University of Rochester, Pennsylvania State University, the University of Montana, the University of San Diego, Syracuse University, York University, and at the meetings of the Modern Language Association of America and the Shakespeare Association of America. Thanks are due to all who heard and questioned. A remarkable gathering of University of California scholars for the four-hundredth anniversary of Shakespeare's birth (held at the San Diego Public Library) gave me the chance to share ideas with a general as well as specialist audience. I thank my UC colleagues who contributed memorably to that event: Heidi Brayman, Frances Dolan, Patricia Fumerton, Jeffrey Knapp, Julia Reinhard Lupton, and Robert Watson.

My work with the Musicians in Ordinary in Toronto (the lutenist John Edwards and the soprano Hallie Fishel) taught me more than any books could about performance practice in early modern England, about the subtleties of Dowland's lyric voices, and about the modern challenges of living with an earlier aesthetic. I thank them for inviting me to perform with them in Toronto and for their unforgettable concerts and lectures at my classes and conferences at UCSD.

Bradin Cormack, William Germano, Kenneth Gross, Timothy Hampton, James Shapiro, and Deanne Williams read versions of this book in progress. They challenged its arguments and honed its scholarship. Working through their responses has made this a better book than I could have imagined it to be.

Notes

PREFACE

1. In R. A. Foakes, *Samuel Taylor Coleridge's Criticism of Shakespeare* (Detroit: Wayne State University Press, 1989), 50.

2. Edward Dowden, *Shakespeare* (New York: Appleton, 1878), 55.

3. Sarah Beckwith, *Shakespeare and the Grammar of Forgiveness* (Ithaca, NY: Cornell University Press, 2012), 1.

4. A full bibliographical review of scholarship and criticism through the early 2000s is available in Raphael Lyne, *Shakespeare's Late Work* (Oxford: Oxford University Press, 2007), 156–59. More recent studies that have influenced my work include the following: Russ McDonald, *Shakespeare's Late Style* (Cambridge: Cambridge University Press, 2006); Gordon McMullan, *Shakespeare and the Idea of Late Writing: Authorship in the Proximity of Death* (Cambridge: Cambridge University Press, 2007); and Beckwith, *Shakespeare and the Grammar of Forgiveness.* More specialized accounts that address changes in the Shakespearean mode in the early 1600s include A. R. Braunmuller, "Shakespeare's Late Style," in *The Oxford Handbook of Shakespeare's Poetry,* ed. Jonathan F. S. Post (Oxford: Oxford University Press, 2013), 43–61; and Bart van Es, "Late Shakespeare and the Middle Ages," in *Medieval Shakespeare: Pasts and Presents,* ed. Ruth Morse et al. (Cambridge: Cambridge University Press, 2013), 37–51. For the idea of an "archipelagic" English and the broader political and social contexts for Jacobean Shakespeare, see John Kerrigan, *Archipelagic English: Literature, History, and Politics,*

1603–1707 (Oxford: Oxford University Press, 2008). Classic studies of the relationships of drama and the state in the Jacobean period remain Stephen Orgel, *The Illusion of Power* (Berkeley: University of California Press, 1975); and Jonathan Goldberg, *James I and the Politics of English Literature* (Stanford, CA: Stanford University Press, 1981).

5. Bart van Es, "Reviving the Legacy of Indoor Performance," in *Moving Shakespeare Indoors: Performance and Repertoire in the Jacobean Playhouse,* ed. Andrew Gurr and Farah Karim-Cooper (Cambridge: Cambridge University Press, 2014), 237.

6. The sense of Shakespeare as returning, late in his career, to early works for revision and recasting stands behind Emrys Jones, *Scenic Form in Shakespeare* (Oxford: Clarendon Press, 1971). For the Shakespearean career narrative as one self-conscious of its closure, see McMullan, *Shakespeare and the Idea of Late Writing.* For the notion that the late plays turn to more elaborate metaphors and rarified locutions, see Simon Palfrey, *Late Shakespeare: A New World of Words* (Oxford: Clarendon Press, 1997); and McDonald, *Shakespeare's Late Style.*

7. Such a sensibility informs Lyne, *Shakespeare's Late Work.* For the challenges to late twentieth-century theatrical performance, see Roger Warren, *Staging Shakespeare's Late Plays* (Oxford: Clarendon, 1990).

8. Lucy Munro, "Emotions in Stranglehold," *Times Literary Supplement,* January 22, 2016, 18.

9. Lyne, *Shakespeare's Late Work,* 42.

10. Ibid., 43.

11. Jonathan Bate, *Shakespeare and Ovid* (Oxford: Clarendon Press, 1993), 267.

12. For a history of critical responses to the "lyric," see *The Lyric Theory Reader,* ed. Virginia Jackson and Yopie Prins (Baltimore: Johns Hopkins University Press, 2014). For broader theoretical questions about lyric as a genre in history, see Jonathan Culler, *Theory of the Lyric* (Cambridge, MA: Harvard University Press, 2015).

13. Helen Vendler, *The Art of Shakespeare's Sonnets* (Cambridge, MA: Harvard University Press, 1997), 2.

14. *Cymbeline,* ed. Roger Warren (Oxford: Oxford University Press, 1998), 133.

15. And for the common reader as well. See, most famously, Francis Meres's 1598 remark that "the sweete wittie soule of Ovid lives in Mellifluous & hony-tongued Shakespeare," and the discussions in Patrick Cheney, *Shakespeare, National Poet-Playwright* (Cambridge: Cam-

bridge University Press, 2004), 49–73; Colin Burrow, *Shakespeare and Classical Antiquity* (Oxford: Oxford University Press, 2013); as well as Bate, *Shakespeare and Ovid.*

16. See Philip Hardie, *Ovid's Poetics of Illusion* (Cambridge: Cambridge University Press, 2002).

17. Diana Poulton, *John Dowland,* rev. ed. (Berkeley: University of California Press, 1982). Additional scholarship may be found in Peter Holman, *Dowland Lacrimae (1604)* (Cambridge: Cambridge University Press, 1999), and in the articles in the special issue of *Early Music* 41.2 (2013), devoted to Dowland on the 450th anniversary of his birth. See, too, Christian Kelnberger, *Text und Musik bei John Dowland* (Passau: Verlag Karl Stutz, 1999), a book based on the author's University of Munich dissertation and one that goes beyond Poulton in, among other things, identifying the strong Petrarchanism of Dowland's lyrics and analyzing the forms of notation and instrumentation through which Dowland's vocal and instrumental compositions would have been disseminated. Kelnberger also includes a complete edition of the lyrics from all four of Dowland's volumes printed in his lifetime, with textual and critical annotations.

18. Michael Gale, "John Dowland, Celebrity Lute Teacher," *Early Music* 41.2 (2013): 205–18, quoted at 213.

19. Ibid.

20. See Robin Headlam Wells, "Dowland, Ficino and Elizabethan Melancholy," in *Elizabethan Mythologies: Studies in Poetry, Drama and Music* (Cambridge: Cambridge University Press, 1994), 189–224.

21. Kirsten Gibson, "'How hard an enterprise it is': Authorial Self-Fashioning in John Dowland's Printed Books," *Early Music History* 26 (2007): 43–90.

22. Tiffany Stern, "The Second Blackfriars Playhouse as a Place of Nostalgia," in *Moving Shakespeare Indoors,* ed. Gurr and Karim-Cooper, 107.

23. Gibson, "'How hard,'" 80.

24. These quotations from Dowland's prefaces, and the material behind my summary, are in Poulton, *John Dowland,* 289–91. The phrase *Cucullus non facit Monachum,* while a commonplace, probably owes its early modern English circulation to Erasmus's *Colloquies,* and while it appears in writings by Thomas Nashe and Richard Greene, it is best known to Shakespeareans for its appearance in *Twelfth Night* (1.5.52) and in *Measure for Measure* (5.1.271).

25. I do not presume to cover all the possible sources for the lyrical, Ovidian, and musical Shakespeare in the late plays. I stress a line of influence and resonance through Golding, Dowland, Chaucer, and the early dramas in the Shakespeare canon. On occasion, I will call attention to the ways in which visions of pastoral, for example, echo the idioms of Spenser, Sidney, and the earlier Elizabethans. But there are features of many other Elizabethan plays (some hovering around Shakespearean contribution) that shape ideas of music, ravishment, historical distance, and pastoral poetics, for example: *Sir Clyomon and Sir Clamydes, The Thracian Wonder, Locrine,* and *Mucedorus.* For scholarship exploring some of these relationships, see Jerry H. Bryant, "*The Winter's Tale* and the Pastoral Tradition," *SQ* 14 (1963): 387–98; L. G. Salingar, "Time and Art in Shakespeare's Romances," *Renaissance Drama* 9 (1966): 3–35; and Ruth Morse, "Shakespeare and the Remains of Britain," in *Medieval Shakespeare: Pasts and Presents,* ed. Ruth Morse et al. (Cambridge: Cambridge University Press, 2013), 119–37.

CHAPTER ONE

1. Quotations in this and the following paragraph are from the *OED,* s.v. "*lyric* (*n*)." For extended discussions of the form and genre in the period, see Heather Dubrow, *The Challenges of Orpheus: Lyric Poetry and Early Modern England* (Baltimore: Johns Hopkins University Press, 2007), and her earlier distillation, "Lyric Forms," in Arthur F. Kinney, ed., *The Cambridge Companion to English Literature, 1500–1600* (Cambridge: Cambridge University Press, 2000), 178–99.

2. Gavin Alexander, "Song in Shakespeare: Rhetoric, Identity, Agency," in Post, ed., *Oxford Handbook of Shakespeare's Poetry,* 247–64, this quotation from 260.

3. George Puttenham, *The Arte of English Poesie* (London, 1589), facsimile reprinting, ed. Baxter Hathaway (Kent: Kent State University Press, 1970), 246.

4. David Orr, "Flying on the Reflected Sky," *New York Times Book Review,* July 20, 2012, BR22.

5. Jonathan Culler, *Theory of the Lyric* (Cambridge, MA: Harvard University Press, 2015), 37.

6. Seth Lerer, "Medieval English Literature and the Idea of the Anthology," *PMLA* 118 (2003): 1251–67.

7. See, too, Jeffrey Todd Knight, *Bound to Read: Compilations, Collections, and the Making of Renaissance Literature* (Philadelphia: University of Pennsylvania Press, 2013).

8. See Raymond Southall, *The Courtly Maker* (Oxford: Blackwell, 1964); Paul G. Remley, "Mary Shelton and Her Tudor Literary Milieu," in Peter C. Herman, ed., *Rethinking the Henrician Era* (Urbana: University of Illinois Press, 1994), 40–77; Seth Lerer, *Courtly Letters in the Age of Henry VIII* (Cambridge: Cambridge University Press, 1997), 143–57.

9. E. Hyder Rollins, *Tottel's Miscellany,* 2 vols. (Cambridge, MA: Harvard University Press, 1928). Recent scholarship includes the essays in Stephen Hamrick, ed., *Tottel's Songes and Sonettes in Context* (Burlington, VT: Ashgate, 2013); J. Christopher Warner, *The Making and Marketing of Tottel's Miscellany, 1557* (Burlington, VT: Ashgate, 2013); Matthew Zarnowiecki, *Fair Copies: Reproducing the English Lyric from Tottel to Shakespeare* (Toronto: University of Toronto Press, 2014).

10. Compare Zarnowiecki's point that Tottel effectively replaces the historical authors (notably Wyatt and Surrey) with a more general, unnamed "lover" figure: "Tottel employs a new kind of textual reproduction, which pursues both textual conservation and textual mutation" (*Fair Copies,* 28).

11. Paul Marquis, *Richard Tottel's Songes and Sonettes, The Elizabethan Version* (Tempe, AZ: ACMRS, 2007), lxii.

12. Text and discussion in Colin Burrow, ed., *The Complete Sonnets and Poems* (Oxford: Oxford University Press, 2002).

13. Ibid., 80.

14. Material in this and the next three paragraphs adapts and revises a few sentences from Seth Lerer, "Hamlet's Poem to Ophelia and the Theater of the Letter," *ELH* 81 (2014): 841–64.

15. Marvin Rosenberg, *The Masks of Hamlet* (Cranbury: Associated University Presses, 1992), 381.

16. Material in this and the next paragraph adapts and revises a few sentences from Seth Lerer, "Cultivation and Inhumation: Some Thoughts on the Cultural Impact of *Tottel's Miscellany,*" in Hamrick, ed., *Tottel's Songes and Sonettes in Context,* 147–61.

17. See Ross W. Duffin, *Shakespeare's Songbook* (New York: Norton, 2004), 211–14.

18. Bate, *Shakespeare and Ovid,* 91.

19. Hardie, *Ovid's Poetics of Illusion,* 259. See, too, his reading of Ceyx and Alcyone, 272–85.

20. Quoted and discussed in Maria Ruvoldt, *The Italian Renaissance Imagery of Inspiration: Metaphors of Sex, Sleep, and Dreams* (Cambridge: Cambridge University Press, 2004), 177. See the discussions throughout

177–85 for the representations of Morpheus as mask-maker in the period of Michelangelo.

21. Colin Burrow, "'Full of the Maker's Guile': Ovid on Imitating and on the Imitation of Ovid," in Philip Hardie et al., eds., *Ovidian Transformations: Essays on the Metamorphoses and Its Reception* (Cambridge: Cambridge Philological Society, 1999), 271–87, this quotation from 278.

22. See John Fyler, *Chaucer and Ovid* (New Haven, CT: Yale University Press, 1979); Deanne Williams, *The French Fetish from Chaucer to Shakespeare* (Cambridge: Cambridge University Press, 2006), 24–27.

23. Among the many studies, see Muriel Bradbrook, "What Shakespeare Did to Chaucer's *Troilus and Criseyde*," *Shakespeare Quarterly* 9 (1958): 311–19; Ann Thompson, *Shakespeare's Chaucer: A Study in Literary Origins* (Liverpool: University of Liverpool Press, 1978); E. Talbot Donaldson, *The Swan at the Well: Shakespeare Reading Chaucer* (New Haven, CT: Yale University Press, 1985); Sherron Knopp, "Poetry as Conjuring Act: *The Franklin's Tale* and the *Tempest*," *Chaucer Review* 38 (2004): 337–54; James Simpson and Sarah Beckwith, eds., "Premodern Shakespeare," special issue of *Journal of Medieval and Early Modern Studies* 40.1 (2010); Seth Lerer and Deanne Williams, "What Chaucer Did to Shakespeare: Books and Bodkins in *Hamlet* and the *Tempest*," *Shakespeare* 8 (2012): 398–410. On the impact of Chaucer editions in the late sixteenth and early seventeenth centuries, see Tim William Machan, "Speght's *Works* and the Invention of Chaucer," *TEXT* 8 (1994): 145–70.

24. See the discussion in Raphael Lyne, *Ovid's Changing Worlds: English Metamorphoses, 1567–1632* (Oxford: Oxford University Press, 2001), 27–79.

25. Ibid., 45.

26. Burrow, "'Full of the Maker's Guile,'" 278.

27. All Chaucer quotations are from Larry D. Benson, general ed., *The Riverside Chaucer*, 3rd ed. (Boston: Houghton Mifflin, 1987).

28. The verb "to harp," meaning to dwell upon in speech or writing, does not appear until the middle of the sixteenth century. The *OED* (s.v. "*harp* [v.])," def. 2, 3a) does not record its full, figurative meaning (that is, without the word "string") until 1562, from *Apol. Private Masse*, "The great matter you harp on." The next quotation is dated 1604, from *Hamlet*, when Polonius remarks, "Still harping on my daughter." Based on this lexicography, Golding's use of the verb here is both strikingly new and purposefully resonant with its mythological contexts.

29. This passage is quoted and discussed in Amanda Eubanks Winkler, *O Let Us Howle Some Heavy Note: Music for Witches, the Melancholic, and the Mad for the Seventeenth-Century English Stage* (Bloomington: Indiana University Press, 2006), 6.

30. Joseph Ortiz, *Broken Harmony: Shakespeare and the Politics of Music* (Ithaca, NY: Cornell University Press, 2011), 6–8, from which I quote Peacham's lines.

31. Embedded, here and throughout my book, is an engagement with music and lyric in Shakespeare that relies on a range of scholarship: Peter Seng, *The Vocal Songs in the Plays of Shakespeare* (Cambridge, MA: Harvard University Press, 1967); Wilfrid Mellers, *Harmonious Meeting: A Study of the Relationship between English Music, Poetry and Theatre, c. 1600–1900* (London: Dennis Dobson, 1965); Winifred Maynard, *Elizabethan Lyric Poetry and Its Music* (Oxford: Clarendon Press, 1986); Robin Headlam Wells, *Elizabethan Mythologies* (Cambridge: Cambridge University Press, 1994); David Lindley, *Shakespeare and Music* (London: Thompson Learning, 2006); Erin Minear, *Reverberating Song in Shakespeare and Milton* (Farnham: Ashgate, 2011).

32. Kirsten Gibson, "'How hard an enterprise it is': Authorial Self-Fashioning in John Dowland's Printed Books," *Early Music Histo*ry 26 (2007): 43–89; this from 78, 80.

33. Originally published in Thomas Campion, *Poemata* (London, 1595). I quote from the edition and (my modernized) translation in Poulton, *John Dowland,* 46.

34. See Martha Maas and Jane Snyder, *Stringed Instruments of Ancient Greece* (New Haven, CT: Yale University Press, 1989), 79–112. For the lexicography, see Charlton T. Lewis and Charles Short, *A Latin Dictionary* (Oxford: Clarendon Press, 1879), s.v. "*chelys.*"

35. For the lexicography and references to literary passages behind this and the following paragraph, see Lewis and Short, *A Latin Dictionary,* s.v. "*mulceo*" and "*permulceo.*"

36. Thomas More, *Utopia,* ed. and trans. Edward Surtz, S.J., and J. H. Hexter, in *The Complete Works of St. Thomas More,* vol. 5 (New Haven, CT: Yale University Press, 1965). These passages can be found in Latin and modern English on 236–37. For Ralph Robinson's revised 1556 translation, I use the edition of Edward Arber (London: Constable, 1906).

37. Richard Barnfield, *Poems In divers humors* (London, 1598), reprinted in *The Passionate Pilgrim* (1599) as the eighth poem in the book. Text and discussion in Burrow, ed., *Complete Sonnets and Poems,* 348–49.

38. The twentieth item in the *First Booke of Songs* (London: Peter Short, 1597). Here, and throughout, I quote from Nadal's slightly modernized editions.

39. See the discussion in Holman, *Dowland Lacrimae (1604).*

40. Poulton lists over a dozen references and allusions to *Lacrimae* in the poetry and drama of the first three decades of the seventeenth century (*John Dowland,* 132–33). Further research is revealing. Dowland references come increasingly to appear in comic moments that set Dowland's work in the mouths of clowns or rustics, fools, and animals. Perhaps the strangest of these appearances comes in the scene among the kitchen help in the Fletcher-Chapman-Middleton-Jonson play *The Bloody Brother,* when the Cook boasts of his own stovetop metamorphoses. There, he announces that he will make "pigs speak French at table," "a dish of calves-feet dance the Canaries," "a calves head speak an Oracle," and finally, "Arion, like a Dolphin, playing Lachrymae" (2.ii). Poulton quotes only a small portion from this play (132). The text is usually dated to the end of the first quarter of the sixteenth century; its earliest production was at the Globe in 1633. My text is *Rollo, Duke of Normandy: Or, the Bloody Brother* (London: R. Holt for Dorman Newman, 1686). Readers of Shakespeare will remember this last phrase from *Twelfth Night,* where the figure of the ancient poet Arion, emerging from the sea astride a dolphin, evokes the power of the musical imagination. And, in *Midsummer Night's Dream,* a mermaid on a dolphin figures forth an image of an almost-Orphic musicality. See *Twelfth Night,* 1.2.14–15: "Where, like Arion on the dolphin's back, / I saw him hold acquaintance with the waves." In *Midsummer Night's Dream,* Oberon recalls how he once "heard a mermaid on a dolphin's back / Uttering such dulcet and harmonious breath / That the rude sea grew civil at her song" (2.1.150–52).

41. Steven W. May, "Popularizing Courtly Poetry: *Tottel's Miscellany* and Its Progeny," in Mike Pincombe and Cathy Shrank, eds., *The Oxford Handbook of Tudor Literature, 1485–1603* (Oxford: Oxford University Press, 2009), 432.

42. In Poulton, *John Dowland,* 275; *Third and Last Booke of Songes or Aires . . .* (London: P. S. for Thomas Adams, 1603). For the bibliographical and textual issues surrounding the book's publication, see Poulton, *John Dowland,* 274–87.

43. See the text, discussion, and reproduction of the original printing in Anthony Rooley, "John Dowland and the Emblem Tradition," *Early Music* 41 (2013): 273–80.

44. Poulton, *John Dowland,* 86–88.

45. In Holman, *Dowland Lachrimae (1604),* 4.

46. Charlton Hinman, *The Printing and Proof-Reading of the First Folio of Shakespeare* (Oxford: Clarendon Press, 1963); Peter W. M. Blayney, *The First Folio of Shakespeare* (Washington, DC: Folger Library, 1991); Anthony J. West, *The Shakespeare First Folio: The History of the Book* (Oxford: Oxford University Press, 2001); Emma Smith, *The Making of Shakespeare's First Folio* (Oxford: Bodleian Library, 2016).

47. Here and throughout, I quote from the First Folio's prefatory material from the facsimile of the copy in Trinity College, Cambridge, in Stephen Orgel and A. R. Braunmuller, eds., *The Complete Pelican Shakespeare* (Harmondsworth: Penguin, 2002).

48. See the summary of criticism in Kiernan Ryan, ed., *Shakespeare: The Last Plays* (London: Longman, 1999), 4–12. See, more pointedly, Stephen Orgel's summary of evidence and scholarship on the placement of *The Tempest:* "All this reduces the evidentiary value of the play's place in the Folio to practically nothing" (Orgel, ed., *Tempest,* 59). In reviewing the place of *The Winter's Tale,* Orgel recalls the fact that the preceding play, *Twelfth Night,* ends on a recto and *The Winter's Tale* begins on the following recto. Thus: "it has been deduced that the copy for the play arrived late at the printer's, after the setting of the section of histories was already in progress. If this is the case, the fact that the play was placed last has as little significance as the fact that the *Tempest* was placed first" (Orgel, ed., *Winter's Tale,* 81).

49. See Andrew Murphy, *Shakespeare in Print: A History and Chronology of Shakespeare Publishing* (Cambridge: Cambridge University Press, 2003), 42–51.

50. Smith, *Making,* 29–30.

51. See Valerie Wayne, "The First Folio's Arrangement and Its Finale," *Shakespeare Quarterly* 66 (2015): 389–408. Wayne systematically reviews the arguments for and against coherent ordering in the Folio, and she makes the largely bibliographical case that I summarize in this paragraph.

52. Alfred W. Pollard, *Shakespeare Folios and Quartos: A Study in the Bibliography of Shakespeare's Plays, 1594–1685* (London: Methuen, 1909), 123–24; quoted and discussed in Wayne, "First Folio's Arrangement," 392–93 and throughout.

53. Leah Marcus, *Puzzling Shakespeare: Local Reading and Its Discontents* (Berkeley and Los Angeles: University of California Press, 1988), 109.

54. Henry Peacham, *The Compleat Gentleman* (London, 1622). I quote from the edition based on the 1634 edition, ed. G. S. Gordon (Oxford: Clarendon Press, 1906), 54.

55. These lines come from the famous song beginning "In darkness let me dwell," originally published in Robert Dowland, *A Musicall Banquet* (London: Printed for Thomas Adam, 1610).

56. Bate, *Shakespeare and Ovid,* 217–18.

57. Smith, *Making,* 161–64, with the reproduction of Cary's annotations to the list of actors at plate 31.

58. Smith, *Making,* 164.

CHAPTER TWO

1. See John B. Bender, "The Day of the Tempest," *ELH* 47 (1980): 235–58; Stephen Orgel, ed., *The Tempest,* 1–4; David Lindley, ed., *The Tempest* (Cambridge: Cambridge University Press, 2013), 2–3.

2. See Douglas Bruster, "Local *Tempest:* Shakespeare and the Work of the Early Modern Playhouse," *Journal of Medieval and Renaissance Studies* 25 (1995): 33–53, reprinted in Patrick M. Murphy, ed., *The Tempest: Critical Essays* (New York: Routledge, 2001), 257–75; on Blackfriars and the Globe as potential performance sites, see 264. See, too, Andrew Gurr, *Playgoing in Shakespeare's London* (Cambridge University Press, 1987), on the larger relationships between the spectatorial and the auditory in the late plays, *The Tempest* in particular, and its venues: "From 1610 onwards, Shakespeare abandoned the idea of an auditory [*sic*] in favour of spectators" (93). See, too, the essays collected in Andrew Gurr and Farah Karim-Cooper, eds., *Moving Shakespeare Indoors: Performance and Repertoire in the Jacobean Playhouse* (Cambridge: Cambridge University Press, 2014).

3. In the "Induction" to *Bartholomew Fair,* Jonson states that there will be no "servant-monster" in the play, and goes on that he is "loth to make Nature afraid in his Plays, like those that beget Tales, Tempests, and such like Drolleries," a set of references long taken as a criticism of Shakespeare's play. In the "Prologue" to *Every Man in His Humour,* as printed in the 1616 Folio of Jonson's works, he invites the audience to enjoy a play "Where neither Chorus wafts you o're the seas, / Nor creaking Throne comes down, the boys to please / . . . nor roul'd bullet heard / To say, it Thunders; nor tempestuous Drum / Rumbles, to tell you when the Storm doth come."

4. Thomas Tomkis, *Albumazar,* when the character Antonio describes how he had escaped shipwreck: "The heavens, and seas, and

earth conspir'd against us; / The tempest tore our helm, and rent our tackles, / Broke the main-mast, while all the sea about us / Stood up in watry mountains to overwhelm us." Text from *Albumazar. A Comedy* (London: T. Becket, 1773), 48. *The Sea Voyage,* in A. R. Waller, ed., *Beaumont and Fletcher's Works,* vol. 9 (Cambridge: Cambridge University Press, 1909), opens with the Master commenting on the dangerous sea, with the boat reeling "like a Drunkard" (compare *The Tempest,* when Antonio laments, "We're merely cheated of our lives by drunkards," 1.1.48), and then remarks how he sees devils dancing and a dolphin shot from a wave, "hey day, hey day" (anticipating and displacing Caliban's cries of "High-day! High-day!," 2.2.181).

5. See John Jowett, "Ralph Crane and the Stage Directions in *The Tempest,*" *Shakespeare Survey* 36 (1983): 107–20; Orgel, ed., *The Tempest,* 56–62; Lindley, ed., *The Tempest,* 102–4, and his detailed "Textual Analysis" at 237–68.

6. For the critical tradition of *The Tempest* as a "new world" play, see the foundational essay by Stephen Greenblatt, "Learning to Curse: Aspects of Linguistic Colonialism in the Sixteenth Century," originally published in Fredi Chiappelli, ed., *First Images of America: The Impact of the New World on the Old* (Berkeley and Los Angeles: University of California Press, 1976), 561–80; and the recent review of scholarship and staging in Lindley, ed., *The Tempest,* 58–78.

7. Stephen Orgel, *The Illusion of Power* (Berkeley and Los Angeles: University of California Press, 1975), distilled into Orgel, ed., *The Tempest,* 43–50, especially this maximal statement: "the masque in *The Tempest* is not a court masque, it is a dramatic allusion to one" (43–44).

8. See Bate, *Shakespeare and Ovid,* esp. 239–63; Colin Burrow, *Shakespeare and Classical Antiquity* (Oxford: Oxford University Press, 2013), 128–32; Lindley, ed., *The Tempest,* 4–9.

9. Philip Hardie, *Ovid's Poetics of Illusion* (Cambridge: Cambridge University Press, 2002), 272–82; Burrow, "'Full of the Maker's Guile,'" 271–87; Bate, *Shakespeare and Ovid,* 218n1.

10. David Lindley, *Shakespeare and Music* (London: Thompson Learning, 2006), 1–9.

11. Ibid., 8.

12. Ibid., 231.

13. See Orgel, ed., *The Tempest,* 1–56. For the ways in which the "thematic" of music inflects the play's sense of theatrical representation, see Lindley, *Shakespeare and Music,* 218–33, with special references to the differences between practical and "speculative" music in Renaissance

theory. For a reading of the play as a theatrical engagement with the move from "barbarousness to language," see Simon Palfrey, *Late Shakespeare, a New World of Words* (Oxford: Oxford University Press, 1997), 138–68. For Prospero's island as a "theater itself" and the role of music in creating it, see Ortiz, *Broken Harmony*, 164–79.

14. See Orgel's note, *The Tempest,* 205.

15. For a review of nineteenth- and early twentieth-century imaginations of "Shakespearean autobiography" in the figure of Prospero, see Orgel, ed., *The Tempest,* 10–11. Erich Auerbach, in his Shakespeare chapter in *Mimesis,* clings to a sense of Prospero as Shakespeare himself, offering a farewell to the stage (for a review and critique, see Seth Lerer, "Auerbach's Shakespeare," *Philological Quarterly* 90 [2011]: 21–44). While the many stage figurations of Prospero have presented him, variously, as a magus, a king, a colonist, and an alchemist (see Orgel, ed., *The Tempest,* 80–83), Ralph Fiennes played him as actually looking like Shakespeare in his *Tempest* at the Theatre Royal, Haymarket, in 2014. See Sam Jordinson, "A Real Character: Is Prospero Shakespeare?," *The Guardian,* April 15, 2014.

16. Lindley hints at such a reading, in *Tempest,* 110, note to line 6.

17. Burrow, "'Full of the Maker's Guile,'" 278.

18. "The Booke of the Duchesse," in Larry D. Benson, gen. ed., *The Riverside Chaucer,* 3rd ed. (Boston: Houghton Mifflin, 1987). For an influential interpretation of this section of the poem as an exercise in courtly tact—presenting, in allegorical form, an argument for the poem's dedicatee, John of Gaunt, to accept the death of his wife, Blanche—see A. C. Spearing, *Medieval Dream Poetry* (Cambridge: Cambridge University Press, 1976), 53–58. For more on the place of Ovid's story in Chaucer's poem, see Kathryn L. Lynch, *Chaucer's Philosophical Visions* (Cambridge: D. S. Brewer, 2000), 31–60; and Deanne Williams, "The Dream Visions," in Seth Lerer, ed., *The Yale Companion to Chaucer* (New Haven, CT: Yale University Press, 2006), esp. 149–55.

19. "Sweet" and "sweetness" fill Elizabethan writings about music and desire. They become part of the larger vocabulary of ravishment, not just in English but in Latin. Campion's verses in praise of Dowland repeatedly call his music *suave.* Dowland's *First Book of Songes* of 1597 has lyrics with such opening lines as "Come away, come sweet loue," "Come againe: sweet loue doth now enuite," and "Awake sweet loue thou art returnd." Barnfield's poem from *The Passionate Pilgrim* had opened, "If music and sweet poetry agree," and Dowland's *Second Book*

of Songes from 1600 has a song that opens, "O sweet woods, the delight of solitarinesse," identified as a line taken from Sir Philip Sidney's 1598 edition of *The Countess of Pembrokes Arcadia* (Poulton, *John Dowland,* 262). For Peacham on Luca Marenzio, see Poulton, *John Dowland,* 415. Patrick Hannay's poem, "Seretine and Mariana," appeared in *The Nightingale* (London: Nathaniel Butler, 1622). His work has long been seen as hearkening back to Marlowe's *Hero and Leander* in particular. An especially Dowland-like moment in Marlowe's poem may be: "And now begins Leander to display / Loues holy fire, with words, with sighs and teares, / Which like sweet musicke entered Heroes eares" (*Hero and Leander,* 192–94, in Fredson Bowers, ed., *The Complete Works of Christopher Marlowe,* vol. 2 [Cambridge: Cambridge University Press, 1981]). Roland Greene finds these images of sweetness to be part of a larger sixteenth-century engagement with Petrarch's poetry and with the inheritance of the idioms of things *dolce* in Italian poetry. See *Post Petrarchism: Origins and Innovations of the Western Lyric Sequence* (Princeton, NJ: Princeton University Press, 1991).

20. Phaer's translation of the first seven books of the *Aeneid* appeared in 1558. Written in fourteeners, it was widely praised throughout the 1560s and 1570s. But by the 1610s, its verse form and its diction would have seemed arrestingly old-fashioned. Phaer's vocabulary, in the words of Margaret Tudeau-Clayton, aspired to an "exclusive . . . ornate . . . polished" language. See her "Supplementing the *Aeneid* in Early Modern England: Translation, Imitation, Commentary," *International Journal of the Classical Tradition* 4 (1998): 507–25. See, too, Sheldon Brammall, *The English Aeneid: Translating Virgil, 1555–1646* (Edinburgh: Edinburgh University Press, 2014), esp. 22.

21. Bruster, "Local *Tempest,*" in Murphy, ed., *Critical Essays,* 267–70.

22. The word "playing" appears three times in *The Tempest* and only in stage directions: at 1.2, "Reenter Ariel, invisible, playing and singing"; at 2.1, "Enter Ariel, invisible, playing; solemn music"; and at 5.1, "Here Prospero discovers Ferdinand and Miranda playing at chess."

23. See Deanne Williams, "Enter Ofelia Playing on a Lute," in Kaara L. Peterson and Deanne Williams, eds., *The Afterlife of Ophelia* (London: Palgrave Macmillan, 2012), 119–36.

24. For a close look at Ariel's entrances, songs, and exits as a matter of performance cuing, see Simon Palfrey and Tiffany Stern, *Shakespeare in Parts* (Oxford: Oxford University Press, 2007), 284–88.

25. See the citations in the online Shakespeare Concordance.

26. Poulton, *John Dowland,* 70. Dowland and Johnson are recorded, as well, as playing at James's funeral, May 5, 1625 (Poulton, *John Dowland,* 88).

27. Jonathan Woolfson, "The Renaissance of Bees," *Renaissance Studies* 24 (2009): 281–300.

28. For a recent discovery of another, printed text of this lyric, together with reflections on its cultural importance in the late Elizabethan world, see Samuel Fallon and David Scott Kastan, "Signature Verses," *TLS* (February 5, 2016): 14. Fallon and Kastan identify a printed fragment as coming from the volume *The Muses Garland* (entered in to the Stationer's Register on February 7, 1603), and containing the poem beginning "It was a time, when sillie Bees could speake," attributed to "Ess." The poem, they write, is "associated with Essex in the manuscript tradition." Whatever the authorship of the poem, it is clear that this publication, as they state, offers "the varied forms in which Elizabethan and Jacobean poetry was published," and it serves to illustrate how much this poem, and its amorous/political narrative of bees, was current in the early years of the seventeenth century.

29. Poulton, *John Dowland,* 285.

30. Bruster, "Local *Tempest,*" in Murphy, ed., *Critical Essays,* 270.

31. Burrow, "'Full of the Maker's Guile,'" 278.

32. For an interpretation of Prospero's names for Ariel ("dainty," "chick," "bird," "tricksy") and their possible historical connotations about gender and service, as well as their stimuli for post-Shakespearean performances of the role, see Deanne Williams, "Prospero's Girls," *Borrowers and Lenders,* 9 (2014), available online at http://www.borrowers.uga.edu/1382/show.

CHAPTER THREE

1. Orgel prints a modernized text of Foreman's account from his *Book of Plaies and Notes thereof per formans for Common Pollicie,* Oxford, Bodleian Library, MS Ashmole 208, fols. 201v–202r (Orgel, ed. *Winter's Tale,* 233). An unmodernized edition of the text appears in Robert Kean Turner and Virginia Westling Haas, eds., *A New Variorum Edition of Shakespeare. The Winter's Tale* (New York: Modern Language Association of America, 2005), 606. On the broader question of the play's comic quality, its generic affiliations, and its movement of forgiveness and restoration, see the overview of critical discussion (through the 1980s) in Turner and Haas, *New Variorum,* 717–28. See, too, Palfrey, *Late*

Shakespeare, 232–43; and Sarah Beckwith, *Shakespeare and the Grammar of Forgiveness* (Ithaca, NY: Cornell University Press, 2012), 127–46.

2. Orgel, ed., *Winter's Tale,* 81. For a review of the bibliographical issues surrounding the printing of the play in the First Folio, see Turner and Haas, *New Variorum,* 586–601.

3. On Ralph Crane and his role in preparing the text, see Turner and Haas, *New Variorum,* 598–601.

4. See the broad lines of argument in, most notably, Palfrey, *Late Shakespeare;* Russ McDonald, *Shakespeare's Late Style* (Cambridge: Cambridge University Press, 2006); Gordon McMullan, *Shakespeare and the Idea of Late Writing: Authorship in the Proximity of Death* (Cambridge: Cambridge University Press, 2007); Beckwith, *Shakespeare and the Grammar of Forgiveness.* The most pointed and succinct statement of the place of *The Winter's Tale* in the late plays remains Anne Barton, "Leontes and the Spider: Language and the Speaker in Shakespeare's Last Plays," originally published in Philip Edwards et al., *Shakespeare's Styles: Essays in Honour of Kenneth Muir* (Cambridge: Cambridge University Press, 1980), and frequently reprinted.

5. A. D. Nuttall, "*The Winter's Tale:* Ovid Transformed," in A. B. Taylor, ed., *Shakespeare's Ovid: The Metamorphoses in the Plays and Poems* (Cambridge: Cambridge University Press, 2000), these quotations from 141, 146, respectively.

6. Autolycus makes his brief appearance in Ovid's *Metamorphoses,* book 11, lines 313–17, where he is described as "of crafty nature, well versed in cunning wiles" (*furtum ingeniosus ad omne*) and capable of making white black and black white (*candida de nigris et de candentibus atra / qui facere adsuerat*). Ovid, *Metamorphoses,* ed. and trans. Frank Justus Miller, Loeb Classical Library (London: William Heinemann, 1916), 142–43.

7. See Palfrey's extended discussion, *New World,* 232–34, and his distillation: "The play's arts are thus plotted in its rogue's etymology" (233). For an argument about Autolycus and his ballads as raising political questions about legitimacy and power in a new, Jacobean world of family politics, see Aaron Kitch, "Bastards and Broadsides in *The Winter's Tale,*" *Renaissance Drama* 30 (1999): 43–71.

8. An edited text of the marginalia, together with critical discussion of their potential source and origin, appeared by Akihiro Yamada, *The First Folio of Shakespeare: A Transcript of Contemporary Marginalia* (Tokyo: Yoshido, 1998), and has been digitized online at shakes.meisei-u.ac

.jp/ALL.html#161. I quote from the online edition. Yamada dates the handwriting to the 1620s up to about 1630. See the brief description in Anthony James West, *The Shakespeare First Folio: The History of the Book, Volume 1* (Oxford: Oxford University Press, 2001), 6–7. See, too, the account in Emma Smith, *The Making of Shakespeare's First Folio* (Oxford: Bodleian Library), 164–66, where she suggests that the annotations are by the individual named as an owner of the volume, William Johnstoone [*sic*], and of whom Smith states "we can deduce from spellings and other linguistic forms that he was probably Scottish, and writing in the late 1620s or 1630."

9. Quoted in Poulton, *John Dowland,* 289.

10. See Steve Newman, "Shakespeare's Popular Songs and the Great Temptations of Lesser Lyric," in Jonathan F. S. Post, ed., *The Oxford Handbook to Shakespeare's Poetry* (Oxford: Oxford University Press, 2013), 279: "popular songs . . . in *The Winter's Tale* . . . help to transform tragedy into renewal but also to complicate pastoral structures and lyric temptations."

11. See Gibson, "'How hard.'" For the rise of printed broadside ballads and the changing attitudes toward publication in the popular world, see Natascha Würzbach, *The Rise of the English Street Ballad,* trans. Gayna Walls (Cambridge: Cambridge University Press, 1990). For a variety of perspectives, some scholarly, some more popular, on printing, song, balladeering, and the Shakespearean world, see Jessie Anne Owens, ed., *"Noyses, sounds, and sweet aires": Music in Early Modern England* (Washington, DC: Folger Shakespeare Library, 2006).

12. See Kitch, "Bastards and Broadsides": "The shared anxieties of paternity and print in the play inscribe broader cultural anxieties about printing as a shift in modes of material production. . . . The print/paternity dialectic provides a cultural context from which to analyze plot, character, and generic status in a way that is unique to *The Winter's Tale,* with its multiple investments in forms of print—not only the source text in Robert Greene's romance *Pandosto* but also the broadside ballad as a competing commercial commodity" (44–45).

13. Orgel, ed., *Winter's Tale,* 80. For a comprehensive review of the early performances, responses, and documentation, see Turner and Haas, *New Variorum,* 798–99.

14. Quoted in Poulton, *John Dowland,* 401.

15. Ibid., 53–54.

16. I offer here an approach to pastoral in the play very different (in

scenic emphases and verbal markers) from Jerry H. Bryant, "*The Winter's Tale* and the Pastoral Tradition," *SQ* 14 (1963): 387–98.

17. *Balletts and Madrigals to Five Voyces* appeared in 1598. I quote from the edition printed by Thomas Este (London, 1608), item xxiii.

18. Thomas Nashe, *A Pleasant Comedy, Called Summer's Last Will and Testament* (London: Simon Stafford for Walter Burre, 1600).

19. I quote from Victor Stetkowicz, ed., *Sir Philip Sidney, The Countess of Pembroke's Arcadia* (The New Arcadia) (Oxford: Clarendon Press, 1987), 11.

20. Note the phrasing of Barnabe Barnes in his fourth Spiritual Sonnet, "Thy precious self in sacrifice had'st laide / To my soul's sustenance." From Alexander B. Grossart, ed., *The Poems of Barnabe Barnes* (London, 1875), 163.

21. For a review of critical assessments of Polixenes's and Leontes's language at the play's opening, see Turner and Haas, *New Variorum,* 753–56.

22. The word "grace" shifts in its force and connotation across its twelve appearances in *The Winter's Tale.* At times it is an aspect of character, at times a quality of personal relationships, at times a title, and at times a quality of social performance. Sidney uses the word (and its various formations) to connote a blend of social virtue and artistic finesse. See, for example, this formulation about virtue, social class, and commercial aspiration in versemaking: "base men with servile wits undertake it [i.e., writing poetry], who think it enough if they can be rewarded of the printer. . . . so these men, no more but setting their names to it, by their own disgracefulness disgrace the most graceful poesy." Sir Philip Sidney, *An Apology for Poetry or The Defense of Poesy,* ed. Geoffrey Shepherd, rev. R. W. Maslen (Manchester: Manchester University Press, 1973), 109.

23. *The Merchant of Venice* is one of the First Folio's Comedies, and Shylock's historical reputation would have been one of a comically exaggerated figure. See John Gross, *Shylock: A Legend and Its Legacy* (New York: Touchstone, 1994), who suggests that Shylock would have been created either by the tragedian Richard Burbage or by the "low comedy actor Will Kempe" (105).

24. Critical responses to Leontes have long stressed the ways in which his increasingly incomprehensible speech may mark his inner self: for example, L. C. Knights on the impossibility of making Leontes's speech "conform to ordinary syntactical forms; the point is its

disjointedness" ("Integration in the Winter's Tale," *Sewanee Review* 84 [1976]: 601–2); S. S. Hussey, Leontes "always chooses the worst sense" of words, the "deliberately revolting" (*The Literary Language of Shakespeare,* 2nd ed. [London, 1992], 232).

25. The Folio reads "Holy-Horse." Nicholas Rowe emended to "hobby-horse" in his 1709 edition of the *Works.* Turner and Haas consider any preference of the Folio reading to be "ridiculous" (*New Variorum,* 108), and they review the possibilities of Ralph Crane's role in this mistake.

26. Thomas Weelkes, *Madrigals to 3. 4. 5. & 6. Voices* (London: Tomas Este, 1597), item XI. Nashe's *Summer's Last Will and Testament* calls for "Morris dancers, with the hobby-horse," and the character of Will Summer states: "You, friend with the hobby-horse, go not too fast, for fear of wearing out my Lord's tilestones with your hobnails."

27. The *OED* gives this line from *The Winter's Tale* as the only citation for "flax-wench" (s.v. "*flax,*" C.2, "*flax-wench*"). The *OED* cites Greene for "flax-wife." See R. Greene, *A Notable Discovery of Cozenage* (London: John Wolfe for T. N., 1591).

28. Howard Felperin, "'Tongue-tied, our Queen?' The Deconstruction of Presence in *The Winter's Tale,*" in Felperin, *The Uses of the Canon: Elizabethan Literature and Contemporary Theory* (Oxford: Clarendon Press, 1990), 51–52.

29. *OED,* s.v. "*slippery,*" which records the phrase "slippery as an eel" from Thomas Hoccleve in the early fifteenth century on. By the early seventeenth century, it is apparently proverbial. The *OED* does record Leontes's line about Hermione as testimony to the definition "licentious, wanton, unchaste," offering two other citations from the 1580s and 1590s.

30. For the repeated appearances of the word "mark" as an imperative verb, see the citations in the online Shakespeare Concordance.

31. Ben Jonson, *Epigrammes:* 4, quoted and discussed in Jonathan Goldberg, *James I and the Politics of Literature* (Stanford, CA: Stanford University Press, 1989), 17.

32. Ibid.

33. George Puttenham, *The Arte of English Poesie* (London: Richard Field, 1589), 244.

34. Goldberg, *James I,* 19. The full title of James's work is *Ane Schort Treatise conteining some Reulis and Cautelis to be observit and eschewit in Scottis poesie,* printed in the *Essayes of a Prentise in the Divine Art of*

Poesie (Edinburgh: Thomas Vautroullier, 1585). I use the reprint edited by Edward Arber (London, 1869).

35. See Ronald D. S. Jack, "James VI and Renaissance Poetic Theory," *English* 16 (1967): 208–11. For a broader contextual survey of James's work in the context of sixteenth-century Scottish literary and political theory, see Sarah M. Dunnigan, *Eros and Poetry at the Courts of Mary Queen of Scots and James VI* (London: Palgrave, 2002).

36. I quote from Arber's edition, 59.

37. The textual, linguistic, and interpretive difficulties of this passage are reviewed in Turner and Haas, *New Variorum,* 69–78.

38. I quote from Charles Howard McIlwain, ed., *The Political Works of James I* (Cambridge, MA: Harvard University Press, 1918), 43, 46.

39. Ibid., 52.

40. Ibid., 50.

41. For a modern attempt to double the parts, see the account in Antony Sher, *Players of Shakespeare #5* (Cambridge: Cambridge University Press, 2003), 91–112.

42. *OED,* s.v. "*catch* (*n.*)," def. 14, citing *Grove's Dictionary:* "The catch was for each succeeding singer to take up or catch his part in time." The first citation is from 1601, "Like a singing catch." On the use of the "catch" in *Twelfth Night,* especially the performance in act 2, scene 3 (with the stage direction "Catch, sung"), see Peter J. Seng, *The Vocal Songs in the Plays of Shakespeare: A Critical History* (Cambridge, MA: Harvard University Press, 1967), 101–3.

43. Samuel L. Bethell, ed., *The Winter's Tale,* New Clarendon Shakespeare (Oxford: Clarendon Press, 1956). See, too, David Lindley, *Shakespeare and Music* (London: Thompson Learning, 2006), 166: "Autolycus, entering on to an empty stage, is singing not just to himself, but explicitly to the audience. . . . it becomes a kind of musical soliloquy. . . . The first person pronouns . . . invite us to identify with the singer, while his self-presentation to us asserts Autolycus's own identity with the persona of his song." My only quarrel with Lindley is his statement that Autolycus sings "on the bare Elizabethan stage," for *The Winter's Tale* is unquestionably a Jacobean play.

44. *OED,* s.v. "*doxy.*" The *OED* quotes this line from *The Winter's Tale,* as well as Middleton and Dekker's *Roaring Girl:* "My doxy stayes for me in a bousing ken." For Dekker's poetic use, see the canting song included in *Villaines Discouered by Lanthorne and Candle-light* . . .

(London: John Busby, 1620), with the refrain "yet would he Wap / with a Mort with a Dell, / And an Autem Mort, with a Doxy," Sig. P4v.

45. *OED,* s.v. "*pugging* (*adj.*)," "Of uncertain meaning," quoting this line from *The Winter's Tale.* OED, s.v. "*pug* (*n.* 2)," def. 1.1.b. Thus, I would take the phrase "pugging tooth" as connoting something like "a taste for whores." The word "tooth" had, since Chaucer, been used to evoke a sexual appetite. See *OED,* s.v. "*tooth,*" def. 2.a, quoting the *Contemplations of Bishop Hall* of 1615: "A wanton tooth is the harbinger to luxurious wantonnesse."

46. *OED,* s.v. "*aunt,*" def. 3, "a bawd or procuress," not quoting this passage, but giving the earliest usage as Middleton's *Michaelmas Terme,* 1607: "She demaunded of me whether I was your worships Aunt or no?"

47. Lindley, *Shakespeare and Music,* 164: "a mixture of pastoral images and thieves' slang." See, too, Steve Newman's formulations: Autolycus's phrasing "allies him to a commercial world that would seem alien to pastoral," and the notion that his performances embody an "interpenetration of high and low at the level of the text" ("Shakespeare's Popular Songs," 279–80).

48. Barton, "Leontes and the Spider," in *Shakespeare's Styles,* 148.

49. Orgel, ed., *The Tempest,* 43–44.

50. I rely on the survey in Würzbach, *Rise,* as well as the materials collected in the English Broadside Ballad Archive, available online at ebba.english.ucsb.edu.

51. Ibid., 257.

52. Ibid., 259.

53. Ibid., 264.

54. Würzbach prints the extended episode of Nightingale's entrance in *Bartholomew Fair,* 2.1, in *Rise,* 265–69.

55. See Jonathan Haynes, "Festivity and the Dramatic Economy of Jonson's *Bartholomew Fair,*" *ELH* 51 (1984): 645–68, especially these remarks on the Stage-keeper's introduction, accusing Jonson of failing to portray the Fair in its historical and social accuracy: "His demands modulate from having actual characters transferred from the Fair to the stage, to the reenactment of social rituals characteristic of fair time . . . to fidelity to the popular tradition of the theater. . . . Jonson meets this attempt by the popular tradition to reclaim its own identity . . ." After quoting the responses of the Book-holder to the Stage-keeper, Haynes states: "The opposition between the popular and coterie theaters is perfectly expressed in this moment: groundlings vs. gentlemen; the Stage-

keeper with his memories of an improvisational popular theater vs. the Book-holder and Scrivener, men of the poet's written text . . ." (658–59). The dramatic tensions in *The Winter's Tale* are, I am arguing throughout, not tensions between popular and poetic theater: they are the tensions involved in poetically representing the popular itself.

56. See the discussion in Gibson, "'How hard.'" My quotations from Dowland's publications are from Poulton, *John Dowland,* 219, 344, and 289, respectively.

57. Newman, again: "When Mopsa and Docas ask if [his ballads] are true, Autolycus insists that the latter [the one about the enormous fish] has been attested to by the signatures of five justices and the former [the story of the usurer's wife] by the midwife, 'one Mistress Taleporter,' thereby supplementing print with the 'authority' of handwriting and oral gossip, as the midwife's name richly combines feminine tale-telling with bawdry" ("Shakespeare's Popular Songs," 280).

58. Orgel reprints settings of the songs in *Winter's Tale,* 275–83. The *New Variorum* has different settings on 851–73. Lindley offers the following conjectures of his own, arguing that Autolycus's first sets of songs are a "kind of musical soliloquy . . . speak[ing] exactly to his present situation. . . . This is clarified by the difference of the final song Autolycus sings as he exits after picking the Clown's pocket. 'Jog on, jog on' seems much more likely to have been one whose words and tune would have been familiar to an audience . . . and the absence of a first-person pronoun generalizes its sentiments, so that it seems much more a case of Autolycus appropriating a lyric of good cheer as a song of triumph for the success of his thievery" (164). Such a view implies that Autolycus's songs are not all of a piece: that some are new and unique, and that others are old and familiar (an argument impossible, at present, to confirm on archival grounds).

59. Poulton, *John Dowland,* 266. Christian Kelnberger, *Text und Musik bei John Dowland* (Passau: Verlag Karl Stutz, 1999), 272, associates this song with those of Autolycus but rejects any direct influence of Dowland on Shakespeare here.

60. The *OED* uses this passage to illustrate def. 2.b, "A female human being," tracing a usage from 1547 to 2000. Among these usages, however, "my she" stands alone. I consider this phrasing more appropriate for def. 1.c., "With premodifying adjectives," called obsolete and rare by the *OED,* with examples only from 1567 to 1684 ("cruel she," "proud she," "poore she"). The use of "mart" as a verb appears, according to the

OED, first in 1589, and carries with it a "sexual connotation," as in "Let peasants marte their marriages" (1598, Warner, *Albion's England*) and, later, in this quotation from *Cymbeline:* "If he shall think fit, A saucy Stranger in his Court, to Mart as in a Romish Stew. . . ."

61. Michael Goldman, *Acting and Action in Shakespeare* (Princeton, NJ: Princeton University Press, 1984), 73–74.

62. Simon Smith, "'Pleasing Strains': The Dramaturgical Role of Music in *The Winter's Tale*," *Shakespeare Survey* 67 (2014): 372–83, this quotation from 382.

63. Ibid., 383.

64. Compare Palfrey, *New World:* Autolycus "is obviously much more than a 'sturdy' vagabond, one of the banes of Jacobean England. He is in fact the future as well as the past incarnate. He supplies what the festive crowd want, as if the metamorphosis of their desires: so it is as their future, their ambivalent consequence, that Autolycus achieves first his expropriative triumphs and then his integration and anonymity" (239).

CHAPTER FOUR

1. Wotton's account of the burning of the Globe has been enshrined as the opening editorial move in the following recent editions of the play: John Margeson (Cambridge: Cambridge University Press, 1990), 1; Jay Halio (Oxford: Oxford University Press, 1999), 17; Jonathan Crewe, in Stephen Orgel and A. R. Braunmuller, *The Pelican Shakespeare* (New York: Penguin, 2002), 1169; Stephen Greenblatt, *The Norton Shakespeare* (New York: Norton, 1997), 3111; David Bevington, *The Complete Works* (New York: HarperCollins, 1992), 893.

2. For an incisive argument about the title of the play in its historical and editorial contexts, see Anston Bosman, "Seeing Tears: Truth and Sense in *All Is True*," *SQ* 50 (1999): 459–76.

3. Since the mid-nineteenth century, discussion of the play's integrity has been wrapped up in discussions of its possibly collaborative origins—the argument often deriving from perceptions that the unevenness of language and dramatic pacing must imply a lack of overall Shakespearean control. The range of views goes from James Spedding, "Who Wrote Shakespeare's *Henry VIII*," *Gentleman's Magazine* (August 1850): 115–24 and (October 1850): 381–82; to Samuel Hickson, *Notes and Queries* (August 24, 1851): 198. Peter Alexander, "Conjectural History, or Shakespeare's *Henry VIII*," *Essays and Studies* 16 (1953): 85–120, argued for the authorial integrity of the play, while claiming that its differences

of style could be seen as having an overarching dramatic function. More recently, John D. Cox made the case for dramatic integrity through the uses of masque and pageant in "*Henry VIII* and the Masque," *ELH* 45 (1978): 390–409.

4. See Margeson's edition, 4–14, and Halio's edition, 16–24.

5. Raphael Lyne, *Shakespeare's Late Work* (Oxford: Oxford University Press, 2007); these quotations from 15, 79, and 17, respectively.

6. On the rising use of writing in the administration of Henry VIII, the images of hand and text, and the broader implications of rule by textuality, see the discussions in G. R. Elton, *Policy and Police* (Cambridge: Cambridge University Press, 1972); Jonathan Goldberg, *Writing Matter: From the Hands of the English Renaissance* (Stanford, CA: Stanford University Press, 1990); Seth Lerer, *Courtly Letters in the Age of Henry VIII* (Cambridge: Cambridge University Press, 1997); and the suggestive summary in Bosman, "Seeing Tears," 463–64.

7. On the tensions between writing and performing in Wyatt, see Jonathan Crewe, *Trials of Authorship* (Berkeley and Los Angeles: University of California Press, 1990); and Lerer, *Courtly Letters.* On the self-consciousness of writing and publishing in *Tottel's Miscellany,* together with the elegiac quality of much of that verse, see Seth Lerer, "Cultivation and Inhumation: Some Thoughts on the Cultural Impact of *Tottel's Miscellany,*" in Stephen Hamrick, ed., *Tottel's Songes and Sonettes in Context* (Farnham, Surrey: Ashgate, 2013), 147–61.

8. Letter to Sir Edmund Bacon, in Logan Pearsall Smith, ed., *The Life and Letters of Sir Henry Wotton,* vol. 2 (Oxford: Clarendon Press, 1907), 32–33. For a reading of Wotton's letter as it bears on the uses of royal pageantry and the initial impressions of the play, see Roderick H. McKeown, "Royal Entries and the Form of Pageantry in *All Is True,*" *Shakespeare Survey* 67 (2014): 191–201.

9. From the letter of Henry Bluett to Richard Weeks, dated July 4, 1613, edited and printed in M. J. Cole, "A New Account of the Burning of the Globe," *SQ* 32 (1981): 352. Bluett calls the play "new," but adds that it "had been acted not passing 2 or 3 times before."

10. *OED,* s.v. "*train* (*n.*)," def. I.3.b, "a line of gunpowder," first attested 1522.

11. *OED,* s.v. "*stuff* (*n.*)." In papermaking, not attested until 1745 (def. I.4.c), but see def. I.2.c, "manufactured material," and these quotations: 1555, W. Waterman, trans. J. Boemus, *Fardle of Factions* I.v.52, "They did weare . . . shoes of a certaine kinde of russhes named Papyrus, which

after became stuffe, to geue name to our paper"; 1626, Bacon, *New Atlantis,* "Wee haue also diuerse Mechanicall Arts, which you haue not; And Stuffes made by them; As Papers, Linens, Silks, Tissues; dainty Works of Feathers of wonderfull Lustre; excellent Dies, and many others."

12. Bosman, "Seeing Tears," 461.

13. See Geoffrey Bullough, *Narrative and Dramatic Sources of Shakespeare,* vol. 4 (New York: Columbia University Press, 1962), 437–42, and the notes to the Prologue in the editions of Halio and Margeson. See, too, Isabel Karremann, "Nostalgic Spectacle and the Politics of Memory in *Henry VIII,*" *Shakespeare Survey* 67 (2014): 180–90.

14. Leontes on the "bawdy planet," *Winter's Tale,* 1.2.199. Though a common word, "fellow" appears thirteen times in *The Winter's Tale,* often to mark the bawdy Autolycus and the clowns ("I am a poor fellow," 4.4.625, 633; see, too, 5.5.151–62).

15. For the presence, and manipulation, of Holinshed's *Chronicles* in *Henry VIII,* see material in Bullough, *Narrative and Dramatic Sources,* 444, and the summary accounts in Margeson, 14–22, and Halio, 12–16. On the broader source materials for the play, see Annabel Patterson, "'All Is True': Negotiating the Past in *Henry VIII,*" in R. B. Parker and S. P. Zitner, eds., *Elizabethan Theater: Essays in Honor of S. Schoenbaum* (Newark: University of Delaware Press, 1996), 147–66. On the Cloth of Gold episode and the displays of royal masculinity, see Gordan McMullan, "'Thou has made me now a man': Reforming Man(ner)liness in *Henry VIII,*" in Jennifer Richards and James Knowles, eds., *Shakespeare's Late Plays: New Readings* (Edinburgh: Edinburgh University Press, 1999), 40–56.

16. Enobarbus's speeches beginning "The barge she sat in, like a burnished throne," are at *Antony and Cleopatra,* 2.2.196–245.

17. Corresponding to 1.1.69–72. Halio and Margeson punctuate: "Whence has he that? If not from hell, the devil . . ." But see Margeson's note on the Folio text at 68.

18. Cox, "*Henry VIII* and the Masque," 391.

19. McKeown, "Royal Entries," 200.

20. Raphael Holinshed, *The Chronicles of England, Scotland, and Ireland,* ed. Abraham Fleming, 2nd ed. (London: Henry Denham, 1587), 922.

21. Karremann, "Nostalgic Spectacle," 185.

22. They include Feste in *Twelfth Night,* Ariel in *The Tempest,* Autolycus in *The Winter's Tale,* the dramatis personae closing *Love's Labor's*

Lost, the Fool in *Lear.* The witches sing in *Macbeth,* but they are hardly women. Ophelia has her songs in *Hamlet,* but by this point in the play she is insane. Desdemona has the "Willow Song" in *Othello,* a staging more of inward eroticism than commissioned entertainment. And Hotspur's wife sings in *Henry IV,* but she does so in Welsh (and what she may have sung is unrecorded in the text).

23. The work of Linda Austern is fundamental here: "'Sing Againe Syren': The Female Musician and Sexual Enchantment in Elizabethan Life and Literature," *Renaissance Quarterly* 42 (1989): 420–48; "Art to Enchant," *Journal of the Royal Musical Association* 115 (1990): 191–206; "'Alluring the Auditorie to Effeminacie': Music and the Idea of the Feminine in Early Modern England," *Music and Letters* 74 (1993): 343–54; "'No Women Are Indeed': The Boy Actor as Vocal Seductress in Late Sixteenth- and Early Seventeenth-Century Early Drama," in Leslie C. Dunn and Nancy A. Jones, eds., *Embodied Voices: Representing Female Vocality in Western Culture* (Cambridge: Cambridge University Press, 1994), 83–102. Building on Austern's work, but making the argument for female music's disturbing power on the Jacobean stage of sorcery, is Amanda Eubanks Winkler, *O Let Us Howle Some Heavy Note: Music for Witches, the Melancholic, and the Mad on the Seventeenth-Century English Stage* (Bloomington: University of Indiana Press, 2006).

24. Austern, "Art to Enchant," 204.

25. Austern, "'Sing Againe Syren,'" 435–36.

26. The heading "Song" is from the Folio.

27. Quoted and discussed in Austern, "'Sing Againe Syren," 446–47.

28. The song beginning "In this trembling shadow": in Nadal, ed., *Third and Fourth Books,* 84–86.

29. When Katherine imagines the two cardinals coming in to speak with her, she questions their motives and their sincerity: "But all hoods make not monks." The Latin version of this maxim, *cucullus non facit monachum,* had appeared in *Twelfth Night* and in *Measure for Measure.* But it appears, too, in Dowland's preface to his 1612 collection, *Pilgrime's Solace,* where he criticizes those new, upstart lutenists at James's court: "Now if these gallant young Lutenists be such as they would haue the world beleeue, and of which I make no doubt, let them remember that their skill lyeth not in their fingers endes: *Cucullus non facit Monachum*" (Poulton, *John Dowland,* 290). The maxim is a commonplace, but I find it striking coming at this moment in the play's most powerfully Dowlandian scene of lyrical performance and political intrusion.

30. I quote here directly from the Folio text.

31. Text from Nadal, *Third and Fourth Books*, 83; translation mine.

CHAPTER FIVE

1. I quote from the slightly modernized edition of Foreman's account as printed in Martin Butler, ed., *Cymbeline* (Cambridge: Cambridge University Press, 2005), 3–4.

2. Throughout, I refer to the character by his Folio spelling, "Iachimo," as opposed to Warren's editorial "Giacomo."

3. See Butler, ed., *Cymbeline:* "speakers seem divorced from their own verse, striving after notions that they can barely find words to articulate" (19).

4. Ibid., 23.

5. The range of scholarship and criticism on the play through the mid-1900s is usefully summarized in Warren, ed., *Cymbeline,* with some updating in Butler, ed., *Cymbeline.* Recent studies that have influenced my chapter include: Peggy Munoz Simonds, *Myth, Emblem, and Music in Shakespeare's "Cymbeline": An Iconographic Reconstruction* (Newark: University of Delaware Press, 1992); Bate, *Shakespeare and Ovid*, esp. 215–19; Palfrey, *Late Shakespeare*, 83–99, 126–37, 213–21, 243–50; Patrick Cheney, *Shakespeare, National Poet-Playwright* (Cambridge: Cambridge University Press, 2004), 267–83; Ortiz, *Broken Harmony*, 157–60; Beckwith, *Shakespeare and the Grammar of Forgiveness*, 104–26; Burrow, *Shakespeare and Classical Antiquity*, 83–91, 124–26; Marion Wells, "Philomela's Marks: Ekphrasis and Gender in Shakespeare's Poems and Plays," in Jonathan F. S. Post, ed., *The Oxford Handbook of Shakespeare's Poetry* (Oxford: Oxford University Press, 2013), 205–24, esp. 212–17; J. K. Barret, "The Crowd in Imogen's Bedroom: Allusion and Ethics in *Cymbeline,*" *SQ* 66 (2015): 440–62; Wayne, "First Folio's Arrangement."

6. On Crane's role in preparing the text, see Paul Werstine, "Ralph Crane and Edward Knight," in M. J. Kidnie and Sonia Massai, eds., *Shakespeare and Textual Studies* (Cambridge: Cambridge University Press, 2015), 27–38. Wayne considers *Cymbeline* the "only Crane text among the tragedies" ("First Folio's Arrangement," 401).

7. W. K. Wimsatt, ed., *Dr. Johnson on Shakespeare* (Harmondsworth: Penguin, 1969), 136.

8. Of the twenty-two appearances of the word "garment" in Shake-

speare's plays and poems, eight of them (more than in any other single text) are in *Cymbeline.*

9. Butler, ed., *Cymbeline,* 2.

10. Burrow, *Shakespeare and Classical Antiquity,* 126.

11. See Julia Haig Gaisser, *Catullus and His Renaissance Readers* (Oxford: Clarendon Press, 1993), and discussion, texts, and bibliography in Gaisser, ed., *Catullus in English* (Harmondsworth: Penguin, 2001).

12. Gordon Braden, "'Viuamus, mea Lesiba' in the English Renaissance," *English Literary Renaissance* 9 (1979): 199–224.

13. George Puttenham, in the *Arte of English Poesie,* lists him with Horace as an exemplar of the lyric mode in Latin. See *The Arte of English Poesie* (London, 1589), facsimile reprinting ed. Baxter Hathaway (Kent, OH: Kent State University Press, 1970), book 1, chapter 11, 41. Puttenham also praises Catullus in book 1, chapter 26, in discussing marriage poems (epithalamia). Frank Whigham states that Puttenham "owned a copy of Catullus's poems." See Whigham, ed., *The Art of English Poesy by George Puttenham: A Critical Edition* (Ithaca, NY: Cornell University Press, 2007), 63n128.

14. See Braden, "'Viuamus, mea Lesiba,'" and more speculatively, Jacob Blevins, *Catullan Consciousness and the Early Modern Lyric in England* (Aldershot: Ashgate, 2004).

15. The Folio's "You are a friend" was first emended by Lewis Theobald to "You are afraid." See Butler, ed., *Cymbeline,* 100.

16. Warren, ed., *Cymbeline,* 108.

17. Tiffany Stern, "Sermons, Plays and Note-Takers: *Hamlet* Q1 as a 'Noted' Text," *Shakespeare Survey* 66 (2013): 1–23; "Watching as Reading: The Audience and Written Text in Shakespeare's Playhouse," in Laurie Maguire, ed., *How to Do Things with Shakespeare* (Oxford: Blackwell, 2013), 136–59, especially 142–44.

18. See the review in Barret, "The Crowd in Imogen's Bedroom."

19. See Lindley, *Shakespeare and Music,* 172–75.

20. David Armitage, "The Dismemberment of Orpheus: Mythic Elements in Shakespeare's Romances," *Shakespeare Survey* 39 (1987): 123–33. See, too, Ortiz, *Broken Harmony,* 157–60; Palfrey, *Late Shakespeare,* 83–99.

21. Among the earliest examples, Thomas Hedley's single printed sheet, "The Judgment of Midas," retold the tale in 1552 more like an Aesopic fable than a myth: a brief account, capped by a moral exhortation

not to judge what you do not know. See Thomas Hedley, *Of such as on fanteseye decree & discuss: on other mens works. Lo Ouids tale thus* (London: Harry Stutton, 1552), STC 1896.5. George Turberville's handling of the myth appeared in his "The Lover against one that compared his Mistresse with his Ladie," in *Epitaphes, Epigrams, Songs and Sonnets,* ed. John Payne Collier (privately printed, 1867), 25.

22. See George K. Hunter and David Bevington, eds., *John Lyly: Galatea, Midas* (Manchester: Manchester University Press, 2000).

23. See the discussion in Peter Holland, ed., *Shakespeare: A Midsummer Night's Dream* (Oxford: Oxford University Press, 1994), 74–81, with special reference to the discussion of Midas in Erasmus's *Praise of Folly* (1.2).

24. George Sandys, *Ovid's Metamorphoses Englished,* facsimile reprinting (New York: Garland, 1976).

25. *OED,* s.v. "give (*v.*)," def. 46 and draft additions 2002.

26. The *OED* records contemporary uses of the verb "tune" meaning "to make subservient to one's own ends" (s.v. "tune [*v.*]," def. 2.c).

27. Joshua Sylvester, in his translation of *The Divine Weeks and Workes* of Du Bartas (1605–1606), quoted in Poulton, *John Dowland,* 68.

28. *OED,* s.v. "chaliced," quoting this passage from *Cymbeline* as the first usage (and none others until the mid-nineteenth century). *OED,* s.v. "Mary," subheading "Mary-bud," quoting this passage as the first usage and stating that the term is used "now only in echoes of Shakespeare." *OED,* s.v. "winking (*adj.*)," def. 2, quoting this passage and a passage from Shakespeare's *King John* as the first uses.

29. *OED,* s.v. "penetrate," def. 3, quoting this passage and, earlier, *Two Gentlemen of Verona* as the first appearances. *OED,* s.v. "Horse-hair," quoting this passage from *Cymbeline* in def. 1.a. *OED.*, s.v. "cat-gut," as used for the strings of musical instruments, first cited in 1599. *OED,* s.v. "gut," def. 4.c., used in the plural "for making violin strings," first attested in 1611 in Middleton and Dekker's *Roaring Girl. OED,* s.v. "unpaved," def. 2., called a "nonce-use," with this passage from *Cymbeline* the only quotation.

30. George Sandys, *Ovid's Metamorphoses Englished,* facsimile reprinting (New York: Garland, 1976).

31. Quinn, ed., *Catullus,* poem 85, with commentary on 421–22. The couplet, perhaps the most famous of Catullus's epigrams, influenced later poets from Martial at least through Abraham Cowley. See Sven Lorenz, "Catullus and Martial," in Marilyn B. Skinner, ed., *A*

Companion to Catullus (Oxford: Blackwell, 2007), 418–19. For Cowley's mid-seventeenth-century version, see Gaisser, *Catullus in English,* 35.

32. Most readings of *Cymbeline* stress its political over its aesthetic tenor. See, for example, the concluding remarks in Jonathan Goldberg, *James I and the Politics of Literature* (Stanford, CA: Stanford University Press, 1981), 240–41, suggesting that the play speaks directly to the "images of rule [and the] ruling images of James's reign"; Leah Marcus, *Puzzling Shakespeare,* 109–57, esp. the avowal, "*Cymbeline* demands political interpretation" (137); and the extended engagements in Palfrey, *Late Shakespeare,* 83–99.

33. Ed. Quinn, *Catullus,* poem 3; translation mine. This poem, together with Catullus 2, became famous as the "sparrow" poems, influencing a range of later writers, again from Martial through John Skelton (in his *Phyyllyp Sparowe*), Thomas Campion, and Nahum Tate. See Gaisser, *Catullus in English,* esp. xxix–xxx, 35–37.

34. Another Catullan resonance in the play may be Iachimo's praise of Posthumus in act 1. Speaking to Innogen, he describes his rival: "He sits 'mongst men like a descended god; / He hath a kind of honour sets him off / More than a mortal seeming" (1.6.169–71). These lines recall Catullus's poem 51, the famous translation of Sappho, that begins: "Ille mi par esse deo uidetur, / ille, si fas est, superare diuos, / qui sedens aduersus identidem te spectat et audi / dulce ridentem . . ." I translate: "He seems to me on par with a god, he, if it may be said, seems to surpass the gods, who sitting opposite watches, over and over, you sweetly laughing." In keeping with what I see as the arc of the Catullan imagery of the poem, these lines may gain their force as an example of Iachimo's lyric ventriloquism—a moment when he does not so much praise Posthumus directly, but ironically distances himself from that praise by means of a literary allusion.

35. Facsimile ed., 22.

36. Quoted and discussed in Warren, ed., *Cymbeline,* 274.

37. Ibid.

38. Burrow, *Shakespeare and Classical Antiquity,* 86.

39. I relineate to reaffirm the fourteen-beat line as the governing metrical structure here.

40. Henry Peacham, *The Compleat Gentleman* (London, 1622). I quote from the edition based on the 1634 reprinting, ed. G. S. Gordon (Oxford: Clarendon Press, 1906), 78.

41. Wayne, "First Folio's Arrangement," 406.

EPILOGUE

1. Lois Potter, ed., *The Two Noble Kinsmen,* Arden Shakespeare 3, rev. ed. (London: Bloomsbury, 2015), 58.

2. See Frederick W. Sternfeld, *Music in Shakespearean Tragedy* (London: Methuen, 1963), 23–52; Eubanks Winkler, *O Let Us Howle Some Heavy Note,* 4–76, 92.

3. Relationships between the play and its Chaucerian source motivate much criticism. See, for example, Ann Thompson, *Shakespeare's Chaucer: A Study in Literary Origins* (Liverpool: Liverpool University Press, 1978); E. Talbot Donaldson, *The Swan at the Well: Shakespeare Reading Chaucer* (New Haven, CT: Yale University Press, 1985); Alex Davis, "Living in the Past: Thebes, Periodization and *The Two Noble Kinsmen,*" *Journal of Medieval and Early Modern Studies* 40 (2010): 173–95; Mischa Teramura, "The Anxiety of *Auctoritas:* Chaucer and *The Two Noble Kinsmen,*" *SQ* 63 (2012): 544–76.

4. The Jailer's Daughter and her scenes have sparked a range of recent critical commentary. Some have found in her an earthly lyricism that reveals Shakespeare's unique hand: see Douglas Bruster, "The Jailer's Daughter and the Politics of Madwomen's Language," *SQ* 46 (1995): 277–300. Others have found her scenes to be a kind of Fletcherian ventriloquism of Shakespeare: see Eric Rasmussen, ed., *The Two Noble Kinsmen,* in Jonathan Bate and Eric Rasmussen, eds., *William Shakespeare, Complete Works* (New York: Palgrave, 2007), 2356. Aspects of the character and her scenes that generate interpretations keyed to the historical recovery of gender roles, of madness, and of class distinction include: L. Dawson, *Lovesickness and Gender in Early Modern Literature* (Oxford: Oxford University Press, 2008); Carol Thomas Neely, "Documents in Madness: Reading Madness and Gender in Shakespeare's Tragedies and Early Modern Culture," *SQ* 42 (1991): 315–38; Kaara Peterson, "Fluid Economics: Portraying Shakespeare's Hysterics," *Mosaic* 34 (2001): 35–51.

5. Mary Ellen Lamb, *The Popular Culture of Shakespeare, Spenser and Jonson* (New York: Routledge, 2006), 206.

6. On the status of the 1609 Quarto, its reprintings, and its possible relationships to performance traditions, see the discussions throughout Roger Warren, ed., *A Reconstructed Text of Pericles, Prince of Tyre* (Oxford: Oxford University Press, 2003), and Doreen Delvecchio and Antony Hammond, eds., *Pericles, Prince of Tyre* (Cambridge: Cambridge University Press, 1998). Warren bases his text on the reconstructed ver-

sion of the play by the Oxford edition editors, and he adds material from the prose version of the story from George Wilkins (whom he also lists as coauthor). The Cambridge editors, by contrast, deemphasize the possibilities of collaboration, and seek a text more directly based on the Quarto. Warren prints a diplomatic edition of the Quarto as an appendix, and it is that text that I use here. For broader discussions of *Pericles* in its textual and generic heritage, see Palfrey, *Late Shakespeare,* 57–78.

7. For the status of *Pericles* and *The Two Noble Kinsmen* as "late plays" in the canon of Romances, see Lyne, *Shakespeare's Late Work,* who considers *Pericles* "the first last play," 56, and who locates *The Two Noble Kinsmen* in the broader thematic, textual, and generic forms of the early 1610s (17–19). By contrast, Palfrey devotes an entire chapter to *Pericles,* while excluding both *The Two Noble Kinsmen* and *Henry VIII* (considering a link between the former and *The Tempest* to be "fairly remote," 31).

8. The history of the term "worthy," as both adjective and noun, to connote an old literary authority may start with Chaucer, whose Clerk calls Petrarch "worthy," and the term is picked up in the fifteenth century to characterize Chaucer himself (along with Gower). For example, Robert Henryson begins his *Testament of Cressid* with a paean to "worthy Chaucer." William Caxton printed Chaucer's *Boece,* calling him "digne and worthy." An anonymous writer of the 1540s refers to "worthy Chaucer," as does John Selden in 1612. By 1660, William Winstanley could publish *England's Worthies* as a literary history beginning with Chaucer and Gower. For these references and others, see Caroline Spurgeon, *Five-Hundred Years of Chaucer Criticism and Allusion (1357–1900)* (London: Oxford University Press, 1922). The noun "worthy" connoted distinction from the late fourteenth century, and by the early sixteenth century it was applied to scholars as well as heroes of history and legend (*OED,* s.v. "worthy," def. C.1.d).

9. Bruster, "Jailer's Daughter," 277.

10. Citations here are to signatures in the Quarto and to corresponding scene numbers in Warren's edition.

11. See the competing approaches in Warren, ed., *Pericles,* and in Delvecchio and Hammond, eds., *Pericles.*

12. For the variety of views on Gower's role in the play (his language, his relationship to Pericles, and his status as source material), see Walter F. Eggers Jr., "Shakespeare's Gower and the Role of the Authorial Presenter," *Philological Quarterly* 54 (1975): 434–43; F. David Hoeniger,

"Gower and Shakespeare in *Pericles*," *SQ* 33 (1982): 461–79; Stephen Dickey, "Language and Its Role in *Pericles*," *English Literary Renaissance* 16 (1986): 550–56; Deanne Williams, "Papa Don't Preach: The Power of Prolixity in *Pericles*," *University of Toronto Quarterly* 71 (2002): 595–622.

13. Delvecchio and Hammond, eds., *Pericles,* 88.

14. Orgel's phase comes from "The Poetics of Incomprehensibility," *Shakespeare Quarterly* 42 (1991): 431–47, portions of which are incorporated into the introduction to his edition of *The Winter's Tale,* esp. 10.

15. Lyne, *Shakespeare's Late Work,* 58.

16. In Stephen Orgel and R. A. Braunmuller, eds., *The Complete Pelican Shakespeare* (New York: Penguin, 2002), 605.

17. Ibid., 606; Lyne, *Shakespeare's Late Work,* 59. My comparisons with Pericles and *Lear* deal with the Quarto text, *The History of King Lear,* as edited in Wells and Taylor, *Complete Works,* and cited by scene and line.

18. My comparisons are between *Pericles* and the Quarto version of *King Lear*. I quote from *The History of King Lear* as edited in the Wells and Taylor Oxford *Complete Works.*

19. For arguments that "rough music" connotes ritual and magic performance, akin to the "rough magic" of Prospero, and that the word "rough" should not be emended to "still" as some editors have it, see F. Elizabeth Hart, "Ceremon's 'Rough' Music in 'Pericles,'" *SQ* 51 (2000); 313–31. The word "viol" was changed to "vial" in the Fourth Quarto printing of the play, an emendation supported by Warren, ed., *Pericles* (164), but rejected by Delvecchio and Hammond, eds., *Pericles* (104), who support a reading devoted to the musical imagery of the episode. See also Lyne, *Shakespeare's Late Work,* for whom "the emendation to 'vial' surely makes sense," but goes on: "it is interesting, though, how the simultaneous music and medicine mark a slippage in language" (65).

20. See Dickey, "Language and Its Role in *Pericles,*" 561: "Ceremon restores Thaisa to life with 'air,' that is, music and oxygen, the pun combining the worlds of art and nature whose intersection so often makes for a supernatural moment in the romances."

21. Poulton, *John Dowland,* collects and prints these various appearances: Dowland's dedication of the *Second Book* to Lucy Countess of Bedford (1600), "yet so rare" (249); Henry Peacham's *Compleat Gentleman* (1622), Dowland as a "rare lutenist" (82); William Webbe (1624), introductory verses to Francis Pilkington's *Second Set of Madrigals,* "rare artists" (87); letter of William Browne to Earl of Shrewsbury (1602),

"rare musick and songs" (398); John Webster, *The Devil's Law Case* (1623), "rare consort of musicke" (165).

22. Teramura, "The Anxiety of *Auctoritas,*" 576.

23. See Potter, ed., *Two Noble Kinsmen,* 406–10.

24. See Tim William Machan, "Speght's *Works* and the Invention of Chaucer," *TEXT* 8 (1995): 145–70.

Index